CONTENTS

**Targeting Homework
Year 3 New Edition**

Copyright © 2024 Blake Education
Reprinted 2024

ISBN: 978 1 92572 645 9

Published by Pascal Press
PO Box 250
Glebe NSW 2037
www.pascalpress.com.au
contact@pascalpress.com.au

Author: Frances Mackay
Publisher: Lynn Dickinson
Editors: Vanessa Barker & Ruth Schultz
Cover and Text Designer: Leanne Nobilio
Typesetters: Leanne Nobilio & Maria Biaggini
Proofreader: Tim Learner
Images & Illustrations: Dreamstime (unless otherwise indicated)
Printed by Wai Man Book Binding (China) Ltd

Acknowledgements
Thank you to the publishers, authors and illustrators
who generously granted permission for their work
to be reproduced in this book.

Introduction

Targeting Homework aims to build and reinforce English and Maths skills. This book supports the ACARA Australian Curriculum for Year 3 and helps children to revise and consolidate what has been taught in the classroom. ACARA codes are shown on each unit and a chart explaining their content descriptions is on pages v and vi. The inside back cover (Maths) and front cover (English) show the topics in each unit.

The structure of this book

This book has 32 carefully graded double-page units on English and Maths. The English units are divided into three sections:

★ Grammar and Punctuation

★ Spelling and Phonic Knowledge

★ Reading and Comprehension — includes a wide variety of literary and cross-curriculum texts.

This also includes a Reading Review segment for children to record and rate their home reading books.

The Maths units are divided between:

★ Number and Algebra

★ Measurement and Space

★ Statistics and Probability

★ Problem Solving.

My Book Review

Title _____

Author _____

Rating ☆☆☆☆☆

Comment _____

_____

Assessment

Term Reviews follow Units 1–8, 9–16, 17–24 and 25–32 to test work covered during the term, and allow parents and carers to monitor their child's progress. Children are encouraged to mark each unit as it is completed and to colour in the traffic lights at the end of each segment. These results are then transferred to the Marking Grid. Parents and carers can see at a glance if their child is excelling or struggling!

● **Green** = Excellent — 2 or fewer questions incorrect
● **Orange** = Passing — 50% or more questions answered correctly
● **Red** = Struggling — fewer than 50% correct and needs help

SCORE **/18** (0-6) (8-14) (16-18)   *Score 2 points for each correct answer!*

How to Use This Book

The activities in this book are specifically designed to be used at home with minimal resources and support. Helpful explanations of key concepts and skills are provided throughout the book to help understand the tasks. Useful examples of how to do the activities are provided.

Regular practice of key concepts and skills will support the work your child does in school and will enable you to monitor their progress throughout the year. It is recommended that children complete 8 units per school term (one a week) and then the Term Review. Every unit has a Traffic Light scoreboard at the end of each section.

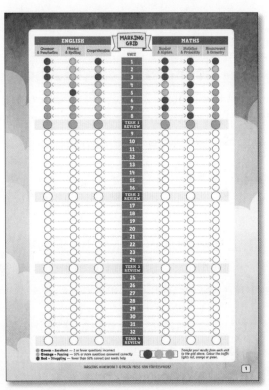

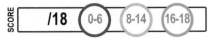

Score 2 points for each correct answer!

You or your child should mark each completed unit and then colour the traffic light that corresponds to the number of correct questions. This process will enable you to see at a glance how your child is progressing and to identify weak spots. The results should be recorded at the end of each term on the Marking Grid on page 1. The Term Review results are important for tracking progress and identifying any improvements in performance. If you find that certain questions are repeatedly causing difficulties and errors, then there is a good reason to discuss this with your child's teacher and arrange for extra instruction in that problem area.

NOTE: The Maths Problem Solving questions do not appear on the Marking Grid as they often have multiple or subjective answers that cannot be easily scored.

Home Reading Journal

Each English unit provides space for your child to log, review and rate a book they have read during the week. These details can then be transferred to the handy Reading Journal Summary on page 146, which can be photocopied and shared with their teacher or kept as a record.

Answers

The answer section on pages 147–162 can be removed, stapled together and kept somewhere safe. Use it to check answers when your child has completed each unit. Encourage your child to colour in the Traffic Light boxes when the answers have been calculated.

TARGETING HOMEWORK 3 © PASCAL PRESS ISBN 9781925726459

Australian Curriculum Correlations: Year 3 English

CODE	CODE DESCRIPTION	Grammar & Punctuation UNITS	Phonic Knowledge & Spelling UNITS	Reading Comprehension UNITS
LANGUAGE				
AC9E3LA02	Understand how the language of evaluation and emotion, such as modal verbs, can be varied to be more or less forceful	10, 19, 29, 32		
AC9E3LA03	Describe how texts across the curriculum use different language features and structures relevant to their purpose	31, 32		8, 30
AC9E3LA04	Understand that paragraphs are a key organisational feature of the stages of written texts, grouping related information together	27, 30		
AC9E3LA06	Understand that a clause is a unit of grammar usually containing a subject and a verb that need to agree	1, 2, 6, 7, 9, 14		
AC9E3LA07	Understand how verbs represent different processes for doing, feeling, thinking, saying and relating	5, 12, 23, 26		
AC9E3LA08	Understand that verbs are anchored in time through tense	14, 15, 28		
AC9E3LA10	Extend topic-specific and technical vocabulary and know that words can have different meanings in different contexts	20, 21, 25		20
AC9E3LA11	Understand that apostrophes signal missing letters in contractions, and apostrophes are used to show singular and plural possession	13, 16, 19, 24, 30	13	
LITERATURE				
AC9E3LE02	Discuss connections between personal experiences and character experiences in literary texts and share personal preferences			12, 15, 18, 22, 23, 24, 25
AC9E3LE03	Discuss how an author uses language and illustrations to portray characters and settings in texts, and explore how the settings and events influence the mood of the narrative	8, 17, 18		9, 11
AC9E3LE04	Discuss the effects of some literary devices used to enhance meaning and shape the reader's reaction, including rhythm and onomatopoeia in poetry and prose			5, 12, 17
LITERACY				
AC9E3LY03	Identify the audience and purpose of imaginative, informative and persuasive texts through their use of language features and/or images			8, 14, 16, 21, 22, 24, 25
AC9E3LY04	Read a range of texts using phonic, semantic and grammatical knowledge to read accurately and fluently, re-reading and self-correcting when required			11, 26
AC9E3LY05	Use comprehension strategies when listening and viewing to build literal and inferred meaning, and begin to evaluate texts by drawing on a growing knowledge of context, text structures and language features			ALL UNITS
AC9E3LY06	Plan, create, edit and publish imaginative, informative and persuasive written and multimodal texts, using visual features, appropriate form and layout, with ideas grouped in simple paragraphs, mostly correct tense, topic-specific vocabulary and correct spelling of most high-frequency and phonetically regular words	1, 2, 3, 4, 6-8, 10, 11, 13, 22, 25, 30		
AC9E3LY09	Understand how to apply knowledge of phoneme–grapheme (sound–letter) relationships, syllables, and blending and segmenting to fluently read and write multisyllabic words with more complex letter patterns		4, 7, 9-15, 17, 18, 20-31	
AC9E3LY10	Understand how to apply knowledge of common base words, prefixes, suffixes and generalisations for adding a suffix to a base word to read and comprehend new multimorphemic words		ALL UNITS	
AC9E3LY11	Use phoneme–grapheme (sound–letter) relationships and less common letter patterns to spell words		1-3, 5, 6, 16-27	
AC9E3LY12	Recognise and know how to write most high frequency words including some homophones		8, 13, 16, 19, 21, 25	
CROSS CURRICULAR COMPREHENSION TEXTS				
HEALTH & PHYSICAL EDUCATION				
AC9HP4P10	Investigate and apply behaviours that contribute to their own and others' health, safety, relationships and wellbeing			29
SCIENCE				
AC9S3H01	Examine how people use data to develop scientific explanations			21
AC9S3U01	Compare characteristics of living and non-living things and examine the differences between the life cycles of plants and animals			1, 4, 11
AC9S3H02	Consider how people use scientific explanations to meet a need or solve a problem			10, 27
HASS INQUIRY SKILLS				
AC9HS3S04	Analyse information and data, and identify perspectives			7, 14, 22
AC9HS3S05	Draw conclusions based on analysis of information			7
HISTORY				
AC9HS3K01	Causes and effects of changes to the local community, and how people who may be from diverse backgrounds have contributed to these changes			23
AC9HS3K02	significant events, symbols and emblems that are important to Australia's identity and diversity, and how they are celebrated, commemorated or recognised in Australia, including Australia Day, Anzac Day, NAIDOC Week, National Sorry Day, Easter, Christmas, and other religious and cultural festivals			6, 19, 28
GEOGRAPHY				
AC9HS3K03	The representation of contemporary Australia as states and territories, and as the Countries/Places of First Nations Australians prior to colonisation, and the locations of Australia's neighbouring regions and countries			3, 9, 31
AC9HS3K04	The ways First Nations Australians in different parts of Australia are interconnected with Country/Place			10, 13
AC9HS3K05	The similarities and differences between places in Australia and neighbouring countries in terms of their natural, managed and constructed features			7, 20
CIVICS & CITIZENSHIP				
AC9HS3K06	Who makes rules, why rules are important in the school and/or the local community, and the consequences of rules not being followed			15

Australian Curriculum Correlations: Year 3 Maths

ACARA CODE	CONTENT DESCRIPTION	Number & Algebra UNITS	Statistics & Probability UNITS	Measurement & Space UNITS	Problem Solving UNITS
NUMBER					
AC9M3N01	Recognise, represent and order natural numbers using naming and writing conventions for numerals beyond 10000	1, 6, 7, 9, 14, 18, 20, 25, 27, 31			25, 27
AC9M3N02	Recognise and represent unit fractions including $\frac{1}{2}$, $\frac{1}{3}$, $\frac{1}{4}$, $\frac{1}{5}$ and $\frac{1}{10}$ and their multiples in different ways; combine fractions with the same denominator to complete the whole	5, 10, 17, 23, 26, 28		22	5
AC9M3N03	Add and subtract two- and three-digit numbers using place value to partition, rearrange and regroup numbers to assist in calculations without a calculator	3, 4, 6, 30, 32			21
AC9M3N04	Multiply and divide one- and two-digit numbers, representing problems using number sentences, diagrams and arrays, and using a variety of calculation strategies	12, 24			12
AC9M3N05	Estimate the quantity of objects in collections and make estimates when solving problems to determine the reasonableness of calculations	14, 22			
AC9M3N06	Use mathematical modelling to solve practical problems involving additive and multiplicative situations including financial contexts; formulate problems using number sentences and choose calculation strategies, using digital tools where appropriate; interpret and communicate solutions in terms of the situation	11, 22			2, 10, 18, 29, 30
AC9M3N07	Follow and create algorithms involving a sequence of steps and decisions to investigate numbers; describe any emerging patterns	2, 6, 28			6, 7
ALGEBRA					
AC9M3A01	Recognise and explain the connection between addition and subtraction as inverse operations, apply to partition numbers and find unknown values in number sentences	6, 21			19
AC9M3A02	Extend and apply knowledge of addition and subtraction facts to 20 to develop efficient mental strategies for computation with larger numbers without a calculator	1, 3, 4, 14, 15			1, 3, 4, 11, 14, 16, 22, 32
AC9M3A03	Recall and demonstrate proficiency with multiplication facts for 3, 4, 5 and 10; extend and apply facts to develop the related division facts	2, 16, 29			31
MEASUREMENT					
AC9M3M01	Identify which metric units are used to measure everyday items; use measurements of familiar items and known units to make estimates			9, 10, 12, 15, 26	17
AC9M3M02	Measure and compare objects using familiar metric units of length, mass and capacity, and instruments with labelled markings			1, 5, 14, 17, 23, 25, 29	
AC9M3M03	Recognise and use the relationship between formal units of time including days, hours, minutes and seconds to estimate and compare the duration of events			27	13, 26
AC9M3M04	Describe the relationship between the hours and minutes on analog and digital clocks, and read the time to the nearest minute			4, 10, 20, 32	15
AC9M3M05	Identify angles as measures of turn and compare angles with right angles in everyday situations			8, 13, 24	24
AC9M3M06	Recognise the relationships between dollars and cents and represent money values in different ways	8		13, 19	8
SPACE					
AC9M3SP01	Make, compare and classify objects, identifying key features and explaining why these features make them suited to their uses			2, 7, 18, 28	23
AC9M3SP02	Interpret and create two-dimensional representations of familiar environments, locating key landmarks and objects relative to each other			3, 11, 16, 19, 21, 30, 31	
STATISTICS					
AC9M3ST01	Acquire data for categorical and discrete numerical variables to address a question of interest or purpose by observing, collecting and accessing data sets; record the data using appropriate methods including frequency tables and spreadsheets		21, 23, 29		
AC9M3ST02	Create and compare different graphical representations of data sets including using software where appropriate; interpret the data in terms of the context		11, 19, 21, 23, 25		20
AC9M3ST03	Conduct guided statistical investigations involving the collection, representation and interpretation of data for categorical and discrete numerical variables with respect to questions of interest		1, 7, 17, 23, 27		
PROBABILITY					
AC9M3P01	Identify practical activities and everyday events involving chance; describe possible outcomes and events as 'likely' or 'unlikely' and identify some events as 'certain' or 'impossible' explaining reasoning		9, 13, 31		
AC9M3P02	Conduct repeated chance experiments; identify and describe possible outcomes, record the results, recognise and discuss the variation		3, 5, 15		

Australian CURRICULUM

TARGETING HOMEWORK 3 © PASCAL PRESS ISBN 9781925726459

MARKING GRID

ENGLISH

Grammar & Punctuation	Phonics & Spelling	Comprehension

MATHS

Number & Algebra	Statistics & Probability	Measurement & Space

UNIT

English			Unit	Maths		
○	○	○	1	○	○	○
○	○	○	2	○	○	○
○	○	○	3	○	○	○
○	○	○	4	○	○	○
○	○	○	5	○	○	○
○	○	○	6	○	○	○
○	○	○	7	○	○	○
○	○	○	8	○	○	○
○	○	○	TERM 1 REVIEW	○	○	○
○	○	○	9	○	○	○
○	○	○	10	○	○	○
○	○	○	11	○	○	○
○	○	○	12	○	○	○
○	○	○	13	○	○	○
○	○	○	14	○	○	○
○	○	○	15	○	○	○
○	○	○	16	○	○	○
○	○	○	TERM 2 REVIEW	○	○	○
○	○	○	17	○	○	○
○	○	○	18	○	○	○
○	○	○	19	○	○	○
○	○	○	20	○	○	○
○	○	○	21	○	○	○
○	○	○	22	○	○	○
○	○	○	23	○	○	○
○	○	○	24	○	○	○
○	○	○	TERM 3 REVIEW	○	○	○
○	○	○	25	○	○	○
○	○	○	26	○	○	○
○	○	○	27	○	○	○
○	○	○	28	○	○	○
○	○	○	29	○	○	○
○	○	○	30	○	○	○
○	○	○	31	○	○	○
○	○	○	32	○	○	○
○	○	○	TERM 4 REVIEW	○	○	○

● **Green** = Excellent — 2 or fewer questions incorrect
● **Orange** = Passing — 50% or more questions answered correctly
● **Red** = Struggling — fewer than 50% correct and needs help

Transfer your results from each unit to the grid above. Colour the traffic lights red, orange or green.

Grammar & Punctuation

AC9E3LA06, AC9E3LY06

Sentences

> A **sentence** is a group of words that states a complete thought. It makes sense on its own.

① **Circle the two sentences.**

   a We went to visit my uncle Jack.

   b in the caravan

   c The ice cream melted in no time.

   d raced along the road

> A **statement** is a sentence that tells us about everyday things, facts and ideas. Statements begin with a capital letter and end with a **full stop (.)**.
>
> A **question** is a sentence that asks for information. It begins with a capital letter and ends with a **question mark (?)**.

② **Circle the two questions.**

   a The sea is bright blue today.

   b Have you been to the circus yet?

   c Why did you put the cat outside?

   d I ran all the way to school.

③ **Circle the capital letter and the question mark.**

   When will you be going on holiday?

Write a full stop or a question mark at the end of each sentence.

④ Are you happy with your new car__

⑤ I like to ride my bike to the park__

⑥ The band played for a long time__

⑦ How many cards do you have__

Use words from the list below to complete the sentences. Put a full stop or a question mark at the end of each one.

Did	Today	How	Why	We

⑧ _____ you visit Tom___

⑨ _____ went fishing yesterday___

⑩ _____ is your arm in a sling___

⑪ _____ is my brother's birthday___

⑫ _____ are you feeling today___

Score 2 points for each correct answer! **SCORE** **/24** (0-10) (12-18) (20-24)

Phonic Knowledge & Spelling

AC9E3LY10, AC9E3LY11,

Vowel sounds – a e i o u

Say each word. What sound does the vowel make? Circle the word in red that has the same vowel sound as the others in the row.

① hat rat flag drag   baby sad cake

② get net best nest   she he men

③ sit knit pink think   gift hide pipe

④ sock rock drop flop   hope hot rope

⑤ sun bun numb crumb   tube tub rule

Choose words from the questions above to complete these sentences.

⑥ Did the bird have any eggs in her _____?

⑦ Many people _____ football is the best sport.

⑧ Do not _____ that glass!

⑨ They want to learn how to _____ scarves.

Making plurals

> To make a word **plural** (more than one) we usually just add –s.
> *Examples:* **nest, nests**   **sock, socks**

Write these words as plurals.

⑩ flag _____

⑪ crumb _____

⑫ rock _____

⑬ gift _____

⑭ net _____

Change the first letter of each word to make a new word.

Some have been done for you.

⑮ bump lump _____ _____ _____

⑯ hill _____ _____ _____ _____

⑰ bent tent _____ _____ _____

⑱ cot not _____ _____ _____

⑲ bang _____ _____ _____ _____

Score 2 points for each correct answer! **SCORE** **/38** (0-16) (18-32) (34-38)

TARGETING HOMEWORK 3 © PASCAL PRESS ISBN 9781925726459

Imaginative text – Narrative
Author – Frances Mackay

Spotty

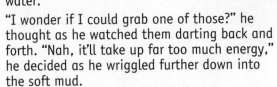

Spotty sat back feeling very pleased with himself. He had just found three fat, juicy slugs to eat, so he settled down at the edge of the dam to watch some flies hovering above the water.

"I wonder if I could grab one of those?" he thought as he watched them darting back and forth. "Nah, it'll take up far too much energy," he decided as he wriggled further down into the soft mud.

Just then, something glistening at the water's edge caught his eye. Spotty hopped over to take a closer look.

"Frogspawn!" he shouted excitedly. "Oh, aren't they cute?" he thought as he peered into the dam. "I once looked like that!"

There were hundreds of them, all sitting in jelly. Inside each egg he could see a tiny black dot that wiggled now and then. Spotty tried to remember what it was like growing up in the dam. He thought back to his life as a tadpole.

"I remember eating just plants at first. It was fun having a long tail and being able to swim around. Then I started to grow back legs and I could cling onto plants. A little while later, my front legs grew and I started eating small bugs in the dam. Then, amazingly, my tail disappeared and I became a froglet! It all seems so long ago now," Spotty sighed.

"Well, good luck, tiny eggs," he whispered. Spotty gave them a little wave before making his way back to his favourite snoozing spot.

Write or circle the correct answers.

① **Where was Spotty?**

a at the pond

b at the dam

c near a river

② **What is Spotty?**

a a frog   b a tadpole   c a froglet

③ **Give one reason why you think Spotty decided not to try and catch a fly.**

_____

_____

④ **What do you think glistening means?**

_____

_____

⑤ **What is frogspawn?**

a weeds in a dam

b baby slugs

c the eggs of a frog

⑥ **What did seeing the frogspawn make Spotty remember?**

a how he learned to catch flies

b what his life was like as a tadpole

c how dangerous life is in a dam

⑦ **Which word in the text means moved 'quickly up and down or side to side'?**

a settled

b wiggled

c peered

⑧ **What do tadpoles eat?**

a fish

b plants and small bugs

c eggs

⑨ **Why do you think Spotty wished the eggs 'good luck'?**

_____

_____

Score 2 points for each correct answer!

SCORE /18   0-6   8-14   16-18

My Book Review

Title _____

Author _____

Rating ☆☆☆☆☆

Comment _____

_____

TERM 1 MATHS

Number & Algebra

AC9M3N01

Numbers to 100

Write the missing numbers in each sequence.

① 11, 12, 13, 14, 15, 16, _____, _____, _____

② 34, 35, 36, _____, _____, _____, 40, 41

③ 30, 29, 28, 27, 26, _____, _____, _____

④ 99, 98, 97, _____, _____, _____, 93, 92

How do you write these numbers using digits? Circle the correct answer.

⑤ twenty-eight   a 82   b 28   c 208

⑥ ninety-nine   a 99   b 909   c 90

⑦ sixty-three   a 603   b 36   c 63

⑧ Which number is 88?
Circle the correct answer.

   a eighty   b eighty-eight

⑨ Which number is 67?
Circle the correct answer.

   a seventy-six   b sixty-seven

Write these numbers in order from smallest to largest.

⑩   45   36   18   60

   _____ _____ _____ _____

⑪   98   84   76   55

   _____ _____ _____ _____

What number is missing from each number sentence? Write in the box.

⑫ 3 + ☐ = 8

⑬ ☐ + 5 = 10

⑭ 15 + 5 = ☐

⑮ 20 − ☐ = 10

Statistics & Probability

AC9M3ST03

Picture graphs

Tom did a survey at school to find out the favourite sports of people in his class.
Here are the results of his survey.

Our favourite sports

= 1 student

Football   Netball   Rugby   Soccer   Swimming   Softball   None

Answer the questions about the graph.

① Which sport was the most popular?
_____

② Which sport was the least popular?
_____

③ How many students liked soccer best?_____

④ How many students liked no sports?_____

⑤ Which two sports had the same number of students who liked them best?
_____ and _____

⑥ Does the graph show how many students liked tennis? _____

⑦ How many students in Tom's class took part in the survey? _____

⑧ How many more students liked football than rugby? _____

⑨ Is it true that more students liked rugby than swimming? _____

Score 2 points for each correct answer!   SCORE /30   0-12 14-24 26-30

Score 2 points for each correct answer!   SCORE /18   0-6 8-14 16-18

TARGETING HOMEWORK 3 © PASCAL PRESS ISBN 9781925726459

Measurement & Space

AC9M3M02

Length

We measure length in centimetres (cm) and metres (m).

$$100 \text{ cm} = 1 \text{ m}$$

A school ruler is usually 30 cm long.

To **estimate** is to make a good guess.

Use this 5 cm line to help you estimate:

```
0    1    2    3    4    5 cm
```

Which is a better estimate for the length of these things? Circle the correct one.

1. TV remote   17 cm   17 m
2. calculator   13 m   13 cm
3. mobile phone   12 cm   12 m
4. school ruler   30 m   30 cm

Estimate the length of these objects to the nearest centimetre. Then measure them to see if you are correct.

5.

    My guess: _____ cm

    Actual length _____ cm

6.

    My guess _____ cm

    Actual length _____ cm

7.

    My guess _____ cm

    Actual length _____ cm

8. The length of this line: ├──────┤

    My guess _____ cm

    Actual length _____ cm

9. The longer side of this book

    My guess _____ cm

    Actual length _____ cm

10. The shorter side of this book

    My guess _____ cm

    Actual length _____ cm

Score 2 points for each correct answer!

SCORE **/20** (0-8) (10-14) (16-20)

Problem Solving

AC9M3A02

Number puzzles

Look at the rows of numbers below.

A	1	1	1	3
B	1	2	1	4
C	2	2	3	7
D	3	1	2	?

1. What number should go at the end of row D? _____

2. Explain how you got your answer.

_____

_____

Look at this number wall.

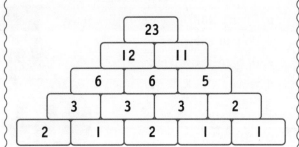

Here's how to work out the numbers in the wall. Start at the bottom row of bricks. To make the number in the row above it, add together the numbers immediately below it.

Starting from the left, **2 + 1** in the bottom row makes **3** in the row above.
1 + 2 in the bottom row makes **3** above.
2 + 1 makes **3** above. **1 + 1** makes **2**.

3. **Make your own number wall.**
Arrange the digits 1 to 5 in the bottom row of bricks. You can't use a digit more than once in this row. Your goal is to get the highest possible number in the top brick.

Try out different combinations using pen and paper. Write your solution here.

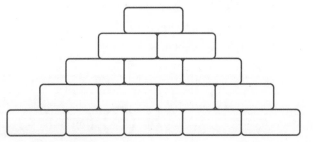

Grammar & Punctuation

AC9E3LA06, AC9E3LY06

Sentences

> **Remember!** A **sentence** is a group of words that states a complete thought. It makes sense on its own.

① **Circle the two sentences.**

   a running down the hill

   b I saw my friends yesterday.

   c next to the back door

   d On Sunday, we are going to the market.

Exclamations

> An **exclamation** is a sentence that shows surprise, fear, happiness or excitement. Exclamations begin with a capital letter and end with an **exclamation mark (!)**.

② **Circle the two exclamations.**

   a I can't wait for my birthday party!

   b Do you know the way to the shop?

   c Our cat is a tabby.

   d Wow — look at that huge dog!

Commands

> A **command** is a sentence that tells you to do something. It begins with a capital letter and ends with a **full stop (.)** or an **exclamation mark (!)**. Commands begin with a doing word or **verb**.
>
> *Examples:* **Drink** your milk. **Wait** for me!

Are these sentences exclamations (E) or commands (C)? Write E or C next to each sentence.

③ Sweep the floor. __

④ This room is a mess! __

⑤ I can't believe I won! __

⑥ Read that book by tomorrow. __

Add a full stop, a question mark or an exclamation mark to complete these sentences.

⑦ Feed the dog before you go__

⑧ Why did you do that__

⑨ That trick is amazing__

⑩ Hurry up and call the police__

Score 2 points for each correct answer! **SCORE /20** (0-8) (10-14) (16-20)

Phonic Knowledge & Spelling

AC9E3LY10, AC9E3LY11

Vowel sounds – a e i o u

Say each word. What sound does the vowel make? Circle the word in red that has the same vowel sound as the others in the row.

① jam slam clap strap tap tape cape

② hen then fetch stretch she jet seen

③ sing wring think wink nice will time

④ toss cross stock flock rock rope nose

⑤ must dust budge nudge cube truck tube

Choose words from the questions above to complete these sentences.

⑥ Spread some _____ on your toast.

⑦ Where did that _____ of sheep go?

⑧ The choir will _____ here tonight.

⑨ The _____ laid her eggs over there.

Adding –ed and –ing

> When a word ends in a short vowel followed by a single consonant, double the last consonant before adding –ed or –ing.
> *Examples:* **clap, clapped, clapping**

Add –ed and –ing to these words.

	–ed	–ing
⑩ slam	_____	_____
⑪ strap	_____	_____
⑫ hop	_____	_____
⑬ skip	_____	_____
⑭ slip	_____	_____

Compound words

> A **compound word** is two words joined together to make one word.
> *Example:* **gold + fish = goldfish**

Make compound words by writing a word from the box on each line. (*Hint:* They are all animals.)

fish	worm	horse	dog	fly	hopper

⑮ butter_____

⑯ sea_____

⑰ grass_____

⑱ jelly_____

⑲ bull_____

⑳ earth_____

Score 2 points for each correct answer! **SCORE /40** (0-18) (20-34) (36-40)

TARGETING HOMEWORK 3 © PASCAL PRESS ISBN 9781925726459

AC9E3LY05

Imaginative text – Humorous narrative
Author – Elizabeth Best
Illustrator – Janine Dawson

Rebel Baby

One day, seeing bare feet waving in the air and the bootees on the ground again, Jack picked them up.

"Hi!" he said. "How's it going?"

The baby ignored him. The reason the baby ignored him was because it was talking into a mobile phone.

"Yes, I'll have half-a-dozen colas. And I'll have a couple of meat pies. Sloppy ones. Just deliver it all to the pram parked outside the store on the corner of Pitt and Stuart Streets. Shove them under the mattress out of sight. And make it snappy, will you?"

Jack could hardly believe his ears. "I thought babies only drank milk," he said.

"I hate milk," the baby said. "Disgusting stuff! How would you like it? A teat stuck in your mouth, 'Drink this!' No choice. No, 'Would you like a lemonade? Or a soda?' No. Just, 'Drink this and like it or lump it!'"

"I'd never thought about that before," said Jack.

Source: *Rebel Baby*, Gigglers, Blake Education.

Write or circle the correct answers.

① What did Jack pick up off the ground when he saw the baby in the pram?

　a a mobile phone

　b bootees

　c a teddy

② Why did the baby ignore Jack?

　a He was drinking some milk.

　b He was talking on a mobile phone.

　c He was sleeping.

③ What did the baby order to eat and drink?

_____

_____

④ Where was the baby's pram parked?

_____

_____

⑤ What did the baby think about milk?

　a He loved it.

　b We are not told.

　c He hated it.

⑥ What is another word for **disgusting**?

　a tasty

　b revolting

　c fresh

⑦ Look at the picture. What was Jack carrying on his back?

_____

⑧ What is **not** unusual about this story?

　a The baby hated milk.

　b The baby was talking on a mobile phone.

　c The baby was in a pram.

Score 2 points for each correct answer! SCORE **/16** 0-6 8-12 14-16

My Book Review

Title _____

Author _____

Rating ☆☆☆☆☆

Comment _____

_____

Number & Algebra

AC9M3A03, AC9M3N07

Counting in twos

① Continue the jumps in twos on the number line.

+2

0 1 2 3 4 5 6 7 8 9 10 11 12 13 14 15

Write the missing numbers.

② | 2 | | | 8 | | | | 18 | |

③ | 10 | | | 16 | 18 | | | 26 | |

④ | 20 | | 16 | | | 10 | | | 2 |

⑤ | | 42 | | 46 | 48 | | | 56 | |

Counting in fives

⑥ Continue the jumps in fives on the number line.

+5

0 1 2 3 4 5 6 7 8 9 10 11 12 13 14 15

Write the missing numbers.

⑦ | 5 | | | 20 | 25 | | | 40 | | 50 |

⑧ | 50 | | 60 | | 70 | | 80 | | 90 | |

⑨ | 50 | 45 | | 35 | | 25 | | 15 | | 5 |

⑩ | | 95 | | 85 | | 75 | | 65 | | 55 |

Counting in twos and fives

Write the answers in the boxes.

⑪ 2 + 2 + 2 + 2 = ☐

⑫ 5 + 5 + 5 + 5 = ☐

⑬ 4 lots of 2 = ☐

⑭ 4 lots of 5 = ☐

⑮ 4 × 2 or 2 × 4 = ☐

⑯ 4 × 5 or 5 × 4 = ☐

⑰ 8 ÷ 4 = ☐

⑱ 20 ÷ 5 = ☐

⑲ Start at **2** on the 100 square.
Count in **twos**.
Colour the numbers in red.

⑳ Start at **5** on the 100 square.
Count in **fives**.
Colour the numbers in blue.

1	2	3	4	5	6	7	8	9	10
11	12	13	14	15	16	17	18	19	20
21	22	23	24	25	26	27	28	29	30
31	32	33	34	35	36	37	38	39	40
41	42	43	44	45	46	47	48	49	50
51	52	53	54	55	56	57	58	59	60
61	62	63	64	65	66	67	68	69	70
71	72	73	74	75	76	77	78	79	80
81	82	83	84	85	86	87	88	89	90
91	92	93	94	95	96	97	98	99	100

㉑ **What do you notice about the patterns you have made on the 100 square?**

_____

_____

Score 2 points for each correct answer!

SCORE **/42**   0-18   20-36   38-42

Statistics & Probability

There are no statistics & probability activities in this unit.

TARGETING HOMEWORK 3 © PASCAL PRESS ISBN 9781925726459

Shapes

Name the shapes in the table. Choose from the words in the box. Then write the number of sides and corners.

| triangle | square | rectangle | pentagon |
| circle | oval | hexagon | |

	Shape	Shape name	Number of sides	Number of corners
①	■			
②	▬			
③	⬠			
④	⬡			
⑤	⬭			
⑥	⬬			
⑦	▲			

More shapes

Here are the names of some more shapes.

| heptagon: 7 sides | octagon: 8 sides |
| nonagon: 9 sides | decagon: 10 sides |

Name these shapes.

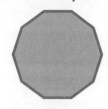 

 ⑧ _____   ⑨ _____

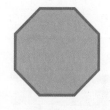 

⑩ _____ ⑪ _____

Score 2 points for each correct answer!

SCORE **/22** (0-8) (10-16) (18-22)

Solving word problems

Solving word problems can be tricky! Read these word problems.

Jamal had 10 football cards. He bought 5 more. How many did he have altogether?
Number sentence: 10 + 5 = ?
Answer: 15

What is five times five?
Number sentence: 5 x 5 = ?
Answer: 25

Eli had 20 shells. He gave 15 away. How many did he have left?
Number sentence: 20 – 15 = ?
Answer: 5

Share 20 grapes equally between 2 people.
Number sentence: 20 ÷ 2 = ?
Answer: 10

Write each word problem as a number sentence to show how you would work out the answer. Then write the answer.

Georgia had 5 birthday gifts. She received 5 more. How many did she have altogether?

① **Number sentence:** _____

② **Answer:** _____

What is six lots of two?

③ **Number sentence:** _____

④ **Answer:** _____

Jack had 20 balloons. Five balloons blew away. How many did he have left?

⑤ **Number sentence:** _____

⑥ **Answer:** _____

Share 18 cupcakes equally between two people.

⑦ **Number sentence:** _____

⑧ **Answer:** _____

Grammar & Punctuation

AC9E3LY06

Phonic Knowledge & Spelling

AC9E3LY10, AC9E3LY11

Nouns

Nouns are the names of things.
Common nouns are words used to name people, animals, places and things.
Examples: girl, builder, hill, city, house, rabbit, cafe, tree, brother, father

Circle the three nouns in each of the sentences below.

1. The elephant picked up the log with his trunk.
2. Our dog chased the cat up a tree.
3. There is a shop and a park near our school.
4. My brother and sister stayed with our uncle.

Proper nouns

Proper nouns are the names of particular people, places, objects and events. Proper nouns start with a **capital letter**.
Examples: Adelaide, Mrs Tyler, Indonesia, Olympic Games, Derwent River

Circle the three proper nouns in each of the sentences below.

5. Jack and Georgia live in Hobart.
6. In August, we are going to Singapore on a Qantas plane.
7. We do our shopping at Coles every Saturday or Sunday.
8. Tenzing Norgay and Edmund Hillary climbed to the top of Mount Everest.

Are these pirate words common or proper nouns? Write CN next to the common nouns and PN next to the proper nouns.

9. Jake ___
10. Captain Hook ___
11. anchor ___
12. flag ___
13. Caribbean ___
14. map ___
15. treasure ___
16. Pacific Ocean ___
17. Jolly Roger ___
18. chest ___
19. parrot ___
20. island ___
21. Blackbeard ___
22. buccaneer ___
23. Atlantic Ocean ___
24. Treasure Island ___

PIRATE PARROT

Vowel sounds – a e i o u

Say each word. What sound does the vowel make? Circle the word in red that has the same vowel sound as the others in the row.

1. catch hatch plant grant ape ant late
2. edge hedge cent went tent he she
3. list mist flip slip trick bike ice
4. lost cost clock block phone across rope
5. bunk trunk bump clump June sun tube

Choose words from the questions above to complete these sentences.

6. They _____ their shoes at the beach.
7. Mia _____ shopping with us yesterday.
8. The elephant's _____ came down with a thump.
9. We are making a _____ to see who can come to my party.

Plurals

Remember!
To make a word **plural** (more than one) you usually just add **–s**.
Examples: plant, plant**s**   clock, clock**s**
For words that end in **s**, **ss**, **sh** or **ch**, you add **–es** to make them plural.
Examples: gas, gas**es**   glass, glass**es**
               dish, dish**es**   church, church**es**

Write these words as plurals.

	one	more than one
10	bus	_____
11	watch	_____
12	class	_____
13	wish	_____
14	princess	_____
15	brush	_____
16	compass	_____
17	patch	_____
18	brooch	_____

Score 2 points for each correct answer! **SCORE** **/48** (0-22) (24-42) (44-48)

Score 2 points for each correct answer! **SCORE** **/36** (0-16) (18-30) (32-36)

TARGETING HOMEWORK 3 © PASCAL PRESS ISBN 9781925726459

Informative text – Report
Author – Frances Mackay

Australia

Australia is divided into six states
and two territories.

Australian Capital Territory (ACT)
South Australia (SA)
New South Wales (NSW)
Tasmania (Tas)
Northern Territory (NT)
Victoria (Vic)
Queensland (Qld)
Western Australia (WA)

The Australian Capital Territory
contains Australia's capital
city, Canberra. The ACT is
approximately 290 kilometres
south of Sydney.

The Northern Territory is right
at the top end of Australia.
Its capital city is Darwin. Alice
Springs is the main inland
town and Uluru (Ayers Rock)
and Kata Tjuta (The Olgas) are
famous landmarks found there.

Queensland is Australia's
second-largest state in size.
Its capital city is Brisbane.
The Great Barrier Reef is found
along the coast of Queensland.

New South Wales sits between
Queensland and Victoria.
Sydney is the capital of New
South Wales and its largest

city. Sydney has the famous
Sydney Harbour Bridge and
Sydney Opera House.

Victoria lies to the south of
New South Wales. The capital
of Victoria is Melbourne, which
is Australia's second-largest
city by population.

South Australia is in the centre
of Australia and sits below the
Northern Territory. Its capital
city is Adelaide.

Western Australia is Australia's
largest state by size. Its capital
city is Perth.

Tasmania is an island to
the south of Victoria. It is
Australia's smallest state by
size. The capital of Tasmania is
Hobart.

Write or circle the correct answers.

① The abbreviation for the Australian
Capital Territory is ACT. What is the
abbreviation for New South Wales?

a QLD

b NSW

c TAS

② What is the capital city of Australia?

a Sydney

b Brisbane

c Canberra

③ Name two well-known landmarks in the
Northern Territory.

_____

④ What is Australia's largest state by size?

_____

⑤ What is the name of Australia's second-
largest city by population?

_____

⑥ What is another word for **approximately**?

a exactly

b about

c located

**What is the capital city of each state and
territory?**

⑦ Australian Capital Territory _____

⑧ New South Wales _____

⑨ Northern Territory _____

⑩ Queensland _____

⑪ South Australia _____

⑫ Tasmania _____

⑬ Victoria _____

⑭ Western Australia _____

*Score 2 points for
each correct answer!*

SCORE **/28** (0-12) (14-22) (24-28)

My Book Review

Title _____

Author _____

Rating ☆☆☆☆☆

Comment _____

_____

Number & Algebra

AC9M3N03, AC9M3A02

Number Splitting

Numbers can be **split** to make them easy to add.
For 35 + 30, split 35 into 30 + 5 and then add.

$$35 + 30$$
$$30 + 30 + 5$$
$$60$$
$$65$$

Complete these number-splitting additions.

(1) 37 + 40 = [30] + [ ] + [7]

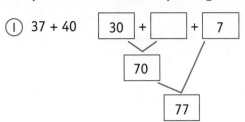

70

77

(2) 43 + 50 = [40] + [ ] + [ ]

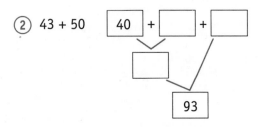

93

(3) 58 + 30 = [ ] + [ ] + [ ]

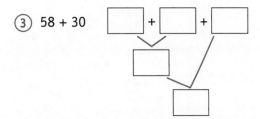

(4) 60 + 73 = [ ] + [ ] + [ ]

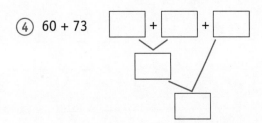

(5) 50 + 58 = [ ] + [ ] + [ ]

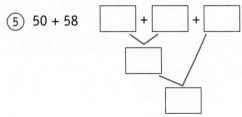

(6) 72 + 90 = [ ] + [ ] + [ ]

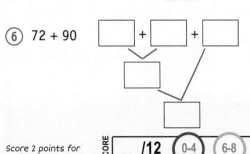

Score 2 points for each correct answer!

SCORE **/12** (0-4) (6-8) (10-12)

Statistics & Probability

AC9M3P02

How likely is it?

Some things are **certain** to happen.
Other things are **unlikely** or **impossible**.

Are these things certain or impossible?
Circle the correct answers.

(1) We will live forever.
  a certain   b impossible

(2) The day after Monday is Tuesday.
  a certain   b impossible

How likely is it that these things will happen when you flip a coin? Circle the correct answer.

(3) You will get a head.
  a very likely   b very unlikely

(4) You will get a tail.
  a very likely   b very unlikely

(5) You will get neither a head nor a tail.
  a very likely   b very unlikely

Show where these things should go on the likely scale. Write the numbers 6, 7, 8, 9 and 10 under the labels.

Likely scale

impossible   very unlikely   likely   very likely   certain

_____   _____   _____   _____   _____

(6) I will grow to be a dinosaur.

(7) Tomorrow I will be older than I am today.

(8) I will do some writing in school today.

(9) We will go on a school trip this year.

(10) Everyone in our class will go to bed at exactly the same time tonight.

Use the marbles to answer the questions. Circle the correct answers.

(11) Which colour marble are you **most likely** to pick without looking?
  a red   b blue   c green

(12) Which colour marble are you **most unlikely** to pick without looking?
  a red   b blue   c green

Score 2 points for each correct answer!

SCORE **/24** (0-10) (12-18) (20-24)

TARGETING HOMEWORK 3 © PASCAL PRESS ISBN 9781925726459

Coordinate grids

This is a **coordinate grid**.

The blue square is located at B5. To find it, go along the bottom to B, then up to 5.

The green triangle is located at E7. Go along the bottom to E, then up to 7.

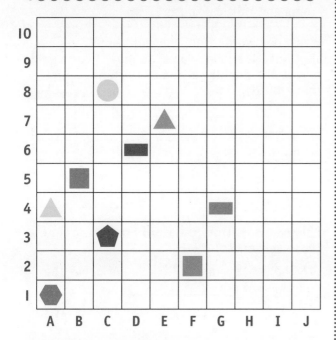

Circle the correct answers.

① **Which shape is at F2?**
   a red rectangle
   b green square
   c yellow circle

② **Which shape is at G4?**
   a yellow triangle
   b blue octagon
   c orange rectangle

③ **Which shape is at C3?**
   a red pentagon
   b yellow circle
   c blue square

Draw these shapes on the coordinate grid.

④ a blue triangle at H10
⑤ a red pentagon at D2
⑥ a yellow rectangle at J6
⑦ a green square at F5
⑧ an orange circle at D8

Score 2 points for each correct answer!

SCORE **/16** (0-6) (8-12) (14-16)

Number clues

Solve these word problems.

① Add two numbers together and the total is 13. The difference between the two numbers is 3. What are the two numbers?

☐ and ☐

② Add two numbers together and the total is 17. The difference between the two numbers is 1. What are the two numbers?

☐ and ☐

③ Double a number then add 3 and the answer is 11. What is the number?

☐

④ Halve a number then add 3 and the answer is 8. What is the number?

☐

⑤ Multiply two numbers together and the answer is 18. The difference between the two numbers is 3. What are the two numbers?

☐ and ☐

⑥ Add two numbers together and the total is 11. Multiply the two numbers together and the answer ends in 0. What are the two numbers?

☐ and ☐

Grammar & Punctuation

AC9E3LY06

Compound nouns

TERM 1 ENGLISH

> **Compound nouns** are two nouns joined together to make one word.
> *Examples*: sea + **shore** = sea**shore**
> toad + **stool** = toad**stool**

Circle the two compound nouns in each sentence.

① Mum got some earrings for her birthday.

② We carried the toolbox into the workroom.

③ A huge sunflower was growing in the greenhouse.

④ Something fell out of the newspaper.

Join the two words together to make compound nouns. Write the new words on the lines. The first words have been done for you.

book + shelf = bookshelf

⑤ case _____

⑥ shop _____

⑦ keeper _____

head + ache = headache

⑧ light _____

⑨ lines _____

⑩ band _____

Write 6 compound nouns using words from the word bank.

water	man	wheel	ball	tooth	rail
basket	brush	melon	snow	arm	lid
chair	way	eye	coat	rain	pit

⑪ _____   ⑭ _____

⑫ _____   ⑮ _____

⑬ _____   ⑯ _____

Commas

> **Commas (,)** are used to show the reader where to make a small break between words. Commas are used to separate items in a list.
> *Example:* I like football, baseball, cricket and hockey.

Add the missing commas in these sentences.

⑰ We bought fruit bread milk and butter at the shop.

⑱ There were trees flowers and statues in the park.

Score 2 points for each correct answer! **SCORE** /36 (0-16) (18-30) (32-36)

Phonic Knowledge & Spelling

AC9E3LY09, AC9E3LY10

Words with double letters

All the words from the word bank below have **double letters** in the middle. Say each word once.

sudden	pepper	ribbon	nugget	soccer
bottle	middle	shuffle	dribble	huddle
sniffle	bubble	ripple	struggle	wriggle
happen	traffic	bitter		

Write two words from the word bank that have the **same vowel sound before the double letters** as each of these words.

① fiddle _____ _____

② letter _____ _____

③ hotter _____ _____

④ puddle _____ _____

⑤ fatter _____ _____

Choose words from the word bank to complete these sentences.

⑥ The police siren could be heard above the sound of the _____.

⑦ The _____ fell down and shattered.

Syllables

> **Syllables** are chunks of sounds in words. We can tell how many chunks of sounds there are in a word by clapping the beats.

Each word from the word bank has 2 syllables. How many syllables do each of these words have?

⑧ phone _____   ⑩ book _____

⑨ rabbit _____   ⑪ netball _____

Plurals

> **Remember!** To make a word plural (more than one) you usually just add **–s**. For words that end in x, z or zz, you add **–es** to make them plural.
> *Examples:* box, box**es**   waltz, waltz**es**
> **NOTE:** Some words do not follow the rules, such as ox (oxen) and quiz (quizzes).

Write these words as plurals.

⑫ fox _____   ⑮ annex_____

⑬ fizz _____   ⑯ fax _____

⑭ topaz _____   ⑰ lynx _____

Score 2 points for each correct answer! **SCORE** /34 (0-14) (16-28) (30-34)

Living Things

All living things can do these seven things:

Glossary table
Author – Frances Mackay

TERM 1 ENGLISH

	Other name	What this means
Movement	moving	All animals can move. Even plants can move, but they move very slowly. Some plants grow towards the light. Plants with petals can open and close them.
Respiration	breathing	Animals breathe in oxygen and breathe out carbon dioxide. Plants do not breathe in the same way as animals — they take in carbon dioxide and give off oxygen.
Sensitivity	responding to things	Plants and animals can respond to things. Humans use five senses — taste, sight, hearing, touch and smell. Plants can respond to light (stems grow towards light) and gravity (roots grow down). Some plants move when you touch them.
Growth	growing	All plants and animals can grow and get bigger. A seed can grow into a tall tree. Animals have babies that grow into adults.
Reproduction	having babies	All plants and animals can make more of themselves. Plants can have seeds. Animals have babies.
Excretion	getting rid of wastes	Humans get rid of waste when they go to the toilet. They also give off waste when they breathe and sweat. Plants give off wastes when they breathe too.
Nutrition	food	All living things need food to grow and stay alive. Green plants can make their own food. Animals eat their food.

Write or circle the correct answers.

① **What is another name for breathing?**

a excretion   b respiration

② **What gas do animals breathe in?**

_____

③ **Name the five senses that humans use.**

_____

_____

④ **What does the word light mean when it is used to describe how plants respond?**

a sunlight   b not heavy

⑤ **True or false? All plants and animals can grow and get bigger.**

a True   b False

⑥ **What is one way that plants can move?**

_____

⑦ **Which of these statements are true?**

a Green plants can make their own food.
b Animals breathe out oxygen.
c All living things need food to stay alive.
d Plants are not able to move.

⑧ **Write one reason why a car is not a living thing.**

_____

⑨ **What does getting rid of wastes mean?**

a losing weight, getting thinner

b doing away with things that are not needed

List the seven things that all living things can do.

⑩ _____

⑪ _____

⑫ _____

⑬ _____

⑭ _____

⑮ _____

⑯ _____

Score 2 points for each correct answer!

SCORE **/32** (0-14) (16-26) (28-32)

My Book Review

Title _____

Author _____

Rating ☆☆☆☆☆

Comment _____

_____

TERM 1 MATHS

Numbers that add up to 10

There are five pairs of numbers that add together to make **10**.

1 + 9   2 + 8   3 + 7   4 + 6   5 + 5

Fill in the missing numbers.

① 5 + ____ = 10

② 4 + ____ = 10

③ 2 + ____ = 10

④ 1 + ____ = 10

⑤ 3 + ____ = 10

⑥ 6 + ____ = 10

⑦ 8 + ____ = 10

⑧ 9 + ____ = 10

⑨ 7 + ____ = 10

Looking for the pairs that add up to 10 can make adding easier.

Examples: 8 + 9 + 2 = ?

First add the 8 and 2 to make 10.
Then add the 9 to make 19.

4 + 9 + 6 + 1 = ?

Add the 4 and 6 (10), then add 9 and 1 (10) to make 20.

Write the answers. Look for pairs that make 10.

⑩ 7 + 6 + 3 = ____

⑪ 5 + 9 + 5 + 1 = ____

⑫ 4 + 7 + 6 = ____

⑬ 8 + 3 + 2 + 7 + 5 = ____

⑭ 1 + 5 + 9 + 5 = ____

⑮ 4 + 9 + 1 + 6 + 7 + 2 + 8 + 3 = ____

Knowing the addition facts helps with subtraction too. Write the answers.

⑯ 10 − ____ = 9

⑰ 10 − ____ = 5

⑱ 10 − ____ = 2

⑲ 10 − ____ = 6

⑳ 10 − ____ = 7

㉑ 10 − ____ = 4

Numbers that add up to 20

These are the addition facts that make **20**.

10 + 10   11 + 9   12 + 8   13 + 7   14 + 6
15 + 5   16 + 4   17 + 3   18 + 2   19 + 1

Write the answers. Use the addition facts for 20 to help.

㉒ 12 + ____ = 20

㉓ 14 + ____ = 20

㉔ 11 + ____ = 20

㉕ 8 + ____ = 20

㉖ 6 + ____ = 20

㉗ 9 + ____ = 20

㉘ 20 − ____ = 12

㉙ 20 − ____ = 14

㉚ 20 − ____ = 11

㉛ 20 − ____ = 8

㉜ 20 − ____ = 6

㉝ 20 − ____ = 9

Write the answers. Look for pairs that make 20.

㉞ 6 + 9 + 14 = ____

㉟ 3 + 8 + 12 = ____

㊱ 15 + 8 + 5 = ____

㊲ 19 + 7 + 1 = ____

㊳ 12 plus 7 plus 8 = ____

㊴ 13 and 4 and 7 = ____

Use number facts to help you add larger numbers.

Examples: 36 + 8 = ?

4   4

Split 8 into two 4s.
Use one 4 to add to the 36. 36 + 4 = 40.
Then add the remaining 4 to 40 to make 44.

64 plus 9 = ?

Split 9 into 6 and 3. 64 + 6 = 70.
Add the remaining 3 to make 73.

Complete these additions.
Show how you worked out the answers.

㊵ 48 + 6

㊶ 83 plus 8

㊷ 79 and 5

㊸ 45 + 9

Score 2 points for each correct answer!

SCORE /86   0-40   42-80   82-86

Statistics & Probability

There are no statistics & probability activities in this unit.

TARGETING HOMEWORK 3 © PASCAL PRESS ISBN 9781925726459

Measurement & Space

AC9M3M04

Time

What is the time? Circle the correct answer.

①
a 12 o'clock
b 8 o'clock
c 20 to 12

②
a $\frac{1}{4}$ past 6
b $\frac{1}{2}$ past 6
c $\frac{1}{4}$ to 6

③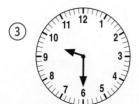
a $\frac{1}{2}$ past 10
b $\frac{1}{2}$ past 9
c $\frac{1}{2}$ past 6

④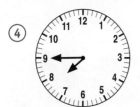
a $\frac{1}{4}$ to 9
b $\frac{1}{4}$ past 8
c $\frac{1}{4}$ to 8

How many minutes?

⑤ 1 hour = _____ mins

⑥ $\frac{1}{2}$ hour = _____ mins

⑦ $\frac{1}{4}$ hour = _____ mins

Circle the matching time.

⑧ 6:15
a 15 minutes to 6
b 15 minutes past 6

⑨ 5:30
a 30 minutes past 5
b 30 minutes to 5

⑩ 6:45
a 15 minutes to 7
b 15 minutes past 6

⑪ 7:25
a 25 minutes past 7
b 25 minutes to 8

Draw the hands on the clock faces to show the times.

⑫ $\frac{1}{2}$ past 10

⑮ 10 past 8
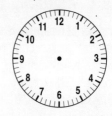

⑬ $\frac{1}{4}$ past 3

⑯ 25 past 11

⑭ $\frac{1}{4}$ to 12

⑰ 25 to 4
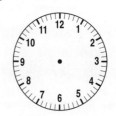

Score 2 points for each correct answer!

SCORE /34 0-14 16-28 30-34

Problem Solving

AC9M3A02

Making links to 20

How many numbers that add up to **20** can you find in the puzzle?

You can add 2, 3 or more numbers together. Any number can be used more than once. You can join them in any direction.

One has been done for you.

10	6	1	2	18	11	4
5	12	11	19	10	15	
13	2	9	7	14	6	3
16	8	9	17	19	2	
1	4	10	5	2	12	9
3	4	8	6	1	7	
18	1	1	10	13	6	3
9	11	4	12	10	18	

TERM 1 ENGLISH

Grammar & Punctuation

AC9E3LA07

Verbs

Every sentence has a **verb**. Verbs are words that tell us what is happening in a sentence. They tell us what the subject of the sentence is doing, thinking, saying and feeling.

Examples: <u>The horse</u> ran down the street.
'The horse' is the subject. What was the horse doing? It **ran**.

Every Saturday, <u>Peter</u> **plays football.**
'Peter' is the subject. What does Peter do? He **plays**.

Underline the subject of each sentence. Then circle the verb.

① The rubber ball rolled down the road.

② Li sings very loudly!

③ Mum shut the front door.

④ Zac hates computer games.

Choose verbs from the box to complete these sentences.

closed	wrote	saw	shaped	bites

⑤ Mrs Baker _____ the door quietly.

⑥ My dog _____ my hand when we play.

⑦ Firstly, the potter _____ the clay with his wet hands.

⑧ The author _____ a story about a lost child.

⑨ At the zoo, we _____ lots of animals from Africa.

Circle the best verb to replace the word in bold.

⑩ Vania **yelled** at him to stop.
   laughed   shouted   sang

⑪ "Lunch is ready," **said** Sara.
   cooked   talked   announced

⑫ The man tried to **hit** the nail with a hammer.
   strike   bend   draw

⑬ I **think** it will rain.
   want   hate   reckon

Phonic Knowledge & Spelling

AC9E3LY10, AC9E3LY11

Long vowel sounds

Say each word from the word bank. Note that each word ends in an **e**. Usually, when a word has an **e** at the end, the e works together with the other vowel to make a **long vowel sound**.

Examples: In the word **game**, the **a** and **e** work together to make the **ae** sound.

The **ae** is split by the letter **m**.

Word Bank

game	flame	tape	shape	face
life	knife	bite	write	mice
hose	close	phone	stone	smoke
tube	cube	cute	flute	rule

Write two words from the word bank that have the same vowel sound as each of these words.

① nine _____ _____

② vote _____ _____

③ snake _____ _____

④ prune _____ _____

Choose words from the word bank to complete these sentences.

⑤ Two fat _____ scurried across the kitchen floor.

⑥ One of the mice hid inside an empty paper towel _____.

⑦ Our cat saw the other mouse and tried to _____ it.

⑧ Mum saw what the cat had done and threw her mobile _____ at it!

Adding –ed and –ing

When a word ends in **e**, you usually take off the e before adding –ing and –ed.

Examples: **close, closed, closing**
phone, phoned, phoning

Add –ed and –ing to these words.

	–ed	–ing
⑨ rule	_____	_____
⑩ vote	_____	_____
⑪ raise	_____	_____
⑫ hope	_____	_____
⑬ race	_____	_____
⑭ move	_____	_____
⑮ taste	_____	_____

Score 2 points for each correct answer! SCORE **/26** 0-10 12-20 22-26

Score 2 points for each correct answer! SCORE **/30** 0-12 14-24 26-30

Imaginative text – Poem
Author – Stewart Mackay

Machines

Moving
Lifting
Folding
Splitting
Inward, outward
Loading, shipping
Digging
Cutting
Slicing
Welding
Upward, downward
Forest felling
Pump it
Push it
Throw it
Roll it
Painting, spraying
Wash it, hose it
Sowing
Reaping
Growing
Crushing
Never ending
Always rushing

③ What types of words does the author use to describe how the machines work?

a nouns

b verbs

c adjectives

④ What is another word for **reaping**?

a cooking

b heating

c gathering

⑤ Which one of these is the odd word out?

a crushing

b smoothing

c squashing

Which four words from the box are verbs that can describe machines?

| like | hit | bang | yell | swim | drill | sing | chop |

⑥ _____ it

⑦ _____ it

⑧ _____ it

⑨ _____ it

Score 2 points for each correct answer!

SCORE **/18** 0-6 8-14 16-18

Write or circle the correct answers.

① Read the poem and clap out the beats in the words. Does the poem use a two-syllable or three-syllable beat?

_____

② What effect does the use of this beat create in the poem?

_____

My Book Review

Title _____

Author _____

Rating ☆☆☆☆☆

Comment _____

_____

Number & Algebra

AC9M3N02

Fractions

> When we share an object into equal parts, each part is called a **fraction**.
>
> *Examples*:
>
>
>
> This circle is cut into 2 equal parts. Each part is a half ($\frac{1}{2}$) of the whole circle.
>
> This circle is cut into 4 equal parts. Each part is a quarter ($\frac{1}{4}$) of the whole circle.

What fraction of the whole shape is the shaded area? Circle the correct answer.

①   a $\frac{1}{4}$ b $\frac{1}{2}$ c $\frac{2}{4}$

②   a $\frac{1}{4}$ b $\frac{2}{4}$ c $\frac{3}{4}$

③   a $\frac{1}{4}$ b $\frac{2}{4}$ c $\frac{3}{4}$

④   a $\frac{2}{4}$ b $\frac{2}{2}$ c $\frac{1}{2}$

Divide (partition) and colour each shape to show the fraction.

⑤ $\frac{2}{4}$ ⑥ $\frac{1}{2}$ ⑦ $\frac{3}{4}$

Fraction number lines

> This number line shows counting in **halves**. The line is divided into **two equal parts**.
>
> 0 $\frac{1}{2}$ 1
>
> This number line shows counting in **quarters**. The line is divided into **four equal parts**.
>
> 0 $\frac{1}{4}$ $\frac{2}{4}$ $\frac{3}{4}$ 1

Mark each fraction on the number line.

⑧ $\frac{1}{2}$ 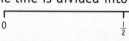 0   1

⑨ $\frac{3}{4}$ 0   1

⑩ $\frac{2}{4}$ 0   1

Statistics & Probability

AC9M3P02

Probability

Use the spinner to answer the questions.

① Is the spinner **more likely** to land on 1 or 3? _____

② Is the spinner **more likely** to land on 1 or 2? _____

③ Which number is the spinner **most likely** to land on? _____

④ Which number is the spinner **least likely** to land on? _____

⑤ How possible is it for the spinner to land on 4? Certain or impossible? _____

> Tarka made a tally chart to show the colours of the counters he had in a box.
>
> | Colour | Tally |
> |--------|-------|
> | red | IIII |
> | blue | II |
> | orange | HHH IIII |
> | green | HHH |

Use the tally chart to answer the question. Write or circle the correct answers.

⑥ How many counters does Tarka have, altogether? ____

Tarka keeps the counters in a box. He took out one counter, without looking.

⑦ What colour is the counter most likely to be?

   a red   b orange   c blue   d green

⑧ What colour is the counter least likely to be?

   a red   b orange   c blue   d green

⑨ Is he more likely to take out a red counter or a blue counter?

   a red   b blue

⑩ How likely is it that he will take out a yellow counter?

   a impossible   c likely

   b unlikely   d certain

⑪ What chance does he have of taking out a green counter?

   a 4 in 20   c 9 in 20

   b 2 in 20   d 5 in 20

TARGETING HOMEWORK 3 © PASCAL PRESS ISBN 9781925726459

Measurement & Space

AC9M3M02

Kilograms (kg) and grams (g)

Mass or **weight** is measured in **grams** and **kilograms**.

A paperclip weighs approximately 1 gram.

A 1 litre bottle of water weighs approximately 1 kilogram.

1 kg = 1000 g 1 kilogram = 1000 grams

$\frac{1}{2}$ kg = 500 g half of a kilogram = 500 grams

$\frac{1}{4}$ kg = 250 g quarter of a kilogram = 250 grams

Circle the correct answer.

① 2000 g = a 2 kg b $2\frac{1}{2}$ kg c 20 kg

② 500 g = a 1 kg b $\frac{1}{2}$ kg c 5 kg

③ 4000 g = a 40 kg b 4 kg c 400 kg

④ 4500 g = a $4\frac{1}{2}$ kg b 45 kg c 4 kg

⑤ 250 g = a 25 kg b $\frac{1}{4}$ kg c $2\frac{1}{4}$ kg

⑥ 1250 g = a $1\frac{1}{4}$ kg b 125 kg c 12 kg

Write the masses in the short way.

⑦ 5 kilograms _____

⑧ 12 kilograms _____

⑨ six kilograms _____

⑩ twenty kilograms _____

⑪ 40 kilograms _____

⑫ thirty kilograms _____

Work out these masses.

⑬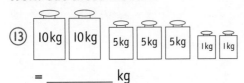

= _____ kg

⑭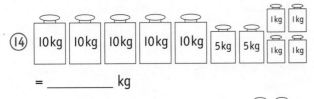

= _____ kg

⑮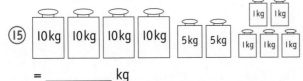

= _____ kg

Colour the weights to show these masses.

⑯ 10kg 10kg 10kg 10kg 10kg 5kg 5kg 1kg 1kg 1kg 1kg

26 kg

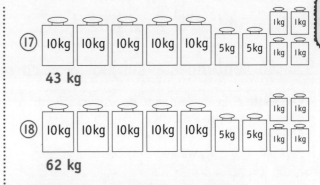

⑰ 10kg 10kg 10kg 10kg 10kg 5kg 5kg 1kg 1kg 1kg 1kg

43 kg

⑱ 10kg 10kg 10kg 10kg 10kg 5kg 5kg 1kg 1kg 1kg 1kg

62 kg

Estimate the mass of each animal. Choose from the masses in the box.

19 g	720 kg	330 g
4 kg	5400 kg	140 000 kg

⑲ _____

㉒ _____

⑳ _____

㉓ _____

㉑ _____

㉔ _____

Score 2 points for each correct answer! **SCORE** /48 0-22 24-42 44-48

Problem Solving

AC9M3N02

The square puzzle

How many different ways can you divide a **square** into **four equal parts**? Use a ruler to help you. Draw your results here.

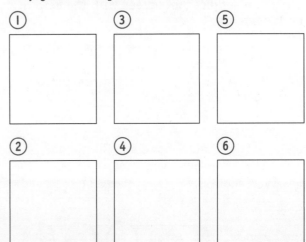

① ③ ⑤

② ④ ⑥

Grammar & Punctuation

AC9E3LA06, AC9E3LY06

Simple sentences – subject & verb

> **Remember!** Every sentence has a subject and a **verb**. A **simple sentence** has <u>one subject</u> and one **verb**.
>
> *Example*: <u>The cows</u> **walked** to the milking shed.
>   <small>subject</small>   <small>verb</small>

Underline the subject in each sentence. Then circle the verb.

1. I bought a new telescope.
2. My uncle rides a scooter.
3. Yesterday, we went to the zoo.
4. A woman on a horse galloped past my car.

Subject–verb agreement

> A **clause** is a group of words that contains a <u>subject</u> and a **verb**. The subject and verb need to agree in number. This means that a <u>singular subject</u> has a **singular verb** and a <u>plural subject</u> has a **plural verb**.
>
> *Examples*: (singular) <u>The mouse</u> **likes** cheese.
>   <u>The girl</u> **is running** fast.
>   (plural) <u>The mice</u> **like** cheese.
>   <u>The girls</u> **are running** fast.

Circle the correct verb to complete each sentence.

5. My dog _____ at cats.
   (*bark   barks*)
6. My sister _____ the best dancer.
   (*is   am*)
7. Josh _____ how to change a tyre.
   (*know   knows*)
8. The children _____ football.
   (*is playing   are playing*)
9. Zara _____ the race.
   (*are watching   is watching*)
10. Cooper and Mica _____ rugby.
    (*likes   like*)

Circle the subject that agrees with the verb in each sentence.

11. _____ works in a cafe on the weekends.
    (*Jai   My sisters*)
12. After school, _____ feeds the animals.
    (*Chloe   my brothers*)
13. _____ belong to us.
    (*Those books   That pencil*)
14. _____ plant flowers in the spring.
    (*My gran   Emily and Dylan*)
15. Every night, _____ sleeps on the bed.
    (*the cat   the cats*)

Score 2 points for each correct answer! **SCORE** /30 (0-12) (14-24) (26-30)

Phonic Knowledge & Spelling

AC9E3LY10, AC9E3LY11

Long vowel sounds

Say each word from the word bank below.

Word Bank

bake	shake	page	stage	late
ride	slide	dine	shine	twice
hole	whole	joke	broke	rose
use	excuse	tune	dune	duke

Write two words from the word bank that have the same vowel sound as these words.

1. fluke _____ _____
2. wrote _____ _____
3. lake _____ _____
4. while _____ _____

Choose words from the word bank to complete these sentences.

5. Please _____ those scuffed shoes.
6. These socks have a _____ in them.
7. Dad was _____ getting home last night.
8. We were going to _____ cupcakes for my birthday.

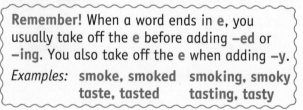

Adding –y

> **Remember!** When a word ends in **e**, you usually take off the **e** before adding **–ed** or **–ing**. You also take off the **e** when adding **–y**.
>
> *Examples*: smoke, smoked smoking, smoky
>   taste, tasted   tasting, tasty

Add –ed to these words.

9. use _____
10. excuse _____
11. dine _____
12. stage _____
13. tune _____
14. joke _____

Add –ing to these words.

15. shake _____
16. make _____
17. slide _____
18. ride _____
19. use _____
20. shine _____

Add –y to these words.

21. rose _____
22. taste _____
23. bone _____
24. slime _____
25. ice _____
26. laze _____

Score 2 points for each correct answer! **SCORE** /52 (0-24) (26-46) (48-52)

AC9E3LY05, AC9HS3K02

Informative text – Report
Author – Carolyn Tate

Anzac Day

Anzac Day is a chance to remember Australians who served and died during war and active duty. It is on 25 April.

Anzac stands for Australian and New Zealand Army Corps. The date marks when soldiers from Australia and New Zealand (Anzacs) left to fight in World War I in 1915.

The soldiers fought at Gallipoli, Turkey, against Turkish soldiers. The battle lasted eight months and more than 8000 Anzacs died. Thousands more were injured.

On Anzac Day, people gather at dawn. They wait in silence for two minutes to remember those who died. A soldier plays the *Last Post* on a bugle.

On Anzac Day, some people wear a red poppy or place poppies on memorials, to show their respect.

Source: *Symbols & Celebrations*, Go Facts, Blake Education.

TERM 1 ENGLISH

Write or circle the correct answers.

① On what date every year does Anzac Day take place?

_____

② What does Anzac stand for?

_____

③ List three things that happen on Anzac Day.

_____

_____

_____

④ What is another word for **respect**?

a regard

b joy

c fear

⑤ What is a **memorial**?

a a paved area in a park

b a statue or structure built to remember an event

c a memory

⑥ Where is Gallipoli?_____

⑦ What happened there during World War I?

_____

_____

_____

⑧ What does the word **marks** mean in this text?

a dirty spots

b commemorates

c lines

Score 2 points for each correct answer! SCORE **/16** (0-6) (8-12) (14-16)

My Book Review

Title _____

Author _____

Rating ☆☆☆☆☆

Comment _____

_____

AC9M3N07, AC9M3A01

TERM 1 MATHS

Numbers to 1000

Write the missing numbers.

① 100, 101, 102, 103, 104, _____, _____, _____

② 523, _____, _____, 526, _____, _____, _____, 530

③ 600, 599, 598, 597, _____, _____, _____, _____

④ 460, 458, 456, 454, _____, _____, _____, 446

How do you write these numbers using digits? Circle the correct answer.

⑤ five hundred and sixty-four
  a 5064   b 564   c 50 064

⑥ eight hundred and eighty
  a 880   b 8008   c 80 080

⑦ one hundred and ninety-nine
  a 109   b 199   c 10 099

Write these numbers in order from smallest to largest.

⑧   682   598   349   872

  _____ _____ _____ _____

⑨   990   900   989   980

  _____ _____ _____ _____

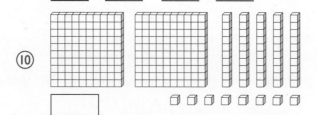

⑩

What numbers do these hundreds, tens and ones make?

⑪ 5 hundreds, 7 tens and 4 ones   _____

⑫ 2 hundreds, 5 tens and 8 ones   _____

⑬ 9 tens + 9 ones   _____

⑭ 1512 tens + 6 ones   _____

Numbers that add up to 100

> Here are some addition facts to **100**.
> 10 + 90   20 + 80   30 + 70   40 + 60   50 + 50

Complete. Use the addition facts to help you.

⑮ 20 + _____ = 100

⑯ 90 + _____ = 100

⑰ 60 + _____ = 100

⑱ 100 − _____ = 70

⑲ 100 − _____ = 20

⑳ 100 − _____ = 50

Write the answers. Look for pairs that make 100.

㉑ 60 + 5 + 40 = _____

㉒ 7 + 80 + 20 = _____

㉓ 70 plus 9 plus 30 = _____

㉔ 50 and 4 and 50 = _____

Adding larger numbers

> Use **partitioning** to help you add larger numbers.
> *Example:*   376 + 9 = ?
>
>   ╱╲
>   4 and 5
>
> Split 9 into 4 and 5. Add the 4 to 376 to make 380. Then add the 5 to 380 to make 385.

㉕   487 + 6 = ?   ㉖   729 + 8 = ?

> Here's another way to use **partitioning** to add larger numbers.
>
>   7 6   +   2 3   = ?
>   ╱ ╲   ╱ ╲
>   70 6   20 3
>   70 + 20 = 90
>   6 + 3 = 9
>   90 + 9 = 99

Add these numbers using partitioning. Show your working out.

㉗ 65 + 32   ㉘ 56 + 33

TARGETING HOMEWORK 3 © PASCAL PRESS ISBN 9781925726459

Addition and subtraction number facts

You can use **addition facts** to help with **subtraction**. If you know that **6 + 7 = 13** then you can easily work out **13 − 7** and **13 − 6** because they are related.

Complete the additions and subtractions.

㉙ 8 + 9 = 17   17 − ☐ = 9

               17 − ☐ = 8

㉚ 9 + 6 = ☐   ☐ − ☐ = 6

               ☐ − ☐ = 9

㉛ 24 + 8 = ☐   ☐ − 8 = ☐

               ☐ − ☐ = 8

㉜ 36 + 9 = ☐   ☐ − 9 = ☐

               ☐ − ☐ = 9

㉝ 47 + 11 = ☐   ☐ − ☐ = 47

               ☐ − ☐ = 11

Write an addition fact that helps with each subtraction.

㉞ 18 − 11   ☐ + 11 = 18

㉟ 27 − 14   ☐ + ☐ = 27

㊱ 36 − 9   ☐ + ☐ = 36

㊲ 23 − 14   ☐ + ☐ = 23

㊳ 101 − 9   ☐ + ☐ = 101

Score 2 points for each correct answer! **SCORE** **/76** (0-34) (36-70) (72-76)

Statistics & Probability

There are no statistics & probability activities in this unit.

Measurement & Space

There are no measurement & space activities in this unit.

Problem Solving

AC9M3N07

Number riddles

What number am I?
Circle the correct answer in the cloud.

①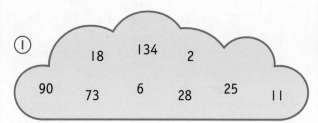

18   134   2
90   73   6   28   25   11

Clues:
- I am an even number.
- I am less than 100 but more than 20.
- Double me is less than 60.

②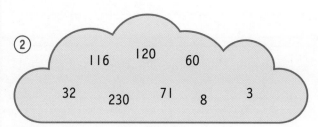

116   120   60
32   230   71   8   3

Clues:
- I am less than 68 + 99.
- I am more than 42 + 12.
- I am an even number less than 62.

③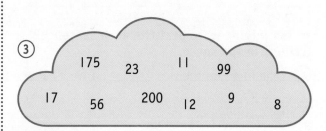

175   23   11   99
17   56   200   12   9   8

Clues:
- I am an odd number.
- I am less than 6 × 2.
- I am a multiple of 3.

④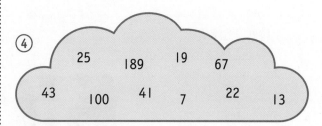

25   189   19   67
43   100   41   7   22   13

Clues:
- I am an odd number.
- I am less than 23 + 18.
- If you add my digits together, you get 10.

TERM 1 ENGLISH

Grammar & Punctuation

AC9E3LA06, AC9E3LY06

Compound sentences

A **compound sentence** is made up of two simple sentences joined by a joining word.

Joining words (also called **conjunctions**) include **and, but, so, because, then** and **while**.

Examples: We can go to the cinema tomorrow **or** we can go next week.

I went to the supermarket **because** I needed some apples.

Join each pair of sentences. Choose from and, but, so or because. Write the new sentence underneath.

① Mum had a bad cold. She could not go to work.

_____

_____

② The man chased the dog. He did not catch it.

_____

_____

③ We went to the park. We walked around the lake.

_____

_____

Which joining word best fits each sentence? Write it in the space.

④ I could go on the ride _____ I were taller.
   (*and   if*)

⑤ Do you like tea _____ coffee?
   (*so   or*)

⑥ I cannot fall asleep _____ I'm in bed.
   (*unless   because*)

⑦ We stayed at the party _____ Dad picked us up. (*or   until*)

⑧ Galahs, cockatoos _____ emus are birds.
   (*but   and*)

⑨ We were late for school _____ we slept in. (*because   if*)

Phonic Knowledge & Spelling

AC9E3LY09, AC9E3LY10

Syllables

Say each word from the word bank below. Clap out the beats of each word as you say it. They each have two beats, or two **syllables**.

Word Bank

tiger	secret	pirate	spider
robot	paper	silent	pretend
stable	staple	rifle	title
nation	station	lotion	notion

Circle the words that have two syllables.

① awake   new   because   potion
② work   trifle   often   mobile
③ table   ale   motion   plate

Choose words from the word bank to complete these sentences.

④ I often put sun _____ on my face.

⑤ I put the _____ outside because it was making cobwebs everywhere.

⑥ The new railway _____ was built in three months.

⑦ Spies carry out top _____ work.

Words ending in –tion

Words that end in **–tion** make a **shun** sound. Read the words from the word bank above that end in **–tion**.

Here are some **–tion** words. Match each word from the box to its meaning. The first one has been done for you.

position	solution	suction
addition	relation	fiction

Meaning		Word
part of a whole		fraction
⑧ stories that are made up		_____
⑨ someone who belongs to your family		_____
⑩ adding things together		_____
⑪ the answer to a problem		_____
⑫ sucking in liquid or air		_____
⑬ the place where something is		_____

Score 2 points for each correct answer! | SCORE | **/18** | 0-6 | 8-14 | 16-18

Score 2 points for each correct answer! | SCORE | **/26** | 0-10 | 12-20 | 22-26

TARGETING HOMEWORK 3 © PASCAL PRESS ISBN 9781925726459

Persuasive text – Discussion
Author – Ian Rohr

Drought in Australia

Many believe that farmers in harsh, dry regions of Australia should quit the land, as it is unsuited to farming. Others believe that changing irrigation practices would help.

Abandon the land

Many have suggested farmers abandon their land, considering them crazy for staying when droughts are inevitable. When it rains, things are good, but in drought farmers get into debt, as they have no crops and their hungry, thirsty livestock need food and water.

If the drought is severe, they may lose their livestock and income. This means borrowing more money.

Changing for the better

There are others who believe things could be better if farmers planted more trees and plants. Farmers would increase the moisture in the soil, as vegetation holds moisture. They also believe water flow on the land is important. By creating creeks and channels similar to pre-European settlement, the land could be irrigated naturally.

Source: *Fire & Drought*, Go Facts, Blake Education.

Write or circle the correct answers.

> A **fact** is something that can be proven to be true.
> *Example*: Florence Nightingale was born on 12 May 1820.
>
> An **opinion** cannot be proven.
> An opinion is a thought or a belief.
> *Example*: Florence Nightingale is a lovely name.

Are these statements facts or opinions?

1. Farmers in harsh, dry regions of Australia should quit the land.   (fact   opinion)

2. Drought occurs in Australia. (fact   opinion)

3. During a drought, farmers may lose their livestock and income.   (fact   opinion)

4. Farmers should only farm in regions that do not experience drought.   (fact   opinion)

5. **What is another word for inevitable?**
   a unlikely
   b certain
   c necessary

6. **List two things that can happen to farmers during a drought.**
   _____
   _____

7. **What is the meaning of debt?**
   a to become rich
   b unhappy
   c to owe money

8. **How might planting more trees help farmers in drought regions?**
   a More wildlife will come to the area.
   b The moisture in the soil will increase.
   c The trees will shade the crops.

9. **The word irrigated means to supply water to crops to help them grow. How could the land be irrigated naturally?**
   _____
   _____

Score 2 points for each correct answer!   SCORE   **/18**   0-6   8-14   16-18

My Book Review

Title _____

Author _____

Rating ☆ ☆ ☆ ☆ ☆

Comment _____
_____

Number & Algebra

AC9M3N01

TERM 1 MATHS

Counting in 10s

0 10 20 30 40 50 60 70 80 90 100

Write the missing numbers.

① 10, 20, 30, 40, 50, 60, ____, ____, ____, 100

② ____, ____, ____, 60, 70, 80, 90

③ 100, 90, ____, ____, ____, 50, 40, 30

Write the correct answers.

④ 50 + 10 = _____   ⑦ 80 − 10 = _____

⑤ 30 + 10 = _____   ⑧ 100 − 10 = _____

⑥ 80 + 10 = _____   ⑨ 10 + 10 = _____

Counting in 100s

Write the missing numbers.

⑩ 100, 200, 300, 400, _____, _____, _____, 800, 900, 1000

⑪ _____, _____, _____, 900, 1000, 1100, 1200

⑫ 800, 700, 600, _____, _____, _____, 200, 100

⑬ 1000, 900, 800, 700, 600, 500, _____, _____, _____, 100

Write the correct answers.

⑭ 400 + 100 = _____   ⑰ 800 − 100 = _____

⑮ 600 + 100 = _____   ⑱ 400 − 100 = _____

⑯ 800 + 100 = _____   ⑲ 1000 − 100 = _____

Numbers larger than 1000

Write how many thousands, hundreds, tens and ones.

	thousands	hundreds	tens	ones
1542	1	5	4	2
3984	3	9	8	4
⑳ 2397				
㉑ 8419				
㉒ 6041				

Write these numbers.

㉓ Five thousands, two hundreds, three tens and four ones = _____

㉔ Eight thousands, four hundreds, zero tens and eight ones = _____

Score 2 points for each correct answer!   SCORE /48 (0-22) (22-42) (44-48)

28

Statistics & Probability

AC9M3ST03

Bar graphs

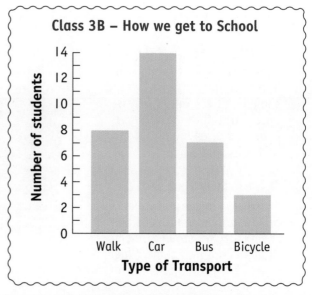

Class 3B – How we get to School

Answer the questions about the bar graph. Circle or write the correct answers.

① How many children walk to school?
a 10   b 8   c 7   d 3

② How many children catch a bus to school?
a 8   b 3   c 7   d 14

③ How do most children in class 3B get to school?
a walk   b car   c bus   d bicycle

④ How many children are there in class 3B?
_____

⑤ Use the information in the box to complete the bar chart.

Pets in Class 3B:
cats: 5   guinea pigs: 2   dogs: 8   no pets: 10

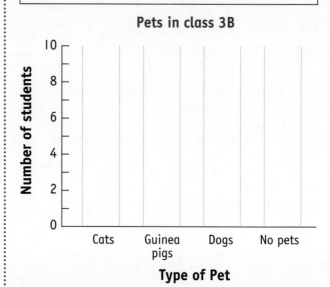

Pets in class 3B

Measurement & Space

AC9M3SP01

3D objects

3D objects have **faces**, **edges** and **vertices**.
  face: the flat part of the surface
  edge: the line where two faces meet
  vertex: the corner (plural is **vertices**)

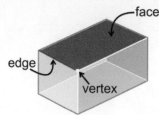

How many faces, edges and vertices do these 3D objects have? Write the correct answers.

3D object	Looks like	Name
		cube

Number of faces	Number of edges	Number of vertices
① _____	② _____	③ _____

3D object	Looks like	Name
		rectangular prism

Number of faces	Number of edges	Number of vertices
④ _____	⑤ _____	⑥ _____

3D object	Looks like	Name
		cone

Number of faces	Number of edges	Number of vertices
⑦ _____	⑧ _____	⑨ _____

3D object	Looks like	Name
		cylinder

Number of faces	Number of edges	Number of vertices
⑩ _____	⑪ _____	⑫ _____

3D object	Looks like	Name
		triangular prism

Number of faces	Number of edges	Number of vertices
⑬ _____	⑭ _____	⑮ _____

3D object	Looks like	Name
		square pyramid

Number of faces	Number of edges	Number of vertices
⑯ _____	⑰ _____	⑱ _____

3D object	Looks like	Name
		sphere

Number of faces	Number of edges	Number of vertices
⑲ _____	⑳ _____	㉑ _____

Score 2 points for each correct answer! SCORE **/42** (0-18) (20-36) (38-42)

Problem Solving

AC9M3N07

Follow the rules

Use the first two numbers in each row to make new numbers. Follow these rules for each column.

A: Add the two numbers.

B: Subtract the second number from the first number.

C: Add 10 to the first number and then subtract the second number.

D: Multiply the first number by 2 and add the second number.

	A	B	C	D
5 and 4				
6 and 3				
7 and 5				
8 and 3				
10 and 9				
6 and 2				
5 and 1				

Grammar & Punctuation

AC9E3LY06, AC9E3LE03

Adjectives

Adjectives are words used to describe people, places and things. They work with a noun to tell us more about what is happening. By saying more about nouns, adjectives help the reader to build up a clear picture of what is being described.

Examples: Compare these two sentences:
The giant stomped into his castle.
The **hideous** giant stomped into his **enormous** castle.
    adjective noun   adjective noun

Types of adjectives

Adjectives can describe:

colour	**blue** sea, **black** cat, **red** flag
size	**huge** dog, **wide** street, **tall** man, **small** mouse
shape	**round** ball, **triangular** sandwiches, **oval** mirror
number	**four** frogs, **many** ships, **few** toys, **ten** toes
sound	**silent** night, **loud** alarm, **quiet** children, **noisy** birds
feelings	**sad** face, **happy** baby, **angry** man, **sleepy** kitten
qualities	**wonderful** party, **lovely** day, **kind** lady, **messy** room

Circle the adjectives in these sentences.

1. Stewart ate a juicy apple.
2. The fluffy rabbit hid in the long grass.
3. Mandy scolded the naughty dog who had dug up her beautiful flowers.
4. The sad dog went and sat in a quiet corner.
5. The huge ship was rolling in the rough sea.
6. The noisy parrots woke the little baby.
7. The old van skidded on the icy road.

Choose an adjective from the word bank to describe each part of the pirate. (Some words can be used more than once.)

Word Bank

red	black	gold	large	shiny	sharp
silver	old	pointy	fancy	wooden	

8. _____ hat
9. _____ telescope
10. _____ cutlass
11. _____ treasure chest
12. _____ jacket

Score 2 points for each correct answer!

SCORE **/24** (0-10) (12-18) (20-24)

Phonic Knowledge & Spelling

AC9E3LY10, AC9E3LY12

Long 'a' sound – ai and ay

Say each word from the word bank. What sound do the letters **ai** make? The **a** and the **i** work together to make one sound — the **long 'a' sound**. The letters **ay** also work together to make the **long 'a' sound**.

Word Bank

main	train	mail	snail
wait	bait	paid	afraid
rain	grain	paint	waist
day	may	pay	say
clay	pray	stay	tray

Choose words from the word bank to complete these sentences.

1. What _____ did you use to catch your fish?
2. Why did you travel by _____ instead of using the car?
3. Who is _____ of spiders?
4. "_____ inside today — or else!" warned Mum.

Homophones

Homophones are words that sound the same but have different spellings and meanings.

Examples: two, to, too here, hear saw, sore

Write words from the word bank that are homophones for these words.

5. waste _____
6. weight _____
7. prey _____
8. male _____
9. reign _____
10. mane _____

Choose the correct homophone for each sentence. Write it in the space.

11. I went _____ the cinema last night.
(*to   two   too*)
12. We had to _____ a diary every day at camp.
(*right   write*)
13. I asked _____ people to my party.
(*eight   ate*)
14. The bridesmaids wore _____ dresses.
(*blew   blue*)
15. Dad bought me some _____ shoes.
(*knew   new*)
16. I tried not to _____ the glass.
(*brake   break*)
17. _____ class went to the circus.
(*Our   Hour*)

Score 2 points for each correct answer!

SCORE **/34** (0-14) (16-28) (30-34)

TARGETING HOMEWORK 3 © PASCAL PRESS ISBN 9781925726459

TERM 1 ENGLISH

Persuasive text – Advertisement

---

www.tiptop.com

MOST LIKELY TO STUDY IN STYLE

BACK TO SCHOOL
Sales — 30% OFF EVERYTHING !

3 Days only! **25–27 January 2018** **10.00 A.M. - 10.00 P.M.**

3 FOR $15!
school books & story books

UP TO 30%
all laptops & tablets

Let's start the school year off in new style

All stock on SPECIAL OFFER — grab a bargain!

Start the school year off with HUGE SAVINGS in our mega 3 DAY SALE.

We hold stock of school uniforms for all the local schools in a full range of sizes.

We also have hoodies, tees, dresses, jeans and trousers — all on special offer.

So come on down to Tip Top TODAY!

NOW ONLY!
$19.00
all girls' & boys' singlets

SPECIAL OFFERS
New limited edition styles!

DRESSES
Pretty party pinafores
All sizes now
ONLY $25

JEANS
Girls' & boys' jeans
All sizes now
ONLY
$30

BUY 1
GET
1 FREE
All tees now ONLY **$25.00**

ONLINE COUPON CODE:
SCHOOL18

Write or circle the correct answers.

① What is the name of the shop having the sale? _____

② For how long does the sale take place?

   a as long as stocks last

   b 3 days

   c the month of January

③ Would the shop be open if you went there at 9.30 am? _____

④ Why do you think the person who created the advertisement used bright colours?

   a because they like bright colours

   b to attract the attention of the reader

   c to design the advertisement quickly

⑤ Who do you think the advertisement is aimed at?

   a children

   b parents of school-age children

   c anyone

⑥ If you purchased a laptop from the sale, what discount would you get? _____

⑦ What can you buy for 'buy one, get one free'? _____

⑧ If you bought 6 books, how much would it cost? _____

⑨ What is on sale for only $19? _____

⑩ What is another word for **mega**?

   a small   b marvellous   c gigantic

⑪ What coupon code do you need to use if you buy online? _____

⑫ 'Tip Top TODAY' is an example of an alliteration, where each word begins with the same letter. What is another example of alliteration in the advertisement?

_____

Score 2 points for each correct answer!

SCORE **/24** 0-10 12-18 20-24

My Book Review

Title _____

Author _____

Rating ☆☆☆☆☆

Comment _____

_____

Number & Algebra

AC9M3M06

TERM 1 MATHS

Money

Australia has six different **coins**, all based on the Australian **dollar**.

 5c   10c   20c

 50c $1 $2

You can make the same amount of money using different coins.

Examples:

 $1

 $1

 $1

Write the coins needed to make these amounts.

① 50c = 20c + 20c + _____

② 50c = 10c + 10c + 10c + 10c + _____

③ 50c = 5c + 10c + 20c + 5c + _____

④ $1 = 50c + 20c + 10c + _____

⑤ $1 = 10c + 10c + 10c + 10c + 10c + _____

⑥ $2 = 50c + 50c + 50c + _____

Are the two groups of coins equal in value? Circle true or false.

⑦   =

                          a true   **b** false

⑧ =

                          a true   **b** false

⑨ =

                          a true   **b** false

⑩  =

                          a true   **b** false

Writing dollars and cents

Money can be written in **words** or as **numbers**.

Examples:

three dollars and ten cents = $3.10

five dollars and five cents = $5.05

fifty cents = $0.50 or 50c

two dollars = $2.00 or $2

Write these amounts as numbers.

⑪ one dollar and fifty cents   = $_____

⑫ seventy cents   = $_____

⑬ four dollars and ten cents   = $_____

⑭ five dollars   = $_____

⑮ three dollars and five cents   = $_____

⑯ ten dollars and ninety-five cents = $_____

Score 2 points for each correct answer!

SCORE /32 (0-14) (16-26) (28-32)

Statistics & Probability

There are no statistics & probability activities in this unit.

Measurement & Space

AC9M3M05

Angles

An **angle** is where **two lines** meet at a **point**.

 A square has 4 angles.

 A triangle has 3 angles.

How many angles do these shapes have?

① _____   ② _____   ③ _____

④ _____   ⑤ _____

TARGETING HOMEWORK 3 © PASCAL PRESS ISBN 9781925726459

Angles can be different sizes.

Examples:

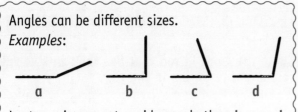

| a | b | c | d |

Laptop **a** is open at a wider angle than **b**, **c** or **d**.
Laptop **d** is open at a wider angle than **b** or **c**.

Number these laptop angles in order of size from smallest to largest.

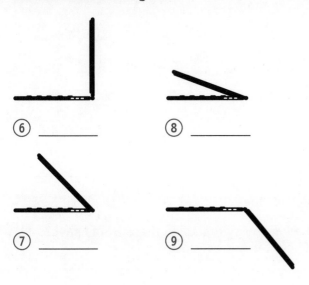

⑥ _____   ⑧ _____

⑦ _____   ⑨ _____

The hands on a clock face make angles. Number these clock face angles in order of size from smallest to largest.

⑩ _____   ⑫ _____

⑪ _____   ⑬ _____

Score 2 points for each correct answer!   **SCORE** **/26** (0-10) (12-20) (22-26)

Cheap Treats Cafe

MENU

Burger	$8.00
Chips	$2.50
Toast	$2.00/slice
Poached egg	$2.00 each
Baked beans	$1.00
Salad	$4.00
Fish fingers	$5.00
Ice-cream	$4.50
Apple pie	$5.00
Orange juice	$1.50
Lemonade	$1.50

Use the menu to answer the questions.

① How much does it cost to buy a burger, chips and a lemonade?

_____

② How much does it cost to buy two poached eggs and two slices of toast?

_____

③ How much does it cost to buy chips and salad?

_____

④ Your friend wants an ice-cream but he only has $2.50. How much more does he need?

_____

⑤ How much does it cost to buy fish fingers, chips, salad and orange juice?

_____

⑥ You have $20. You want to buy a main course, a dessert and a drink. What would you choose?

_____

_____

Grammar & Punctuation

① **Circle the sentence.**

   a are swimming in the sea

   b I am going to Jack's birthday party.

Write a full stop (.), question mark (?) or exclamation mark (!) at the end of each sentence.

② Shut the door, quick___

③ When are you going to Paris___

④ I like chocolate___

Circle the nouns in these sentences.

⑤ Aidan went to school on Monday.

⑥ The black dog chased the cat down Perry Street.

Make four compound nouns using words from the box below.

rain	fly	bow
cup	coat	butter

⑦ _____

⑧ _____

⑨ _____

⑩ _____

⑪ **Add the missing commas in this sentence.**

   We bought carrots potatoes beans bread and milk at the shop.

⑫ **Underline the subject and circle the verb in this sentence.**

   The car raced down the road.

⑬ **Circle the subject that agrees with the verb then write it in the space.**

   _____ are going to London tomorrow.   (*Josh and Mia*   *Ben*)

⑭ **Circle the simple sentence.**

   a Ahmed is five years old.

   b We stayed inside the shop until it stopped raining.

⑮ **Write and, but, so or because to complete this sentence.**

   We could not have cereal _____ we didn't have any milk.

⑯ **Circle the adjectives in this sentence.**

   A green frog was sitting on the muddy log.

Score 2 points for each correct answer!   **SCORE**   **/32**   (0-14)   (16-26)   (28-32)

Phonic Knowledge & Spelling

Circle the word in red that has the same vowel sound as the others in the row.

① rock   sock   drop   hope   hot

② must   budge   nudge   truck   cube

③ life   knife   mice   bit   bite

④ rain   bait   tray   stay   bat

Rewrite these words as plurals (more than one).

⑤ cat_____   ⑦ dish_____   ⑨ table_____

⑥ glass_____   ⑧ box_____   ⑩ match_____

Add –ed and –ing to these words.

	–ed	–ing
⑪ drop	_____	_____
⑫ jump	_____	_____
⑬ race	_____	_____

How many syllables do these words have? Circle the correct answers.

⑭ shopping   1   2

⑮ text   1   2

⑯ laptop   1   2

Add –y to these words.

⑰ slime   _____

⑱ hill   _____

⑲ shake   _____

Write the words from the box next to their correct meanings.

motion	fraction

⑳ part of a whole   _____

㉑ movement   _____

Choose words from the box to complete these sentences.

phone	rule	flame

㉒ The fire was burning with a bright red _____.

㉓ The King had to _____ for forty years before he could retire.

㉔ I had to _____ my uncle if I was going to be late.

TARGETING HOMEWORK 3 © PASCAL PRESS ISBN 9781925726459

Do these words have a long or short vowel sound? Circle the correct answers.

㉕ think   (short   long)

㉖ pain   (short   long)

㉗ fetch   (short   long)

㉘ stray   (short   long)

Circle the double letters in these words.

㉙ sniffle

㉚ soccer

㉛ pepper

Circle the correct homophone for each sentence then write the words.

㉜ I _____ five sandwiches for my lunch.
     (*eight   ate*)

㉝ The wind _____ a tree down.
     (*blue   blew*)

㉞ We couldn't _____ the noise of the traffic.   (*here   hear*)

㉟ I get my _____ and left mixed up!
     (*write   right*)

Score 2 points for each correct answer!   SCORE   **/70**   (0-32) (34-64) (66-70)

Reading & Comprehension

Narrative text – Recount
Author – Frances Mackay

It was a bit difficult when all five children were at home together during the school holidays. The compact house only had four bedrooms, one small one and three big ones.

Mum and Dad had one of the big bedrooms, and David always had the small one. The other boys could have one big room, and the girls had two single beds in the other.

Rusty the dog always got excited when the children came home. He couldn't wait for Max to take him for long walks.

Write or circle the correct answers.

① How many people were in the family? _____

② Did they live in a house or an apartment?

_____

③ How many boys were in the family? _____

④ How many girls were in the family? _____

⑤ Where did David usually sleep?

_____

⑥ When were the children all at home together? _____

⑦ Who is Rusty? _____

⑧ What is another word for **difficult**?

   a easy

   b manageable

   c troublesome

⑨ Name one of David's brothers.

_____

⑩ Tick the correct meaning of the word **compact** in this text.

   a having everything needed in a small space

   b to press down on something

Score 2 points for each correct answer!   SCORE   **/20**   (0-8) (10-14) (16-20)

TERM 1 MATHS

Number & Algebra

Write the missing numbers.

① 12, 14, _____, _____, _____, 22

② 95, 90, 85, 80, _____, _____, _____

③ 900, 800, 700, _____, _____, _____

Write these numbers as digits.

④ fifty-eight _____

⑤ one hundred and twenty-nine _____

⑥ four hundred and six _____

⑦ two thousand, five hundred and fifty _____

What number is missing from each number sentence? Write in the box.

⑧ 5 + 5 + 5 = ☐

⑨ 20 − 2 = ☐

⑩ 6 lots of 2 = ☐

⑪ 2 × ☐ = 10 × 2

⑫ Circle the odd numbers.

   14   8   23   60   75   3   11   92

Write the answers.
Look for pairs that make 10.

⑬ 6 + 8 + 2 + 4 + 5 = _____

⑭ 7 + 9 + 3 + 2 = _____

Complete. Use addition facts to help you.

⑮ 12 + _____ = 20   ⑰ 80 + _____ = 100

⑯ 20 − 15 = _____   ⑱ 100 − 30 = _____

Write these numbers.

⑲ Four thousands, zero hundreds, five tens and nine ones = _____

⑳ Two thousands, nine hundreds, three tens and seven ones = _____

What fraction of these shapes is shaded?

㉑ _____   ㉒ _____

Write the coins needed to make these amounts.

㉓ 60c = 20c + 20c + _____

㉔ 80c = 10c + 10c + 20c + 20c + _____

㉕ 50c = 5c + 10c + 10c + 5c + _____

㉖ $1 = 20c + 20c + 10c + _____

Score 2 points for each correct answer!   SCORE /52   (0-24) (26-46) (48-52)

Statistics & Probability

How likely are these statements?
Circle the correct answer.

① People live in China.
   a impossible   c likely
   b unlikely   d certain

② I will live on the moon tomorrow.
   a impossible   c likely
   b unlikely   d certain

③ I will win the lottery.
   a impossible   c likely
   b unlikely   d certain

④ A surfer will wear a wetsuit.
   a impossible   c likely
   b unlikely   d certain

⑤ Friday is the day after Thursday.
   a impossible   c likely
   b unlikely   d certain

Answer the questions about this bar graph.

Class 3C – Types of Homes We Live In

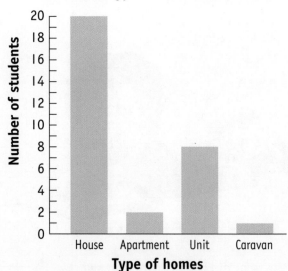

Circle or write the correct answers.

⑥ How many children live in an apartment?
   a 20   b 2   c 8   d 1

⑦ How many children live in a caravan?
   a 20   b 2   c 8   d 1

⑧ What type of house do most of the children in 3C live in?
   a caravan   b apartment   c unit   d house

⑨ How many children in 3C took part in the survey? _____

⑩ How many more children live in a house than in a unit? _____

Score 2 points for each correct answer!   SCORE /20   (0-8) (10-14) (16-20)

TARGETING HOMEWORK 3 © PASCAL PRESS ISBN 9781925726459

Measurement & Space

Which measurement is longer?
Circle the correct answer.

①   8 cm   or   8 m

②   20 mm   or   20 m

③   6 cm   or   6 mm

What are the names of these shapes?
Circle the correct answer.

④   a rectangle   b circle   c square

⑤   a square   b triangle   c rectangle

⑥   a pentagon   b hexagon   c oval

How many sides do these shapes have?

⑦   rectangle _____

⑧   square   _____

⑨   triangle   _____

⑩   pentagon   _____

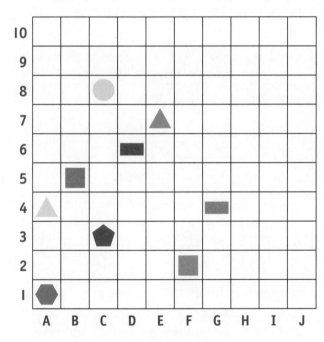

Answer the questions about this coordinate grid. Circle the correct answer.

⑪   **Which shape is at C3?**

    a   red rectangle

    b   green square

    c   red pentagon

⑫   **What are the coordinates of the red rectangle?**

    a   G4   b   D6   c   A4

What is the time? Circle the correct answer.

⑬

   a   12 o'clock

   b   5 o'clock

   c   25 past 12

⑭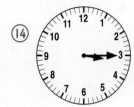

   a $\frac{1}{4}$ past 3

   b $\frac{1}{2}$ past 3

   c $\frac{1}{4}$ to 3

Circle the correct answer.

⑮   1000 g =   a   1 kg   b   1$\frac{1}{2}$ kg   c   10 kg

⑯   500 g =   a   1 kg   b $\frac{1}{2}$ kg   c   5 kg

⑰   **Which picture does not show halves?**

   a   b   c   d

Complete the information.

3D object: Looks like:

⑱   **Name:** _____

⑲   **Number of faces:** _____

⑳   **Number of edges:** _____

㉑   **Number of vertices:** _____

㉒   **Is this 3D object a prism or a pyramid?** _____

Number these book angles in order from the smallest to the largest.

㉓ _____   ㉕ _____

㉔ _____   ㉖ _____

Score 2 points for each correct answer!   **SCORE**   **/52**   (0-24)   (26-46)   (48-52)

Grammar & Punctuation

AC9E3LA06

Subject and object

Remember! All sentences have a **subject** and a **verb**. Many sentences also have an **object**. The subject does the action and the object receives the action. The object usually follows the verb.

Example: <u>The dog</u> **chased** *the cat.*
    subject   verb   object

The dog chased (who?) the cat.

Underline the object in these sentences. (*Hint:* Ask 'who' or 'what' after the verb to find the object.)

① I ate a meat pie.

② The farmer planted a wheat crop.

③ After school, we baked some cakes for Mum.

④ In the story, there was a scary monster frightening the people.

⑤ Liam and Jake are playing football in the park.

Choose objects from the box below to complete the sentences.

| a tiny ball | the lily pad | a new car |
| porridge | the sky | |

⑥ There was an enormous frog sitting on
_____.

⑦ My grandad eats _____ for breakfast every day.

⑧ Last night, a shooting star zoomed across
_____.

⑨ The huge dog was playing with
_____.

⑩ Sophia bought _____ yesterday.

Phonic Knowledge & Spelling

AC9E3LY09, AC9E3LY10

Words that end in y

Say each word from the word bank. Listen to the different end sounds of the words.

Word Bank

bay	boy	valley	buy	key
city	baby	body	pony	jelly
lazy	busy	ugly	tidy	pretty
carry	hurry	study	bury	enjoy

Choose words from the word bank to complete these sentences.

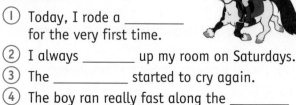

① Today, I rode a _____ for the very first time.

② I always _____ up my room on Saturdays.

③ The _____ started to cry again.

④ The boy ran really fast along the _____ street.

Plurals – y after a vowel

When a word ends in a y after a vowel (**ay, ey, oy** or **uy**), just add **–s** to make the plural (more than one).

Examples: **day, days**   **valley, valleys**
        boy, boys   **buy, buys**

Rewrite these words as plurals.

⑤ bay _____   ⑨ monkey _____

⑥ key _____   ⑩ delay _____

⑦ toy _____   ⑪ trolley _____

⑧ guy _____   ⑫ convoy _____

Plurals – y after a consonant

When a word ends in a y after a consonant, change the y into i and add **–es** to make the plural.

Examples: **pony, ponies**   **baby, babies**
        city, cities   **jelly, jellies**

Write these words as plurals.

⑬ party _____   ⑰ family _____

⑭ lady _____   ⑱ enemy _____

⑮ ferry _____   ⑲ fairy _____

⑯ army _____   ⑳ factory _____

Score 2 points for each correct answer! **SCORE** /20 (0-8) (10-14) (16-20)

Score 2 points for each correct answer! **SCORE** /40 (0-18) (20-34) (36-40)

TARGETING HOMEWORK 3 © PASCAL PRESS ISBN 9781925726459

Imaginative text – Narrative
Author – Lisa Thompson, **Illustrator** – Brenda Cantell

Taste of Thailand

The market was hot, steamy and crowded. Everyone was talking fast and loud. Meh haggled for a good price and paid them in *baht*, Thai money. They bought herbs, spices, fruit and vegetables. Some of the fruit Lulu and Ben had never heard of before, like rambutans, mangosteens and pomelos.

Ben held up a large spiky fruit. "What's this?" he asked.

"That is durian. It's very good. You must try."

It didn't smell so good, but if you held your nose it was delicious!

"Now we go to the *klongs*," said Meh quickly.

Meh led them along crowded laneways jammed with motorbikes and three-wheeled

taxis called *tuk-tuks*. They passed dusty shops with birds in cages, people wanting to tell your fortune and a shop that sold nothing but images of Buddha.

Then they hit water. They stepped aboard a longboat. It twisted and turned down one klong after another. They passed other longboats filled with fruits and vegetables.

Source: *Taste of Thailand*, SWAT, Blake Education.

TERM 2 ENGLISH

Write or circle the correct answers.

What three adjectives are used to describe the market?

① _____

② _____

③ _____

④ **What does the word haggled mean?**

a waited   b negotiated a lower price

⑤ **In what country was the market?**

a We are not told.   b Thailand

List four fruits that Lulu and Ben had never heard of.

⑥ _____

⑦ _____

⑧ _____

⑨ _____

⑩ **Which one of these is the odd word out?**

a delicious   c disgusting

b tasty   d scrumptious

List three things other than food that Lulu and Ben saw near the market.

⑪ _____

⑫ _____

⑬ _____

⑭ **What is another word for klongs?**

a boat   b bridge   c waterways

⑮ **Look at the picture. This is a three-wheeled taxi. What is it called?**

_____

Score 2 points for each correct answer!

SCORE /30   0-12   14-24   26-30

My Book Review

Title _____

Author _____

Rating ☆☆☆☆☆

Comment _____

_____

Number & Algebra

AC9M3N01

Numbers to 10 000

This number line counts from 1000 to 1010 (one thousand to one thousand and ten).

1000 1001 1002 1003 1004 1005 1006 1007 1008 1009 1010

Continue counting by writing the missing numbers from this number line.

1011 1012 1013 1014 1 2 3 4 1019 1020 1021

① _____
② _____
③ _____
④ _____

Write these numbers in words.

⑤ 1015 = _____
⑥ 1016 = _____
⑦ 1017 = _____
⑧ 1018 = _____

Write the numbers in order from smallest to largest.

⑨ 1000, 1006, 1009, 1002

_____

⑩ 6022, 6012, 6002, 6023

_____

⑪ 9200, 9100, 9400, 9300

_____

Write the missing numbers.

⑫ 1000, 1001, 1002, 1003, _____, _____, _____

⑬ 5002, 5000, 4998, 4996, _____, _____, _____, 4988

Write the number.

⑭ The first even number after 1010

_____

⑮ Double 3333 _____

⑯ The number that is two hundred less than 7246 _____

Statistics & Probability

AC9M3SP01

Spinner results

Amy spun this spinner 50 times and recorded her results in a tally chart.

red	blue	green
卌 |||	卌 卌 卌 |||	卌 卌 卌 卌			

Use Amy's spinner and her tally chart to answer the questions.
Write or circle the correct answers.

① Does the spinner have an equal chance of landing on any colour?
 a yes   **b** no

② Which colour came up the most in Amy's experiment? _____

③ Which colour came up the least?

_____

④ Is there just as much chance of the spinner landing on blue as green?
 a yes   **b** no

⑤ What are the chances of the spinner landing on green?
 a certain   **b** likely
 c unlikely   **d** impossible

⑥ What are the chances of the spinner landing on red?
 a certain   **b** likely
 c unlikely .   **d** impossible

⑦ What are the chances of the spinner landing on yellow?
 a certain   **b** likely
 c unlikely   **d** impossible

⑧ If Amy spun the same spinner 50 more times, what are the chances of her getting similar results?
 a certain   **b** likely
 c unlikely   **d** impossible

Measurement & Space

AC9M3M01

Measuring litres and millilitres

> **Capacity** is the amount a container can hold. When we measure capacity, we use **millilitres** and **litres**.
>
> 1000 millilitres = 1 litre
>
> 500 millilitres = $\frac{1}{2}$ litre
>
> 250 millilitres = $\frac{1}{4}$ litre

How many litres?

1. 2000 millilitres = _____

2. 500 millilitres = _____

3. 250 millilitres = _____

> When we write **millilitres** in the short form, we use **mL**.
>
> 30 millilitres = 30 mL
>
> 375 millilitres = 375 mL

Write these amounts in the short form.

4. 25 millilitres = _____

5. 135 millilitres = _____

6. 250 millilitres = _____

7. 550 millilitres = _____

8. 984 millilitres = _____

This measuring jug has 2 litres of orange juice in it.

How much orange juice is in these jugs? Circle the correct answers.

9.

   a 2 litres   b 1 litre   c 3 litres

10.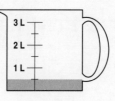

   a 1 litre   b $\frac{1}{4}$ litre   c $\frac{1}{2}$ litre

Colour each measuring jug to show the amount.

11. 2 litres

12. $1\frac{1}{2}$ litres

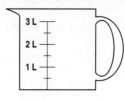

13. $2\frac{1}{2}$ litres

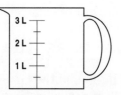

Score 2 points for each correct answer!

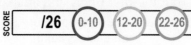

SCORE /26   0-10   12-20   22-26

Problem Solving

AC9M3SP01

Joining triangles

Equilateral triangles have three equal sides.

How many ways can you join four **equilateral** triangles?

You must match an edge to an edge.

Here is one way:

Use this grid to draw your results.

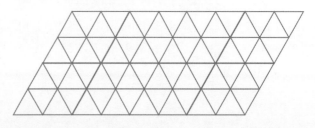

TARGETING HOMEWORK 3 © PASCAL PRESS ISBN 9781925726459

TERM 2 MATHS

Grammar & Punctuation

AC9E3LA02, AC9E3LY06

TERM 2 ENGLISH

Modal verbs

Modal verbs show how likely something is to happen, or how important it is that it happens. They include should, could, will, must, and might.

Example:
You <u>must</u> stay out of the haunted house.

Underline the modal verb in each sentence.

① We should leave before dark.

② If you try it, you might like it.

③ We will have pies for dinner.

④ We could go to the movies.

Articles – a, an, the

The words **a**, **an** and **the** come before nouns. These words are called **articles**. They are often the first words in a noun group.

Examples: **the** oldest man on the street
an ancient building
a bright yellow flower

The word **the** relates to a particular person or thing. It tells people who or what is being spoken about. **The** is called the **definite article**.

A and **an** are used more generally. They do not relate to a particular person or thing.
A and **an** are called **indefinite articles**.

A is used before a singular noun.
Examples: **a** fat cat, **a** tall building

An is used before a singular noun beginning with a vowel.
Examples: **an** umbrella, **an** elephant

Choose a, an or the to complete these sentences.

⑤ She wore _____ expensive dress to the party.

⑥ Max is _____ smallest dog in _____ street.

⑦ _____ bright sun was blinding _____ young driver.

⑧ Please have _____ slice of cake and _____ biscuit.

⑨ I want to see _____ elephant in _____ wild.

⑩ Mum cut up _____ apple and _____ orange for me to eat.

Phonic Knowledge & Spelling

AC9E3LY09, AC9E3LY10

ee and eer words

Say each word from the word bank. What sound do the letters **ee** make?

The words that end in **eer** are pronounced 'ear' (like the ear on your head).

Word Bank

feet	meet	green	queen
need	speed	keep	steep
kneel	wheel	reef	beef
deer	peer	cheer	steer
jeer	veer	sheer	sneer

Write words from the word bank to complete these sentences.

① Early morning is the best time to see a _____ in the forest.

② We really _____ a new computer at home.

③ The _____ mountain pass was very windy.

④ The _____ stew was already cooking when we arrived.

Syllables

All the words in the word bank have one syllable. Here are some compound words containing **ee** or **eer**. Write the number of syllables that each word has.

⑤ goalkeeper _____   ⑨ wheelbarrow _____

⑥ reindeer _____   ⑩ buccaneer _____

⑦ cheerfulness _____   ⑪ speedway _____

⑧ beehive _____   ⑫ mountaineer _____

Rhyming words

Write words from the word bank that rhyme with these words.

⑬ greet   m_____   ⑰ steel   wh_____

⑭ sleep   s_____   ⑱ seen   qu_____

⑮ leer   p_____   ⑲ street   f_____

⑯ career   ch_____   ⑳ peep   k_____

AC9E3LY05, AC9S3H02, AC9HS3K04

Imaginative text – Traditional Aboriginal tale
Author – Reproduced courtesy of www.emudreaming.com

Walu, the Sun-woman

Arnhem Land

The Yolngu people of Arnhem Land in the far north of Australia tell a story about Walu, the Sun-woman, to explain the apparent daily movement of the sun across the sky.

Each morning, Walu, the Sun-woman, lights a small fire, creating dawn. She decorates herself with red ochre, some of which spills onto the clouds, creating the red sunrise. She then lights her torch, made from stringy-bark tree, and travels across the sky from East to West, carrying daylight in the form of her blazing torch.

As she descends at the end of her journey, some of the ochre again dusts the clouds to create the red sunset. On reaching the western horizon, she puts out her torch and starts the long journey underground back to the morning camp in the East.

Tick the correct box or write the answers about the text.

1 **Where do the Yolngu people live?**

_____

2 **What do you think red ochre is?**

a red jewels

b a crumbly red rock used for painting

3 **According to this traditional tale, what creates daylight?**

a a blazing torch

b the sun

4 **Walu travels from East to:**

a North

b West

Find the words in the text that have these meanings.

5 to move downwards   d_____

6 to make something
more attractive   d_____

7 very hot   b_____

8 to make   c_____

9 journeys   t_____

10 **Which one of these is the odd word out?**

a creating   c destroying

b making   d inventing

11 **What was Walu's torch made from?**

_____

12 **What does the word horizon mean?**

a where the sky appears to meet the land
or sea

b hillside

Score 2 points for each correct answer!   SCORE /24   0-10   12-18   20-24

My Book Review

Title _____

Author _____

Rating ☆ ☆ ☆ ☆ ☆

Comment _____

_____

Number & Algebra

AC9M3N02

Fractions

When we **share** an object into **equal parts**, each part is called a **fraction**.

Examples:

This circle is cut into 3 equal parts.

Each part is a third ($\frac{1}{3}$) of the whole circle.

This circle is cut into 5 equal parts.

Each part is a fifth ($\frac{1}{5}$) of the whole circle.

What fraction of the whole shape is the shaded area? Circle the correct answers.

①

a $\frac{1}{3}$ b $\frac{1}{2}$ c $\frac{2}{3}$

②

a $\frac{1}{5}$ b $\frac{2}{5}$ c $\frac{3}{5}$

③

a $\frac{1}{3}$ b $\frac{2}{3}$ c $\frac{3}{3}$

④

a $\frac{2}{5}$ b $\frac{3}{5}$ c $\frac{4}{5}$

⑤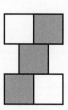

a $\frac{2}{5}$ b $\frac{3}{5}$ c $\frac{4}{5}$

⑥

a $\frac{1}{3}$ b $\frac{2}{3}$ c $\frac{3}{3}$

Divide (partition) and colour each shape to show the fraction.

⑦  $\frac{2}{5}$

⑧ $\frac{1}{3}$

Fraction number lines

This number line shows **counting in thirds**. The line is divided into **three equal parts**.

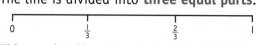

This number line shows **counting in fifths**. The line is divided into **five equal parts**.

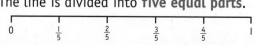

Mark each fraction on the number line.

⑨ $\frac{2}{3}$ 0 ———————————— 1

⑩ $\frac{2}{5}$ 0 ———————————— 1

⑪ $\frac{4}{5}$ 0 ———————————— 1

Score 2 points for each correct answer! SCORE /22 (0-8) (10-16) (18-22)

Statistics & Probability

There are no statistics & probability activities in this unit.

Measurement & Space

AC9M3M04

Analogue and digital time

When we tell **digital time**, we say the **hour** first and then the **minutes** past the hour.

Examples:

In **analogue** time, write this time as $\frac{1}{2}$ **past 9**.

In **digital** time, write this time as **9:30**.

In **analogue** time, write this time as **1 o'clock**.

In **digital** time, write this time as **1:00**.

TARGETING HOMEWORK 3 © PASCAL PRESS ISBN 9781925726459

Write these analogue times as digital times.

①

_____

②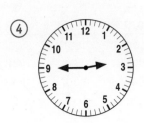

_____

③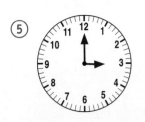

_____

④

_____

⑤

_____

True or false?

Circle the correct answer.

⑥ 9:15 is the same as $\frac{1}{4}$ past 9.

   a true   **b** false

⑦ 8:30 is the same as 30 minutes past 8.

   a true   **b** false

⑧ 6:28 = 28 minutes to 6

   a true   **b** false

⑨ $\frac{1}{4}$ to 10 = 9:50

   a true   **b** false

⑩ 6 minutes past 3 is the same as 3:06.

   a true   **b** false

⑪ 8:45 = $\frac{1}{4}$ to 9

   a true   **b** false

Word problems

Answer these problems.
Show your working out.

① A baker baked 5 trays of cupcakes. Each tray had 6 cupcakes on it. How many cupcakes did he bake in total?

_____

② Two dogs had 10 puppies each. How many puppies altogether?

_____

③ How many wheels are there on four cars?

_____

④ Peta runs 3 kilometres every day. How far does she run in one week?

_____

⑤ A multipack of chocolate bars holds 8 bars. How many bars of chocolate are there in 5 multipacks?

_____

⑥ At the zoo, Amy saw five elephants walking in a line. How many elephant legs did she see altogether?

_____

⑦ How many elephant ears did Amy see?

_____

TERM 2 MATHS

Score 2 points for each correct answer! **SCORE** /22 (0-8) (10-16) (18-22)

UNIT 11

Grammar & Punctuation

AC9E3LY06

Pronouns

Pronouns are words that are used to take the place of nouns.

Example: <u>Ted</u> **went fishing. He caught a big fish.**
　　　　　noun　　　　　　　　pronoun

The <u>noun</u> 'Ted' has been replaced by the **pronoun** 'he'.

Personal pronouns take the place of the names of people, places, animals and things. Like nouns, they can be **singular** or **plural**.

Singular pronouns: I, me, you, he, she, it, him, her

Plural pronouns: we, us, they, them, you

Circle the pronouns in these sentences.

① He asked them to stop teasing her.

② "You can come with us," he said.

③ Last week, they came to the park with us.

④ She asked me to come to her party.

⑤ I tried tennis, but I didn't continue playing it.

Circle and write the correct pronoun for each sentence.

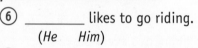

⑥ _____ likes to go riding.
　　(He　Him)

⑦ He asked _____ to go with him.
　　(I　me)

⑧ _____ are going on holiday next week.
　　(Them　They)

⑨ Come to the swimming pool with _____.
　　(us　we)

⑩ The cat chased a mouse and caught _____. (them　it)

Write personal pronouns to complete these sentences.

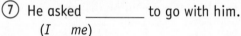

Emily raced home as fast as _____ ⑪ could. She wanted to get home before _____ ⑫ brother so she could wrap a present for _____ ⑬ and get the party food ready. Emily had invited five of _____ ⑭ brother's friends and _____ ⑮ were arriving at 5 o'clock, so _____ ⑯ didn't have much time. In _____ ⑰ hurry, Emily tripped over a mat and dropped the birthday cake. Luckily, _____ ⑱ landed on the table and wasn't ruined!

Score 2 points for each correct answer! **SCORE** /36 (0-16) (18-30) (32-36)

Phonic Knowledge & Spelling

AC9E3LY09, AC9E3LY10

ea and ear words

Say each word from the word bank. What sound do the letters **ea** make?
The words that end in **ear** are pronounced 'ear' (like the ear on your head).

Word Bank

seat	heat	neat	team	dream
meal	steal	beak	speak	leaf
dear	clear	near	spear	fear
tear	hear	rear	gear	drear

Choose words from the word bank to complete these sentences.

① "Please _____ up so I can _____ you," said Mum.

② My friend has a _____ of spiders.

③ It was very windy, so we ate our _____ inside.

④ We have every type of camping _____ we could ever want.

Compound words

Make compound words by writing a word from the box on each line.

| land | mint | work | let | some | worm |

⑤ fear _____　⑧ spear _____

⑥ meal _____　⑨ team _____

⑦ dream _____　⑩ leaf _____

Plurals – words ending in f and fe

To make the plural of many words that end in **f** or **fe**, change the **f** or **fe** to **v**, then add **–es**.
Examples: loa**f**, loa**ves**　　wi**fe**, wi**ves**

Write these words as plurals.

⑪ leaf _____

⑫ sheaf _____

⑬ half _____

⑭ calf _____

⑮ knife _____

⑯ life _____

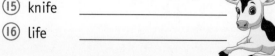

Score 2 points for each correct answer! **SCORE** /32 (0-14) (16-26) (28-32)

TARGETING HOMEWORK 3 © PASCAL PRESS ISBN 9781925726459

TERM 2 ENGLISH

Informative text – Report
Author – Ian Rohr

Super Squid

You're on a boat at sea. Suddenly, an enormous creature with two tentacles and eight long arms covered in suckers rises from the water. It's a giant squid! Sailors long ago thought that giant squid were 'monsters' that would grab them and pull them under the sea.

These super-sized squid roam the depths of the world's oceans. Because they can live in seas up to 1,000 metres deep, we don't know much about them.

Sometimes dead giant squid, or parts of them, are washed ashore. Scientists study these parts. They think that some giant squid could be up to 18 metres long and weigh up to 900 kilograms! Submersibles that can travel into very deep waters may soon allow scientists to study living giant squid.

The eyes of a giant squid are the largest in the animal kingdom. Each is as big as a human head!

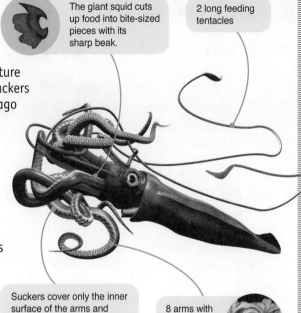

The giant squid cuts up food into bite-sized pieces with its sharp beak.

2 long feeding tentacles

Suckers cover only the inner surface of the arms and tentacles. They 'suck' onto prey to give the giant squid a good grip.

8 arms with two rows of suckers on the inside

Source: *Biggest, Highest, Fastest*, Brainwaves, Blake Education.

Write or circle the correct answers.

1. **Read the first two sentences again. What effect do you think the author was trying to create?**

   a He wanted to frighten the reader.

   b He wanted to create an exciting beginning so the reader would read on to find out more.

   c He wanted to write about giant squid.

2. **What is another word for tentacles?**

   a long body parts used for feeling or feeding

   b arms

3. **Why don't we know much about giant squid?**

   a They are too scary to get close to.

   b They live in very deep water and it's difficult for scientists to travel there.

4. **An average eight-year-old child weighs approximately 25 kilograms. How many times heavier does a giant squid weigh?**

   a 5 times heavier

   b 36 times heavier

Find the words in the text that have these meanings.

5. huge   e_____

6. to wander around   r_____

7. an animal part that clings by using suction   s_____

8. on the seashore   a_____

9. a body part used to cut up food   b_____

10. **What is a submersible?**

    a a boat that can travel underwater

    b a diving platform

Score 2 points for each correct answer! **SCORE** /20 (0-8) (10-14) (16-20)

My Book Review

Title _____

Author _____

Rating ☆☆☆☆☆

Comment _____

Number & Algebra

AC9M3N06

Multiplying and dividing by 2, 3, 5 and 10

TERM 2 MATHS

Number facts

$5 \times 2 = 10$ $2 \times 5 = 10$

$10 \div 2 = 5$ $10 \div 5 = 2$

Here are some number equations and different ways to solve them.

$$\_\_\_ \times 2 = 10$$

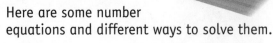

- How many lots of 2 are there in 10?
- Divide 10 by 2.
- What do you double to make 10?
- What do you multiply by 2 to make 10?

$$10 \div \_\_\_ = 2$$

- How many lots of 2 are there in 10?
- $2 \times$ what $= 10$?
- What do you multiply 2 by to make 10?

Complete each fact family.

1. $6 \times \_\_\_ = 18$
2. $3 \times 6 = \_\_\_$
3. $18 \div 3 = \_\_\_$
4. $18 \div \_\_\_ = 3$
5. $4 \times 5 = \_\_\_$
6. $5 \times \_\_\_ = 20$
7. $20 \div 5 = \_\_\_$
8. $\_\_\_ \div 4 = 5$
9. $3 \times 10 = \_\_\_$
10. $\_\_\_ \times 3 = 30$
11. $30 \div \_\_\_ = 10$
12. $\_\_\_ \div 10 = 3$

Complete these multiplications.

13. $4 \times 2 = \_\_\_$
14. $\_\_\_ \times 2 = 12$
15. $7 \times \_\_\_ = 14$
16. $4 \times 3 = \_\_\_$
17. $\_\_\_ \times 3 = 15$
18. $8 \times \_\_\_ = 24$
19. $4 \times 5 = \_\_\_$
20. $\_\_\_ \times 5 = 30$
21. $3 \times \_\_\_ = 15$
22. $4 \times 10 = \_\_\_$
23. $\_\_\_ \times 10 = 60$
24. $9 \times \_\_\_ = 90$

Complete these divisions.

25. $10 \div 2 = \_\_\_$
26. $20 \div \_\_\_ = 10$
27. $\_\_\_ \div 2 = 8$
28. $9 \div 3 = \_\_\_$
29. $18 \div \_\_\_ = 6$
30. $\_\_\_ \div 3 = 6$
31. $25 \div 5 = \_\_\_$
32. $30 \div \_\_\_ = 6$
33. $\_\_\_ \div 5 = 4$
34. $50 \div 10 = \_\_\_$
35. $70 \div \_\_\_ = 7$
36. $\_\_\_ \div 10 = 3$

Answer these number problems. Show your working

37. Jake has 15 chocolate bars to share equally with his 4 friends. How many chocolate bars does each friend have, including Jake?

_____

38. There are 9 rabbits in a burrow. How many rabbit ears are there altogether?

_____

39. Julia earned $3 selling ice-creams. Lee earned three times as much as Julia. How much did Lee earn?

_____

40. Spiders have 8 legs. There were 10 spiders in our hallway. How many spider legs altogether?

_____

Score 2 points for each correct answer!

SCORE /80 0-38 40-74 76-80

Statistics & Probability

AC9M3ST02

Comparing tally charts

The local council carried out a traffic survey. They recorded the type and number of vehicles that went past Hightown School within half an hour at two different times of day.

They recorded the results in these tally charts.

Table 1
Monday 8.30–9.00 am

Vehicle	Tally
🚗	卌 卌 卌 卌 卌 卌 卌 卌 Ⅲ
🚌	ⅢⅠ
🚚	卌 Ⅲ
🏍	Ⅲ Ⅰ
🚲	卌 卌

Table 2
Monday 9.30–10.00 am

Vehicle	Tally
🚗	卌 卌 卌 卌 Ⅲ
🚌	Ⅱ
🚚	卌 卌 卌
🏍	Ⅱ
🚲	ⅢⅠ

Use the the tally charts to answer the questions. Write or circle the correct answers.

① At which time of day was the traffic outside the school busier?

_____

② Why do you think it was busier at this time?

 a Most people get up early.

 b People are travelling to work or school at that time.

 c The school was open.

③ How many cars passed the school 8.30–9.00 am? _____

④ How many cars passed the school 9.30–10.00 am? _____

⑤ How many buses passed the school 8.30–9.00 am? _____

⑥ How many buses passed the school 9.30–10.00 am? _____

⑦ At what time of day did the smaller number of motorbikes go by? _____

⑧ At what time of day did the smaller number of trucks go by? _____

⑨ What would be a good reason for the council to carry out this survey?

 a to decide if a pedestrian crossing is needed outside the school

 b to make sure no vehicles had an accident outside the school

Score 2 points for each correct answer! SCORE **/18** (0-6) (8-14) (16-18)

Measurement & Space

AC9M3SP02

3D shapes and 2D faces

① A **cube** has:

 ____ faces

 ____ vertices

 ____ edges

② A **cone** has:

 ____ faces

 ____ vertices

 ____ edges

③ A **cylinder** has:

 ____ faces

 ____ vertices

 ____ edges

④ A **rectangular prism** has:

 ____ square faces

 ____ rectangular faces

 ____ vertices

 ____ edges

⑤ A **square-based pyramid** has:

 ____ square faces

 ____ triangular faces

 ____ vertices

 ____ edges

Score 2 points for each correct answer! SCORE **/10** (0-2) (4-8) (10)

Problem Solving

AC9M3A02

Number square puzzles

Use the 100 square to solve these puzzles.

1	2	3	4	5	6	7	8	9	10
11	12	13	14	15	16	17	18	19	20
21	22	23	24	25	26	27	28	29	30
31	32	33	34	35	36	37	38	39	40
41	42	43	44	45	46	47	48	49	50
51	52	53	54	55	56	57	58	59	60
61	62	63	64	65	66	67	68	69	70
71	72	73	74	75	76	77	78	79	80
81	82	83	84	85	86	87	88	89	90
91	92	93	94	95	96	97	98	99	100

① Write the palindromes you can find. A palindrome is a number that is the same forwards and backwards, such as 55 and 101.

_____

② Which numbers have digits that add up to 9?

_____

③ Colour all the odd numbers.

Grammar & Punctuation

AC9E3LA07

Saying verbs

> **Saying verbs** show how people say things.
> *Examples*: Holly screamed a warning.
> "Where are your shoes?" asked Dad.

Look at these saying words that have similar meanings.

cried			
	sobbed	screamed	bellowed
	yelled	bawled	whined
	screeched	wailed	howled

laughed			
	chuckled	giggled	sniggered
	snickered	cackled	chortled

Choose suitable saying verbs from the boxes above to complete these sentences.

① "Ha, ha, I have you now," _____ the evil witch.

② "I fell over and scraped my knee," _____ the little girl.

③ The two boys _____ at the clown's tricks.

④ The baby _____ so loudly it woke up the whole house.

Circle the odd word out.

⑤ answered   replied   laughed   responded

⑥ whispered   yelled   murmured   sighed

⑦ groaned   moaned   whined   giggled

Speech marks

> Writers tell us what people say to each other by using **speech marks ("...")**. The speech marks go at the beginning and end of what was said. The first spoken word always has a **capital letter**, and a **comma** marks off the spoken words from the rest of the sentence.
>
> *Examples*: Gemma said, "We would love to go to the party."
>
> "We would love to go to the party," said Gemma.
> speech   capital   comma speech
> marks   letter   marks
>
> **NOTE:** If the sentence has a **question mark (?)** or an **exclamation mark (!)**, do not use a comma.

Punctuate these sentence by adding the missing speech marks and commas.

⑧ You're out! yelled the umpire.

⑨ I can't walk any further wailed Ruby.

⑩ Those monkeys are really funny laughed Ahmed.

Phonic Knowledge & Spelling

AC9E3LY09, AC9E3LY10

oa and ow words

**Say each word from the word bank.
What sound do the letters oa and ow make?**

Word Bank

boat	oat	coast	toast
load	toad	coach	moan
low	slow	mow	grow
blow	arrow	narrow	follow

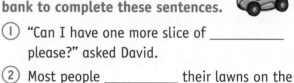

Choose words from the word bank to complete these sentences.

① "Can I have one more slice of _____ please?" asked David.

② Most people _____ their lawns on the weekend.

③ Few people are lucky enough to have their own tennis _____.

④ There are many different types of flowers that will _____ here.

Adding –ed and –ing

**Add –ed and –ing to these verbs.
The first one has been done for you.**

		–ed	–ing
	float	floated	floating
⑤	load	_____	_____
⑥	coach	_____	_____
⑦	poach	_____	_____
⑧	moan	_____	_____
⑨	groan	_____	_____
⑩	mow	_____	_____
⑪	row	_____	_____
⑫	follow	_____	_____

NOTE: grow, grew, gr**ow**ing   bl**ow**, blew, bl**ow**ing

Compound words

Write eight compound words using the word boat and a word from the box.

house	shed	sail	paddle
yard	builder	speed	row

⑬ _____   ⑰ _____

⑭ _____   ⑱ _____

⑮ _____   ⑲ _____

⑯ _____   ⑳ _____

Imaginative text – Narrative
Author – Tracy Hawkins
Illustrator – John Yahyeh

Liar, Liar, Pants on Fire

Ben sat in the car staring out the window at the sports field. He twisted his lip nervously one way, then another. He could see the boys in his hockey team arriving at the field for their game.

"C'mon Ben, you'll be late if you don't get a move on," said his mother. She dragged the big goalie bag from the boot of the car.

"I'm coming," said Ben, clambering out of the car. He picked up his hockey stick and grabbed the handles of the bag. He pulled it across the grass to join the other boys.

"Hey Ben, are you ready for the big game?" asked Coach. He ruffled Ben's hair with his hand. Coach had selected Ben to be the team's goalie for this week.

"Yep," said Ben, trying to sound like he was excited as he patted his hair back down on his head.

Inside his head a small voice teased, "Liar, liar, pants on fire. You're not ready. Go on, tell him the truth."

Ben looked up at his coach and smiled. He put on his best happy face. This wasn't easy when it felt like rats were gnawing away at his guts. He didn't want to be the goalie and he wasn't at all happy.

Source: *Yellow-Bellied Goalie*, Gigglers, Blake Education.

TERM 2 ENGLISH

Write or circle the correct answers.

① **What sport does Ben play?**

_____

② **The author begins the story by telling us that Ben 'twisted his lip nervously one way, then another'. Immediately, we know that Ben was feeling:**

a happy   b worried   c sad

③ **What is another word for clambering?**

a hopping   b running   c climbing

④ **'Liar, liar, pants on fire' is a common saying. People say it when someone gets caught out in a lie. Why do you think Ben said this to himself?**

a He pretended he was happy about being goalie when he wasn't.

b He said it to try and cheer himself up.

⑤ **Ben was so worried about being goalie that day that 'it felt like rats were gnawing away at his guts'. What do you think this expression means?**

a He was carrying his pet rats that were scratching him.

b He was so worried that his stomach was hurting.

⑥ **What did the small voice in Ben's head want him to tell Coach?**

_____

⑦ **This text extract tells us the beginning of the story. The full story ends with the words, 'Being a goalie wasn't so bad after all. Maybe, just maybe, he would give it another go next week.' What does this tell us about what happened next?**

a Ben runs back home because he is too scared to play.

b Ben plays the game and turns out to be a good goalie.

Score 2 points for each correct answer!

SCORE 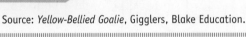 /14   0-4   6-10   12-14

My Book Review

Title _____

Author _____

Rating ☆ ☆ ☆ ☆ ☆

Comment _____

_____

AC9M3N04

UNIT 12	Number & Algebra

Doubling numbers

Doubling a number is the same as **multiplying** the number **by 2**.

Examples:
double 2 = 4
double 8 = 16
double 10 = 20

To double larger numbers, split the number to make it easier.

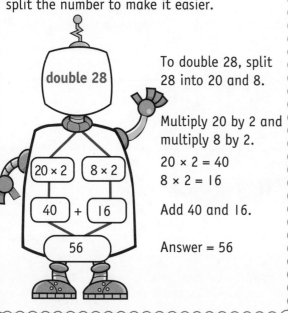

To double 28, split 28 into 20 and 8.

Multiply 20 by 2 and multiply 8 by 2.
20 × 2 = 40
8 × 2 = 16

Add 40 and 16.

Answer = 56

Halving numbers

Halving numbers is the same as **dividing** a number **by 2**.

Examples:
half of 4 = halve 4 = 2
half of 16 = halve 16 = 8
half of 20 = halve 20 = 10

To find half of larger numbers, split the number to make it easier.

To halve 28, split 28 into 20 and 8.

Divide 20 by 2 and divide 8 by 2.
20 ÷ 2 = 10
8 ÷ 2 = 4

Add 10 and 4.

Answer = 14

Complete the doubling robots.

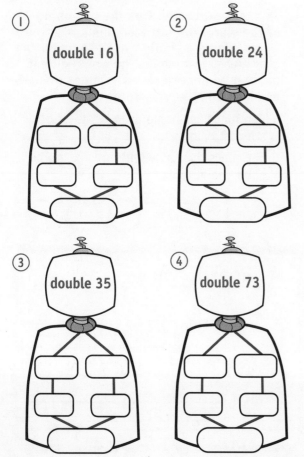

① double 16

② double 24

③ double 35

④ double 73

Complete the halving robots.

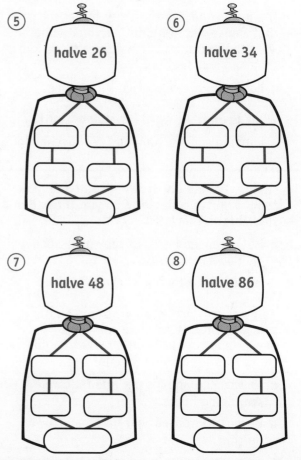

⑤ halve 26

⑥ halve 34

⑦ halve 48

⑧ halve 86

TARGETING HOMEWORK 3 © PASCAL PRESS ISBN 9781925726459

Multiplying by 10 and 100

The easy way to **multiply** a number **by 10** is to add a zero to the end.

$5 \times 10 = 50$ $120 \times 10 = 1200$

The easy way to **multiply** a number **by 100** is to add two zeros to the end.

$5 \times 100 = 500$ $120 \times 100 = 12\,000$

Write the answers.

⑨ $4 \times 10 =$ _____   ⑬ $56 \times 10 =$ _____

⑩ $4 \times 100 =$ _____   ⑭ $56 \times 100 =$ _____

⑪ $12 \times 10 =$ _____   ⑮ $130 \times 10 =$ _____

⑫ $12 \times 100 =$ _____   ⑯ $130 \times 100 =$ _____

Score 2 points for each correct answer! | **SCORE** **/32** | 0-14 | 16-26 | 28-32

Statistics & Probability

There are no statistics & probability activities in this unit.

Measurement & Space

AC9M3M01

Units of measurement

Measurement units can be written in **long form** or **short form**.

Long form	Short form
kilogram	kg
gram	g
metre	m
centimetre	cm
litre	L
millilitre	mL

Write the correct measurement unit in long form and short form.

① The length of a path

_____, _____

② The amount of liquid in a cup

_____, _____

③ The length of a leaf

_____, _____

④ The mass of a flower

_____, _____

⑤ The length of a flea

_____, _____

⑥ The water in a bathtub

_____, _____

⑦ The mass of a bag of sugar

_____, _____

Score 2 points for each correct answer! | **SCORE** **/14** | 0-4 | 6-10 | 12-14

Problem Solving

AC9M3N04

What number am I?

① • Double the number is less than 50.
   • Half the number is more than 10.
   • The number is not the highest or lowest possible.
   • The number does not have two digits the same.

   The number is ☐.

② • Double the number is more than 60.
   • Half the number is less than 18.
   • The number is not an even number.
   • The number is not the highest or lowest possible.

   The number is ☐.

③ • Half the number is less than 50.
   • The number is more than double 34.
   • Both digits in the number are the same and both are even.

   The number is ☐.

④ • The number is in the 3s counting sequence.
   • The number is less than 50.
   • The number has two digits that are both the same.

   The number is ☐.

TARGETING HOMEWORK 3 © PASCAL PRESS ISBN 9781925726459

TERM 2 MATHS

Grammar & Punctuation

AC9E3LY06, AC9E3LA11

Possessive pronouns

Remember! Pronouns are words that are used to take the place of nouns.
Possessive pronouns show ownership.
Examples: That is **my** football.
We gave **our** old toys to the charity shop.

Possessive pronouns can be **singular** or **plural**.
Examples: (singular) my, mine, your, yours, her, hers, his, its
(plural) our, ours, your, yours, their, theirs

Choose possessive pronouns from the box above to complete these sentences.

① Ella forgot _____ homework and had to run back home to get it.

② Where did you buy _____ shoes?

③ The boys had to tidy up _____ bedroom.

④ My friend's dog Max loves to chase _____ tail.

⑤ We moved into _____ new house last week.

⑥ Are those pencils _____ or _____?

its and it's

Watch out! Don't confuse **its** and **it's**.

It's is a **contraction**. A contraction is when two words have been shortened to make one word. An **apostrophe (')** replaces any missing letters.

It's is short for **it is**.
The apostrophe replaces the letter i.
Example: **It's** my birthday today.
= **It is** my birthday today.

Its is a **possessive pronoun**.
It does not need an apostrophe.
Example: The cat licked **its** paw.

NOTE: **It's** can also mean **it has**.
Example: **It's** been good to see you.

Write it's or its to complete these sentences.

⑦ The dog wagged _____ tail when I arrived.

⑧ Do you think _____ going to rain tomorrow?

⑨ "Come on, _____ time to go," said Dad.

⑩ The horse cut _____ leg on the barbed wire fence.

⑪ That tree loses _____ leaves in autumn.

Score 2 points for each correct answer! **SCORE** **/22** (0-8) (10-16) (18-22)

Phonic Knowledge & Spelling

AC9E3LA11, AC9E3LY09, AC9E3LY10, AC9E3LY12

Contractions

Look at each word in the word bank. They are all **contractions**, where two words have been shortened to make one word. These shortened words are often used in speaking.
Examples: **doesn't** = does not
"He **doesn't** like me," said Jack.

they've = they have
"**They've** been there before," she said.

Word Bank

I'd	I've	you've	they've	I'm
you're	we're	he's	she's	it's

Choose words from the word bank to complete these sentences.

① _____ caught a cold so _____ staying in bed today.

② I want to go inside as _____ cold out here.

③ Let's run so _____ not late for the movie.

④ _____ not the type of person who would hurt an animal.

NOTE: won't is a tricky contraction — it is short for will not.

Write the contractions from the box next to their meanings.

shouldn't	we're	I'll	could've
she's	you're	that's	you've

⑤ she is _____

⑥ you have _____

⑦ that is _____

⑧ should not _____

⑨ we are _____

⑩ I will _____

⑪ could have _____

⑫ you are _____

Tricky homophones

Remember! Homophones are words that sound the same but have different spellings and meanings. Look at these tricky homophones.
Examples: they're, their, there   you're, your

Write the correct homophones from the brackets to complete these sentences.

⑬ _____ going on holiday tomorrow. (There, They're)

⑭ Is that _____ bag over there? (your, you're)

⑮ The dog was gnawing _____ bone. (its, it's)

Score 2 points for each correct answer! **SCORE** **/30** (0-12) (14-24) (26-30)

TARGETING HOMEWORK 3 © PASCAL PRESS ISBN 9781925726459

Informative text – Report
Author – Frances Mackay and Neil Johnson

Welcome to Country

A 'Welcome to Country' is a ceremony performed by Aboriginal or Torres Strait Islander peoples to welcome others to their traditional lands. It is held at the beginning of important events to recognise and show respect to the traditional owners and Elders of the area where the event is held. It should be conducted by an Elder or recognised community spokesperson of the region.

A 'Welcome to Country' can include traditional singing, dancing or smoking ceremonies. A smoking ceremony involves burning various native plants to produce smoke and is believed to cleanse the area and ward off evil spirits. Smoking ceremonies are only performed by Indigenous peoples with special cultural knowledge.

Procedures for welcoming visitors to the traditional lands of Aboriginal and Torres Strait Islander

peoples began thousands of years ago. When people would leave their lands and cross into someone else's country, they would ask permission before crossing the border. Once permission was granted to enter, the owners of that country would welcome them.

Source: *Australian History Centres*, Blake's Learning Centres, Blake Education.

TERM 2 ENGLISH

Write or circle the correct answers.

① **What is the meaning of ceremony?**

a an important event

b story

② **What is another word for traditional?**

a new

b exciting

c established

③ **Why is a 'Welcome to Country' ceremony held?**

_____

_____

④ **Who conducts the 'Welcome to Country' ceremony?**

_____

⑤ **In this text, what is an Elder?**

a an old person

b a person who is recognised as having special knowledge about customs and traditions

⑥ **What happens in a smoking ceremony?**

_____

_____

⑦ **Which one of these is the odd word out?**

a cleanse   c pollute

b purify   d clean

⑧ **Which word is opposite in meaning to permission?**

a consent   b refusal   c agreement

Score 2 points for each correct answer! SCORE **/16** 0-6   8-12 14-16

My Book Review

Title _____

Author _____

Rating ☆ ☆ ☆ ☆ ☆

Comment _____

_____

Number & Algebra

AC9M3M06

Using coins

Here are the six Australian coins:

5c   10c   20c   50c $1 $2

Work out how much each set of coins is worth.

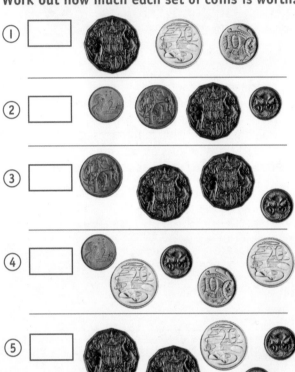

① [ ]

② [ ]

③ [ ]

④ [ ]

⑤ [ ]

Spending money

Jasmine bought a book that cost $4.50.
She paid $5. How much change did she get?

How will you work out the answer?
One way is to ask: How much do I add to
$4.50 to make $5.00?

Another way is to subtract $4.50 from $5.00.

Either way, the answer is 50 cents.

Work out the change.

⑥ Cost of pencil: $2.50
   Paid: $3.00   Change = _____

⑦ Cost of game: $8.00
   Paid: $10.00   Change = _____

⑧ Cost of notepad: $3.40
   Paid: $4.00   Change = _____

Making money amounts

⑨ Draw three coins that make $1.15.

⑩ Draw four coins that make $1.20.

⑪ Draw five coins that make $3.10.

Score 2 points for
each correct answer!   SCORE   **/22**   (0-8) (10-16) (18-22)

Statistics & Probability

AC9M3P01

Rolling dice

Did you know that one dice is
actually called a **die**? The **plural** of
die is **dice**.

A die is a cube with **six** sides. Each of the sides
has dots that show the numbers from **1 to 6**.

If we roll a die, we have a 1 in 6 chance of
rolling any of the numbers from 1 to 6.
We call this an **equal chance**.

**Are these statements true or false when you
roll one die? Circle the correct answer.**

① **There is a 1 in 6 chance of rolling a 4.**
   a True   b False

② **There is a 1 in 6 chance of rolling a 6.**
   a True   b False

③ **The chance of rolling a 2 is the same as
   the chance of rolling a 3.**
   a True   b False

④ **A 5 is always rolled more times than a 6.**
   a True   b False

⑤ **If there are two dice, there is a better
   chance of rolling a double 6 than a double
   2.** a True   b False

Toby rolled a die 60 times and recorded the
number he rolled each time. Here are his results.

Number rolled	1	2	3	4	5	6
Number of times	11	9	10	11	9	10

**Answer the questions about Toby's results.
Circle the correct answers.**

⑥ Did the dice roll the different numbers fairly
   evenly?
   a yes   b no

TERM 2 MATHS

⑦ If Toby repeats the activity, what are the chances that his results will be similar?

   a certain   **c** likely
   b unlikely   **d** impossible

⑧ How likely is it that Toby will roll a 0?

   a certain   **c** likely
   b unlikely   **d** impossible

⑨ If Toby does 10 more rolls, how likely is he to roll a number from 1 to 6?

   a certain   **c** likely
   b unlikely   **d** impossible

⑩ If a die had two 4s on it and no 3, how likely are you to roll a 4?

   a double the chance   **b** even chance

Score 2 points for each correct answer! **SCORE** /20   (0-8)   (10-14)   (16-20)

Measurement & Space

AC9M3M05

Quarter turns

The hands of a clock move in a **clockwise direction**. The long hand starts at 12 and moves around the clock to the **right** as the minutes pass.

When the long hand reaches the 3, it has moved a quarter of the way around the clock. We call this a **quarter turn**.

If the long hand on the clock moved a quarter turn, what time would the clock show? Circle the correct answer.

①

②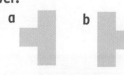

a 7:30 **b** 7:15 **c** 7:45   **a** 8:30 **b** 8:15 **c** 8:45

If you turned this shape a quarter turn to the right, what would it look like? Circle the correct answer.

③

④

        a   **b**   **c**

Turns to the left are in the anticlockwise direction. Which angle shows a quarter turn anticlockwise? Circle the correct answer.

⑤

   a   **b**   **c**   **d**

⑥

   a   **b**   **c**   **d**

Score 2 points for each correct answer! **SCORE** /12   (0-4)   (6-8)   (10-12)

Problem Solving

AC9M3M03

Calendar problem solving

Use the calendar to solve these puzzles.

JANUARY 2018

S	M	T	W	T	F	S
	1	2	3	4	5	6
7	8	9	10	11	12	13
14	15	16	17	18	19	20
21	22	23	24	25	26	27
28	29	30	31			

① On which day of the week is the first day of this month?

   _____

② How many Sundays are in this month?

   _____

③ Jake has to visit the dentist on 8 January. His next appointment is on 26 January. How many days are there between these appointments? _____

④ Georgia decided to have her party 6 days before her actual birthday so that all her friends could come. Her party was on 27 January. What date was her birthday?

   _____

⑤ Lee is flying to London on 28 January. His friend is flying to London 7 days later. On what date is his friend flying? _____

⑥ Mia was born on 23 January. Her sister's birthday is 12 days earlier. What date is her sister's birthday? _____

Grammar & Punctuation

AC9E3LA06, AC9E3LA08

Verb groups

A **verb group** has more than one verb. It is made up of a main verb and a helper verb.

Example: **Sara is eating her lunch.**

helper verb   main verb

The helper verb is called an **auxiliary verb**.

Underline the verb groups in these sentences.

① I will visit my uncle this Saturday.

② My dad has eaten his lunch.

③ Jai is riding his bike into town.

④ Talia can run very fast.

⑤ Ben was playing in the garden.

Helper verbs – time

Some helper verbs tell us about **time** — whether things are happening in the **present**, the **past** or the **future**.

Examples: Ian **is** riding his bike. (present)

Ian **was** riding his bike. (past)

Ian **will** ride his bike. (future)

Underline the verb groups in these sentences. Circle whether they are happening in the present, past or future.

⑥ I will see you tomorrow.

(*present   past   future*)

⑦ Yang is reading a book.

(*present   past   future*)

⑧ We are waiting for Jayne to arrive.

(*present   past   future*)

⑨ Dad was singing in the shower.

(*present   past   future*)

⑩ The two girls were playing in the park.

(*present   past   future*)

Score 2 points for each correct answer! **SCORE** **/20** (0-8) (10-14) (16-20)

Phonic Knowledge & Spelling

AC9E3LY09, AC9E3LY10

Letter team oo

Say each word from the word bank. They all contain the letter team **oo**, which makes a short sound.

Word Bank

look	cook	book	foot
good	stood	wool	door
crook	shook	stood	chook

Choose words from the word bank to complete these sentences.

① We went for a long walk, which made my left _____ ache.

② The _____ took one _____ at the burnt dessert and almost fainted!

③ "Alright, I'm coming as soon as I finish reading this _____."

④ The sneaky _____ was caught by the police.

Opposites

A **prefix** is a letter or group of letters that is added to the beginning of a word.

The prefix **un–** means 'not' or 'the opposite of'.

Examples: hook, **un**hook
happy, **un**happy
comfortable, **un**comfortable

Add the prefix un– to these words then write their meanings from the box.

not safe	not healthy	not kind
not known	not sure	not able

⑤ ____kind   _____

⑥ ____able   _____

⑦ ____sure   _____

⑧ ____safe   _____

⑨ ____known   _____

⑩ ____healthy   _____

Compound words

Make compound words by joining book to these words.

⑪ let   _____

⑫ case   _____

⑬ shop   _____

⑭ keeper   _____

⑮ mark   _____

Score 2 points for each correct answer! **SCORE** **/30** (0-12) (14-24) (26-30)

TARGETING HOMEWORK 3 © PASCAL PRESS ISBN 9781925726459

AC9E3LY03, AC9E3LY05, AC9HS3S04

Persuasive text – Editorial
Author – Frances Mackay and Eileen Jones

City Centres for the People: It's About Time We Got Our Roads Back!

Do cars belong in the city? City centres are busy places. This means we need to do all we can to feel safe there.

As the number of cars increases, so does the number of health problems. The amount of people with asthma has gone up 40% in the past ten years. Obesity, heart disease and diabetes have also increased.

This must prove that the car is partly to blame. Cars bring traffic, air pollution and senseless accidents. If cars are so harmful, then why not keep them away from these crowded areas? We can try walking, which doesn't kill anyone, or even a cheap bus ride. It's better than risking death every time we venture into the city.

Many busy cities around the world have introduced park-and-ride programs. Cars park outside of the city and regular buses take people into the city centre. This helps the city to become as car-free as possible.

Fred Holden is the Fair Go Party's spokesperson on transport. This week he said, "There are 200 needless, appalling road accidents in city centres every day. Something must change."

Holden is right. Asthma, obesity, injuries and deaths tell us that people and cars just do not mix.

Our government needs to ban cars NOW!

TERM 2 ENGLISH

Write or circle the correct answers.

1. **The author begins the text with a question, 'Do cars belong in the city?' Why do you think the author has done this?**

   a The author likes to start with a question.

   b To make the reader curious about the issue.

Are these statements facts or opinions?

2. City centres are busy places.
   (fact   opinion)

3. Our government needs to ban cars NOW!
   (fact   opinion)

4. **In this text, what is the meaning of venture?**

   a to go   b to walk   c to leave

5. **The words 'needless, appalling road accidents' are an example of emotive language. The author has used this to stir up strong feelings about the issue. Which of these is another example of emotive language?**

   a risking death every time we venture into the city

   b Many busy cities around the world have introduced park-and-ride programs.

6. **What is the point of view of the author?**

   a The author wants cars to remain in city centres.

   b The author wants cars banned from city centres.

7. **What audience do you think this text is aimed at?**

   a young children

   b people concerned about health and safety

   c bus drivers

8. **Which one of these is the odd word out?**

   a venture   c rest

   b journey   d travel

9. **Which word is opposite in meaning to needless?**

   a necessary   b useless   c pointless

10. **Who is Fred Holden?**

_____

Score 2 points for each correct answer! | **SCORE** | **/20** | 0-8 | 10-14 | 16-20

My Book Review

Title _____

Author _____

Rating ☆☆☆☆☆

Comment _____

_____

Place value

Example:
One thousand, six hundreds, four tens, three ones is 1643.

Write these expanded numbers in their **short form**.

1. Two thousands, three hundreds, five tens, six ones is _____
2. Four thousands, six hundreds, five tens, three ones is _____
3. Six thousands, four tens, eight ones is _____
4. Three thousands, three hundreds, five ones is _____
5. Four thousands, six hundreds, eight tens is _____

Write these numbers as **numerals**.

6. Four thousand, six hundred and seventy-eight _____
7. Five thousand, three hundred and sixty-six _____
8. Two thousand, six hundred and eight _____
9. Seven thousand, seven hundred and seventy _____
10. Eight thousand and sixty-five _____

More than, less than

Write the number that matches the description.

11. 2000 more than 3576 _____
12. 100 more than 4578 _____
13. 10 more than 6379 _____
14. 1 more than 3699 _____
15. 10 more than 4992 _____
16. 100 more than 3956 _____
17. 1000 more than 9998 _____
18. 100 less than 3156 _____
19. 1000 less than 16 378 _____
20. 10 000 less than 112 458 _____

True or false?

Circle the correct answer.

21. 27 is closer to 30 than it is to 20.
    a true   b false
22. 56 is closer to 70 than it is to 50.
    a true   b false
23. 65 is the same distance from 60 as it is from 70.
    a true   b false
24. 73 is closer to 75 than it is to 70.
    a true   b false
25. 65 cents is closer to 90 cents than it is to 50 cents.
    a true   b false
26. 99 cents is close to $1.
    a true   b false
27. 79 cents is closer to $1 than it is to 50 cents.
    a true   b false
28. $99.99 is closer to $100 than it is to $99.
    a true   b false

Making estimates

An **estimate** is an approximate answer that makes calculations easier but is close enough to the real answer. For example, 48 + 98 is difficult to work out quickly. 50 + 100 = 150 is easier. So 150 is an estimate for 48 + 98.

Make estimations for these equations.
(Your estimations should end in a zero.)

29. 53 + 103   Estimate: _____
30. 503 – 99   Estimate: _____
31. 303 – 286   Estimate: _____
32. 453 + 43   Estimate: _____
33. 49 × 2   Estimate: _____
34. 97 × 8   Estimate: _____
35. 604 ÷ 6   Estimate: _____

Score 2 points for each correct answer!   SCORE   /70   0-32   34-64   66-70

Statistics & Probability

There are no statistics & probability activities in this unit.

Measurement & Space

AC9M3M02

Height

Height is measured in **centimetres** (cm).

This is the Chan family.

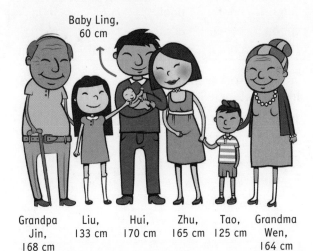

Baby Ling, 60 cm

Grandpa Jin, 168 cm

Liu, 133 cm

Hui, 170 cm

Zhu, 165 cm

Tao, 125 cm

Grandma Wen, 164 cm

Answer these questions about the Chan family.

① Who is the tallest? _____

② Who is the shortest? _____

③ What height is Grandma Wen? _____

④ How much taller than Tao is Liu? _____

⑤ Who is taller: Zhu or Grandma Wen?

_____

⑥ Who is 2 cm shorter than Hui?

_____

⑦ Who is 40 cm taller than Tao? _____

⑧ How much shorter is Grandma Wen than Grandpa Jin?

_____

⑨ How much does Baby Ling need to grow to become 1 m tall?

_____

⑩ Who is closest to 150 cm?

_____

⑪ Who is between 120 cm and 130 cm?

_____

Read the heights on these height measurers. Write the heights in cm.

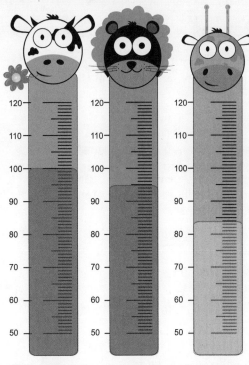

⑫ cow = _____ cm

⑬ lion = _____ cm

⑭ giraffe = _____ cm

Score 2 points for each correct answer! **SCORE** /28 0-12 14-22 24-28

Problem Solving

AC9M3A02

Crack the secret code

a	b	c	d	e	f	g	h
4	0	2	1	7	3	8	0
i	j	k	l	m	n	o	p
0	9	6	2	3	8	1	0
q	r	s	t	u			
4	9	7	6	0			
v	w	x	y	z			
5	4	1	6	7			

Use the code to solve these secret messages. Add up the numbers for each letter in the message to work out the secret number.

① Meet me today _____

☐+☐+☐+☐+☐+☐+☐+☐+☐+☐+☐

② By the river _____

☐+☐+☐+☐+☐+☐+☐+☐+☐

③ Do not be late _____

☐+☐+☐+☐+☐+☐+☐+☐+☐+☐+☐

TERM 2 MATHS

Grammar & Punctuation

AC9E3LA08

Verb tenses

> **Verbs** tell us when things are happening.
> **Tense** refers to the point in time they are happening.
> *Examples:*
> **now** (present tense) **He opens the door.**
> **yesterday** (past tense) **He opened the door.**
> **tomorrow** (future tense) **He will open the door.**

Underline the verbs in these sentences.
Circle the verb tenses.

① Leo sings in a choir.
(*present   past   future*)

② The shop will close soon.
(*present   past   future*)

③ Dad washed our clothes on Monday.
(*present   past   future*)

④ I am doing my homework.
(*present   past   future*)

⑤ A horse galloped through the park.
(*present   past   future*)

Past tense – adding –ed

> **–ed** is added to many verbs to show the **past tense**.
> *Examples:*
> (present tense) play   walk   jump
> (past tense) play**ed**   walk**ed**   jump**ed**

Write the past tense of these verbs.

⑥ work _____   ⑩ wait _____
⑦ talk _____   ⑪ listen _____
⑧ push _____   ⑫ clean _____
⑨ ask _____   ⑬ look _____

Future tense – adding 'will'

> **'will'** is added to verbs to show the **future tense**.
> *Examples:*
> (present tense) play   walk   jump
> (past tense) **will** play   **will** walk   **will** jump

Add **will** to the verbs in these sentences to show future tense.

⑭ Freya _____ **show** you how to cook spaghetti.

⑮ Our class _____ **play** football this afternoon.

⑯ I _____ **eat** my apple after lunch.

⑰ _____ you **carry** my bag for me?

Score 2 points for each correct answer!
SCORE /34 (0-14) (16-28) (30-34)

Phonic Knowledge & Spelling

AC9E3LY09, AC9E3LY10

Letter team oo

Say each word from the word bank.
They all contain the letter team
oo that makes a long sound.

Word Bank

moon	noon	pool	cool	food
hoop	snoop	boot	shoot	roof
loose	goose	balloon	spooky	rooster

Choose words from the word bank to complete these sentences.

① It costs a lot of money to send a rocket to the _____.

② There were eleven _____ ghosts at the Halloween party.

③ Fruit is a healthy _____ to eat.

④ We sat by the _____ sipping fruit juice.

Plurals of words ending in f

> **Remember!** To make the plural of many words that end in **f**, change the **f** to **v**, then add **–es**.
> *Examples:* **shelf, shelves   thief, thieves**
> However, some words keep the **f** (or **ff**) and just add **–s** to make the plural.
> *Examples:*
> **roof, roofs**   **gulf, gulfs**
> **reef, reefs**   **cuff, cuffs**
> **cliff, cliffs**   **wharf, wharfs or wharves**
> **dwarf, dwarfs**   **hoof, hoofs or hooves**
> **proof, proofs**

Complete these sentences by using plurals of words ending in **f, fe** or **ff**.

Snow White and the seven d_____ ⑤
chased after the th_____ ⑥ who had
stolen six l_____ ⑦ of bread and four
sharp k_____ ⑧ from their kitchen.
They raced along the tops of the c_____ ⑨
overlooking the sea, trying not to slip on the wet
l_____ ⑩ that had fallen from the trees.
But it was no use, as the th_____ ⑪ got
away and Snow White and the d_____ ⑫
had to go without their supper.

Score 2 points for each correct answer!
SCORE /24 (0-10) (12-18) (20-24)

TARGETING HOMEWORK 3 © PASCAL PRESS ISBN 9781925726459

Informative text – Report
Author – Hazel Edwards and Goldie Alexander

A rule for a successful team — follow the rules.

Team Rules

In sport, rules help competitors on all teams to play the game properly. When all players stick to the rules, it makes the competition fairer. Everyone has a better time. Most sports have someone who is on neither team to act as a referee or an umpire. It is their job to watch the game carefully and make sure none of the competitors break the rules. Often there are consequences for breaking the rules, such as a free pass for the other team or being taken out of the game for a short time.

Sports teams aren't the only teams to be governed by rules. Other teams use rules to make sure people on a team and people around them are kept safe and happy. Organisations and clubs also use rules to make sure everyone can work together well without causing problems. Some examples of other teams' rules include:

- washing hands before preparing food
- arriving on time for meetings or band practice
- returning equipment or tools after you've used them
- wearing appropriate safety gear, such as helmets or covered shoes
- taking turns to speak.

Source: *Teamwork*, Health & Understanding, Blake Education.

TERM 2 ENGLISH

Write or circle the correct answers.

① **What is another word for competitors?**

   a athletes   b players   c winners

② **'When all players stick to the rules, it makes the competition fairer.' What does this sentence mean?**

   a When all players keep to the rules, each team has an equal chance of winning.

   b Players cannot win if they cheat.

③ **What does a referee or an umpire do?**

   _____

   _____

④ **Give an example from the text of a consequence for breaking a rule.**

   _____

   _____

⑤ **Why do you think a club rule might include 'washing hands before preparing food'?**

   a People like to have clean hands.

   b Germs are carried on hands and washing them might prevent people from getting ill after eating the food.

   c All clubs must have rules about washing hands.

⑥ **Which one of these is the odd word out?**

   a incorrect   c proper

   b suitable   d appropriate

⑦ **Why do teams other than sports teams use rules?**

   _____

   _____

   _____

Score 2 points for each correct answer!

SCORE **/14**

My Book Review

Title _____

Author _____

Rating ☆☆☆☆☆

Comment _____

_____

Number & Algebra

AC9M3A02

Doubles

When we double a number, we add that number twice.

Examples:
double 5 = 5 + 5 = 10
double 6 = 6 + 6 = 12

Double these numbers.

① double 4 = _____
② double 2 = _____
③ double 6 = _____
④ double 8 = _____
⑤ double 9 = _____
⑥ double 7 = _____

⑦ double 40 = _____
⑧ double 20 = _____
⑨ double 60 = _____
⑩ double 80 = _____
⑪ double 90 = _____
⑫ double 70 = _____

⑬ double 400 = _____
⑭ double 200 = _____
⑮ double 600 = _____
⑯ double 800 = _____
⑰ double 900 = _____
⑱ double 700 = _____

Near doubles

When adding numbers that follow each other, you can use **doubles** to help you.

We know that double 5 or 5 + 5 = 10.

5 + 6 is the same as doubling 5 and adding 1.

5 + 5 + 1 = 10 + 1 = 11

Use the doubling + 1 method to work out these additions. Show your working out.

⑲ 7 + 8 =
_____

⑳ 8 + 9 =
_____

㉑ 4 + 5 =
_____

㉒ 6 + 7 =
_____

Doubles in the tens

This doubling method can be used for numbers in the **tens**.

We know that double 50 or 50 + 50 = 100.

50 + 60 is the same as doubling 50 and adding 10.

50 + 50 + 10 = 100 + 10 = 110

Use the doubling + 10 method to work out these additions. Show your working out.

㉓ 70 + 80 =
_____

㉔ 40 + 50 =
_____

㉕ 80 + 90 =
_____

㉖ 60 + 70 =
_____

Doubles in the hundreds

Doubling + 100 can be used to add numbers in the hundreds. We know that double 500 or 500 + 500 = 1000.

500 + 600 is the same as doubling 500 and adding 100.

500 + 500 + 100 = 1000 + 100 = 1100

100 + 100 = ?

Use the doubling + 100 method to work out these additions. Show your working out.

㉗ 700 + 800 =
_____

㉘ 400 + 500 =
_____

㉙ 800 + 900 =
_____

㉚ 600 + 700 =
_____

Score 2 points for each correct answer!

SCORE | /60 | 0-28 | 30-54 | 56-60

Statistics & Probability

AC9M3P02

Chance experiment

Tracy had a bag of coloured marbles. There were 5 red ones, 3 blue ones and 2 green ones. She did an experiment to see which colour she was most likely to pull out of the bag, without looking. Each time she took out a marble, she put it back in the bag before pulling out the next one. She did this 40 times.

Here are her results.

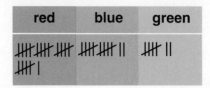

red	blue	green
ЖЖ ЖЖ ЖЖ Ж I	ЖЖ ЖЖ II	ЖЖ II

Use Tracy's experiment and results to answer the questions. Write or circle the correct answers.

① **Which colour was pulled out the most?**

_____

TARGETING HOMEWORK 3 © PASCAL PRESS ISBN 9781925726459

② **Which colour was pulled out the least?**

_____

③ **What chance does Tracy have of pulling out a green marble?**

a 3 in 10 chance
b 1 in 10 chance
c 2 in 10 chance

④ **What chance does Tracy have of pulling out a red marble?**

a 5 in 10 chance
b 3 in 10 chance
c 2 in 10 chance

⑤ **How likely is it that Tracy will pull out a red marble?**

a certain   b likely
c not likely   d impossible

⑥ **How likely is it that Tracy will pull out a yellow marble?**

a certain   b likely
c not likely   d impossible

Score 2 points for each correct answer! **SCORE** **/12** (0-4) (6-8) (10-12)

Measurement & Space

AC9M3M01

Mass
....

~~~
Mass or weight is measured in grams and kilograms.
~~~

How much does each item weigh? Circle the correct answers.

①

a 50 g   b 250 g   c 2500 g   d 25 g

②

a 1 g   b 10 kg   c 1 kg   d 100 kg

If this mass 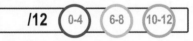 **is 250 g, how much do these items weigh?**

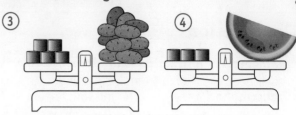

③   ④

_____   _____

Read the scales to find out how much each package weighs. Circle the correct answers.

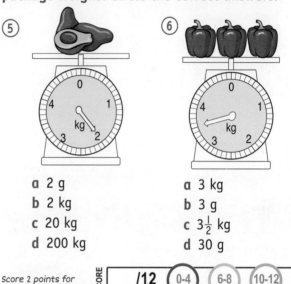

⑤   ⑥

a 2 g   a 3 kg
b 2 kg   b 3 g
c 20 kg   c 3½ kg
d 200 kg   d 30 g

Score 2 points for each correct answer! **SCORE** **/12** (0-4) (6-8) (10-12)

Problem Solving

AC9M3M04

Time puzzle
....

Find a pathway through the clock maze. Start at 12 o'clock and move forward in time until you reach 6 o'clock. You must always move forward in time, you cannot go backwards in time.

Grammar & Punctuation

AC9E3LA11

Contractions

> **Remember! Contractions** are two words that have been shortened to make one word. An **apostrophe (')** replaces the missing letters.
> *Examples*: **we've = we have let's = let**

Write the contractions for the words in brackets to complete these sentences.

① _____ coming to your party?
  (*Who is*)

② She _____ sing very well.
  (*can not*)

③ I _____ be able to see you today.
  (*will not*)

④ _____ better go before _____ dark.
  (*We had   it is*)

⑤ _____ the best cake _____ eaten!
  (*That is   I have*)

⑥ We _____ been there if the car _____ broken down.
  (*would have   had not*)

Circle the contractions that makes sense in these sentences and are spelled correctly. Write the words.

⑦ That _____ seem right!
  (*dosen't   doesn't   isn't   is'nt*)

⑧ Remi _____ go to gym last night.
  (*won't   didnt   didn't   could've*)

⑨ I _____ tell you what happened.
  (*isn't   carnt   isnt   can't*)

⑩ _____ be alright after _____ eaten.
  (*He'll   hes   he's   Hell*)

Score 2 points for each correct answer! **SCORE** **/20** (0-8) (10-14) (16-20)

Phonic Knowledge & Spelling

AC9E3LY11

Letter team -dge

**Say each word from the word bank.
They all contain the letter team -dge, which makes a soft g sound like the letter sound j.**

Word Bank

badge	dodge	edge	fridge	lodge
smudge	trudge	hedge	ridge	judge
ledge	cartridge	porridge	knowledge	

Choose words from the word bank to complete these sentences.

① I like to sit on the _____ of a riverbank all by myself.

② You will have to make _____ for breakfast yourself today.

③ The player had to _____ to the right to avoid being hit.

④ We had to _____ through thick forest to get to the lake.

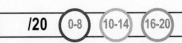

Adding –ing

Add –ing to these words.

⑤ trudge _____
⑥ smudge _____
⑦ dodge _____
⑧ judge _____
⑨ edge _____
⑩ lodge _____

Little words

Find 8 little words in the word acknowledgement.
Example: **now**

acknowledgement

⑪ _____   ⑮ _____
⑫ _____   ⑯ _____
⑬ _____   ⑰ _____
⑭ _____   ⑱ _____

Prefixes: pre–, re–

> When a **prefix** is added to the beginning of a word, it changes its meaning.
> The prefix **pre–** means 'before'.
> *Example:* arrange, prearrange (arrange before)
> The prefix **re–** means 'again'.
> *Example:* build, rebuild   (build again)

Add the prefix pre– to these words.

⑲ judge _____
⑳ view _____
㉑ record _____
㉒ date _____

Add the prefix re– to these words.

㉓ use _____
㉔ turn _____
㉕ write _____
㉖ make _____

Score 2 points for each correct answer! **SCORE** **/52** (0-24) (26-46) (48-52)

TARGETING HOMEWORK 3 © PASCAL PRESS ISBN 9781925726459

TERM 2 ENGLISH

Imaginative text – Anecdote
Author – Merryn Whitfield
Illustrator – Shiloh Gordon

Things Kids Say

Just when you think you are beginning to understand your kids, they come out and say something you would never expect.

That's what happened to me last week.

My four-year-old daughter came to me and asked, "Daddy, I'm bored. Can I play outside now?"

I was a bit worried about this because we had been renovating our veranda and there were still some leftover nails and small pieces of timber lying around. But it was a lovely day for playing outside so I agreed.

"OK, sweetie," I said. "But make sure you don't have bare feet."

Georgia looked carefully at her feet and wiggled her toes. Then she looked at me.

"But Daddy," she said. "I don't have bear feet. I have people feet."

I couldn't help but laugh. "So you do!" I agreed. "But before you go outside, please put some shoes on."

It's times like this when I don't want Georgia to grow up. I enjoy not knowing what she's going to say next!

Source: *Writing Centres: Imaginative Texts*, Blake's Learning Centres, Blake Education.

TERM 2 ENGLISH

Write or circle the correct answers.

1. **What was the purpose of this text?**
   a to tell us about Georgia
   b to make the reader laugh

2. **The author has written the text as if Georgia's father is talking directly to the reader. Why do you think the author did this?**
   a to make the reader feel like a friend who will enjoy hearing the funny story
   b to make the reader feel uncomfortable

3. **What does renovating mean?**
   a repairing
   b painting
   c cleaning

4. **This story is an anecdote. An anecdote is a funny short story about something that happened to the person telling the story. The punchline is the funny part of the story. Write the punchline of this text.**

   _____

   _____

5. **Which one of these is the odd word out?**
   a approved   c disagreed
   b agreed   d allowed

6. **From which character's point of view is the story told?**
   a Georgia   b Georgia's father

7. **Bear and bare are examples of what type of words?**
   a pronouns
   b homophones
   c contractions

Score 2 points for each correct answer!

SCORE /14 (0-4) (6-10) (12-14)

My Book Review

Title _____

Author _____

Rating ☆☆☆☆☆

Comment _____

_____

TERM 2 MATHS

Multiplying by 10

The quick way to **multiply a number by 10** is to add a zero to the end of the number.

Example: 70 × 10 = 700

What you are actually doing is moving all the digits one place to the left and adding a zero in the ones.

H	T	O
	7	0
7	0	0

Complete the number wheels by multiplying the numbers by 10.

①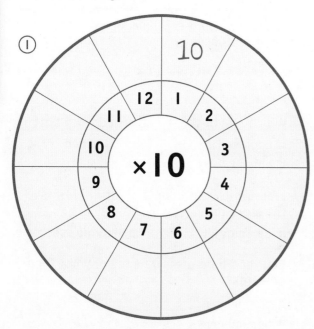

②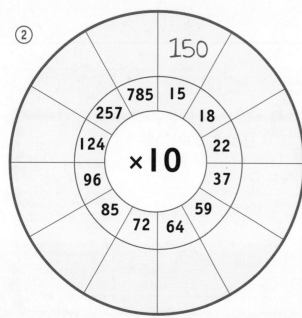

Dividing by 10

When a number ends in zero, the easy way to **divide by 10** is to take off the zero.

Example: 700 ÷ 10 = 70

To divide by 10, move all the digits one place to the right.

H	T	O
7	0	0
	7	0

Write the answers.

③ 60 ÷ 10 = _____   ⑦ 450 ÷ 10 = _____

④ 80 ÷ 10 = _____   ⑧ 670 ÷ 10 = _____

⑤ 40 ÷ 10 = _____   ⑨ 6000 ÷ 10 = _____

⑥ 130 ÷ 10 = _____   ⑩ 4560 ÷ 10 = _____

Quick way to multiply by 5

When you know how to multiply a number by 10, you can use this to help you multiply by 5.

Examples:

4 × 5 = ?
Multiply 4 × 10: **40**
Halve the answer because 5 is half of 10.
Half of 40 is **20.**
4 × 5 = 20

24 × 5 = ?
Multiply 24 × 10 = **240**
Halve the answer.
Half of 240 is **120.**
24 × 5 = 120

Use this quick method of multiplying by 5 to solve these.

⑪ 8 × 5 = _____   ⑭ 50 × 5 = _____

⑫ 9 × 5 = _____   ⑮ 120 × 5 = _____

⑬ 23 × 5 = _____   ⑯ 400 × 5 = _____

Score 2 points for each correct answer!

SCORE **/32** (0-14) (16-26) (28-32)

Statistics & Probability

There are no statistics & probability activities in this unit.

TARGETING HOMEWORK 3 © PASCAL PRESS ISBN 9781925726459

Treasure map

> To read a **coordinate grid**, first read the letter along the bottom (horizontal axis), then read the number up the side (vertical axis).
>
> A good way to remember how to read coordinates: **Go in the door, then up the stairs.**

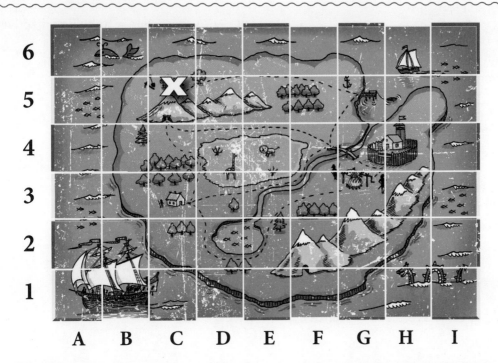

TERM 2 MATHS

Use the treasure map to answer the questions. Circle or write the correct answers.

1. The fort is marked on the map at H4. What can be found at D2?

   a a lake   **b** a mountain   **c** a river

2. What sea creature is at B6?

   a sea serpent   **b** shark   **c** whale

3. What are the map coordinates for the jetty?

   _____

4. What are the people doing at G3?

   a painting a house   **b** cooking a fish

5. What animal is at E4?

   a lion   **b** elephant   **c** snake

6. What can be found at F3?

   a lake   **b** trees   **c** mountain

7. What animal can you see at D4? _____

8. A track is shown on the map with dotted lines (-----). The track goes through a tunnel in a mountain. What are the coordinates of the tunnel? _____

9. The treasure is marked **X** on the map. What are the coordinates?

   a A2   **b** C5   **c** C2

Score 2 points for each correct answer!

SCORE /18   0-6   8-14   16-18

Problem Solving

AC9M3A02

Addition shapes

1. Write these numbers in the circles to make a magic triangle. Each line must add up to the same total. **1 2 3 5 6 7**

   (circles arranged in a triangle)

2. Write these numbers in the magic star. Each line must add up to the same total.
   1 2 3 5 6 7

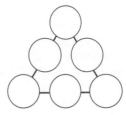

Grammar & Punctuation

① **Circle the adjectives in this sentence.**
The tiny, old lady slipped on the wet floor.

② **Circle the subject and underline the object in this sentence.**
The singer sang a song.

③ **Underline the noun group built around the noun in bold.**
The tall, black **hat** was stolen from the museum.

④ **Circle the pronouns in this sentence.**
He asked me to visit him at his house.

⑤ **Add the missing speech marks, comma and full stop in this sentence.**
You are walking too fast moaned Millie

⑥ **Circle the odd word out.**
yelled   shouted   sighed   screamed

Write its or it's to complete these sentences.

⑦ The cat was licking _____ sore paw.

⑧ _____ cold outside today.

⑨ **Underline the verb group in this sentence. Then circle the correct tense.**
My mother has eaten her lunch.
(*present   past   future*)

Write the future tense of these verbs.

⑩ walk _____

⑪ jump _____

⑫ **Circle the contraction that makes sense in this sentence and is spelled correctly.**
He _____ care!
(*isn't   doesn't   dosen't   isn't*)

Phonic Knowledge & Spelling

Choose the correct homophones for these sentences.

① I _____ he would be late.
(*new   knew*)

② We turned _____ at the lights.
(*right   write*)

Add −y to these words to make adjectives.

③ shine _____

④ crisp _____

⑤ laze _____

Write the plurals of these words.

⑥ toy _____

⑦ baby _____

⑧ city _____

Circle the number of syllables these words have.

⑨ reindeer   (1   2   3)

⑩ wheel   (1   2   3)

⑪ goalkeeper   (1   2   3)

Write the plurals of these words.

⑫ life _____

⑬ roof _____

⑭ leaf _____

Write the contractions of these words.

⑮ she is _____   ⑰ you are _____

⑯ will not_____

Make four compound nouns using the words in the box.

meal	book	let	worm	case

⑱ _____   ⑳ _____

⑲ _____   ㉑ _____

㉒ **Circle the word that has the same oo sound as the words in the box.**

moon spoon	book mood
roof hoof	shook cook

Add −ed and −ing to these words.
                    −ed   −ing

㉓ judge _____ _____

㉔ look _____ _____

㉕ carry _____ _____

㉖ **Add the prefix re− to this word then write its new meaning.**
___write   meaning: _____

Score 2 points for each correct answer! SCORE **/24** (0-10) (12-18) (20-24)

Score 2 points for each correct answer! SCORE **/52** (0-24) (26-46) (48-52)

TARGETING HOMEWORK 3 © PASCAL PRESS ISBN 9781925726459
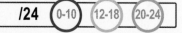

Narrative text – Recount
Author – Frances Mackay

Max took out his money box and counted what he had saved. There was $8.40. Now he could go to the shops and get some ideas.

He walked into a large store and started to look around. He saw a coffee mug and thought that might do. Then he saw a book his mum would like, but he would need another $4.50 for that. Next, he looked at vases, but decided that Mum had plenty. There were some nice fluffy slippers, but they cost twice as much as he could afford.

In the end, Max went back to his first idea.

Write or circle the correct answers.

① What had Max been saving for?

_____

② Who was he buying for? _____

③ How much was the book? _____

④ How much were the slippers? _____

⑤ What is the meaning of **afford**?
a like the look of
b have enough money for

⑥ What is the meaning of the word **saw** in this text?
a to cut wood in half
b past tense of the verb 'see'

⑦ Which word is the odd one out?
a idea   c fact
b thought   d plan

⑧ What did Max buy in the end?

_____

Score 2 points for each correct answer! SCORE **/16**   0-6   8-12   14-16

Number & Algebra

Write these numbers in words.

① 1018

_____

② 24 580

_____

_____

③ Colour this shape to show $\frac{2}{3}$.

Complete.

④ 6 × 2 = _____

⑤ 4 × 3 = _____

⑥ 5 × _____ = 25

⑦ 12 × 10 = _____

⑧ 124 × 10 = _____

⑨ 743 × 100 = _____

⑩ 30 ÷ 5 = _____

⑪ 18 ÷ _____ = 6

⑫ 60 ÷ 10 = _____

⑬ 800 ÷ _____ = 80

⑭ 1300 ÷ 10 = _____

⑮ 4500 ÷ 100 = _____

⑯ **Solve this problem.**

Mandy has 20 cupcakes to share equally with her 4 friends. How many cupcakes do they each get, including Mandy?

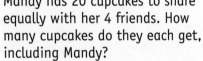

_____

Solve these.

⑰ double 43 = _____

⑱ double 28 = _____

⑲ halve 26 = _____

⑳ halve 48 = _____

Work out the change for these purchases.

㉑ banana: 60 cents   paid $2

change = _____

㉒ cake: $1.83   paid $3

change = _____

Round these numbers to the nearest 10.

㉓ 25 _____

㉔ 68 _____

㉕ 43 _____

Round these numbers to the nearest 100.

㉖ 178 _____

㉗ 323 _____

㉘ 679 _____

Round these numbers to the nearest 1000.

㉙ 1267 _____

㉚ 3954 _____

㉛ 4598 _____

Estimate the differences.

㉜ 69 – 24 estimated difference to the nearest 10 = _____

㉝ 549 – 127 estimated difference to the nearest 100 = _____

㉞ 8678 – 3590 estimated difference to the nearest 1000 = _____

Use the doubling + 1 method to work out these additions. Show your working out.

㉟ 6 + 7 _____

㊱ 8 + 9 _____

Write the numbers.

㊲ the first even number after 2010

_____

㊳ eight thousand, four hundred and thirty-seven

_____

㊴ the number that is two hundred less than 8246

_____

Score 2 points for each correct answer!   SCORE   /78   (0-36) (38-72) (74-78)

72

TARGETING HOMEWORK 3 © PASCAL PRESS ISBN 9781925726459

Statistics & Probability

Sam had a bag of coloured marbles. There were 6 red ones, 4 blue ones and 3 green ones. He did an experiment to see which colour he was most likely to pull out of the bag, without looking. Each time he took out a marble, he put it back in the bag before pulling out the next one. He did this 40 times. Here are his results.

red	blue	green
卌 卌 卌 卌	卌 卌 ||	卌 ||

Use Sam's experiment and results to answer the questions. Write or circle the correct answers.

① Which colour was pulled out the most?

_____

② Which colour was pulled out the least?

_____

③ What chance does Sam have of pulling out a green marble?
  a 6 in 13 chance
  b 1 in 13 chance
  c 3 in 13 chance

④ How likely is it that Sam will pull out a red marble?
  a certain   **b** likely
  c not likely   **d** impossible

⑤ How likely is it that Sam will pull out a yellow marble?
  a certain   **b** likely
  c not likely   **d** impossible

Score 2 points for each correct answer! **SCORE** /10 (0-2) (4-8) (10)

Measurement & Space

How many litres?

① 3000 millilitres = _____ litres

② 500 millilitres = _____ litre

How much juice is in the jug?

③ _____ litres

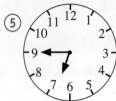

Write these analogue times as digital times.

④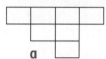

_____

⑤

_____

Circle the correct answers.

⑥ Which net will make a cube?

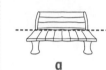
a   **b**   **c**

⑦ Which picture shows halves?

a   **b**   **c**

⑧ Which angle shows a quarter turn clockwise?

a   **b**   **c**

⑨ How much does this tin of paint weigh, in grams? _____

▬ = 500 g
▬ = 1 kg

Use the treasure map to answer the questions. Circle or write the correct answers.

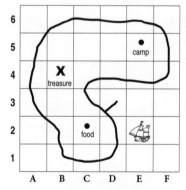

⑩ Where is the pirate ship located?
  a D2   **b** E2   **c** F2

⑪ Is the camp located at E4?
  a Yes   **b** No

⑫ If you are at C5, are you on land or in the sea?
  a land   **b** sea

⑬ What are the coordinates of the treasure, marked **X**?

_____

Score 2 points for each correct answer! **SCORE** /26 (0-10) (12-20) (22-26)

Grammar & Punctuation

AC9E3LE03

Adjectives

> **Remember!** **Adjectives** are words used to describe people, places and things. They work with the <u>noun</u> to tell us more about what is happening.
>
> Adjectives can be used to describe the setting in a story — to help the reader build up a clear picture of what is being described.
>
> *Examples*: The **huge, rickety** <u>door</u> slowly creaked open to reveal a **dark, rat-infested** <u>room</u> covered in **creepy** cobwebs.
>
> **Adjectives** can be placed *before* or *after* the <u>noun</u> they describe.
>
> *Examples*:
> The **dark, rat-infested** <u>room</u> was revealed.
> The <u>room</u> was **dark** and **rat-infested**.

Choose adjectives from the word bank to complete this story setting.

Word Bank

huge	sticky	wooden	spindly
large	old	moth-eaten	loud
dusty	black	terrifying	enormous

The Haunted House

We stepped further into the **h_____** ① **entrance hall.** As our eyes adjusted to the gloom, we began to see more clearly.

A **l_____** ②, **b_____** ③ **piano** stood in one corner, its **s_____** ④ **legs** looking like they would collapse at any minute. In the centre was a **w_____** ⑤ **staircase** covered in **d_____** ⑥ **footprints**, with **s_____** ⑦ **cobwebs** hanging from every step. A **travel trunk**, all **o_____** ⑧ and **d_____** ⑨, stood in the other corner with a **m_____** ⑩ **rug** flung across it. Suddenly we heard a **l_____** ⑪ **sound.** A **t_____** ⑫, piercing scream echoed down the stairs. We stood stock-still, frozen with fear.

TERM 3 ENGLISH

Score 2 points for each correct answer! **SCORE** **/24** (0-10) (12-18) (20-24)

Phonic Knowledge & Spelling

AC9E3LY09, AC9E3LY10, AC9E3LY11

Letter team: ar

Say each word from the word bank. They all contain the letter team **ar**. The letters work together to make the one sound 'ah'.

Word Bank

car	far	star	start	part
yard	hard	guard	bark	shark
farm	dark	spark	smart	march
harvest	parcel	arcade	garden	sharpen

Choose words from the word bank to complete these sentences.

① Our visit to the dairy _____ was great.

② I have a vegetable _____ in my yard.

③ Could you please _____ my pencil?

④ The _____ on the tree was rough.

Write words from the word bank that match these clues.

⑤ g _ _ _ _ _ : someone who protects a person or place

⑥ s _ _ _ _ _ : a tiny flash

⑦ d _ _ _ _ : the opposite of light

⑧ s _ _ _ _ _ : clever

⑨ y _ _ _ _ : a piece of ground near a building

⑩ f _ _ : the opposite of near

Add star to the beginning of these words to make compound words.

⑪ fish _____

⑫ dust _____

⑬ gaze _____

⑭ ship _____

⑮ let _____

⑯ burst _____

⑰ board _____

⑱ light _____

⑲ fruit _____

Score 2 points for each correct answer! **SCORE** **/38**   (0-16)   (18-32)   (34-38)

TARGETING HOMEWORK 3 © PASCAL PRESS ISBN 9781925726459

Imaginative text – Poem
Author – Frances Mackay

The Mighty Volcano

The earth trembles, quivers and shakes
All around slowly awakes
Inside the earth, molten magma stirs
Awaiting the disaster that will occur
Bubble, bubble, pop, pop
Clouds of smoke rise from the vent
Throwing out ash wherever it went
The heat rises, the volcano moans
Out of the crater a bomb is thrown
Bubble, bubble, pop, pop
Molten rocks begin to implode
Violently, the mountain suddenly explodes
Red hot lava finally escapes
Quickly destroying all in its wake
Bubble, bubble, pop, pop
Trees burn, rocks slide
Beware all creatures — there's nowhere
to hide
But slowly the flow begins to subside
Leaving the earth raw and incised
Bubble, bubble, pop, pop
The mighty volcano has had its say
And now lies dormant until another day

Write or circle the correct answers.

1. The word **pop** is an example of
   onomatopoeia — a word that sounds
   like its meaning. Which of these words
   from the text is also an example of
   onomatopoeia?

   a red   b bubble   c trees

2. Why do you think the author has repeated
   the line 'Bubble, bubble, pop, pop'?

   a because she likes the sound of the words

   b to give a rhythm to the poem and to
   create the sounds of the volcano

3. What is another word for **disaster**?

   a fun   b work   c tragedy

4. Which one of these is the odd word out?

   a calm   b burst   c explode

5. **Implode** has the opposite meaning to
   explode. What do you think it means?

   a to collapse inwards

   b to blast outwards

**Use words from the text to label this diagram
of a volcano.**

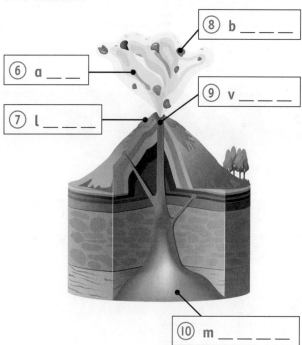

6. a _ _ _
7. l _ _ _ _
8. b _ _ _ _
9. v _ _ _ _
10. m _ _ _ _ _ _

11. What do you think a **dormant** volcano is?

    a a volcano that will not erupt again

    b a volcano that will erupt again one day

Score 2 points for
each correct answer!

SCORE /22   0-8   10-16   18-22

My Book Review

Title _____

Author _____

Rating ☆☆☆☆☆

Comment _____
_____

TERM 3 ENGLISH

Number & Algebra

AC9M3N02

Finding a half

To find a half ($\frac{1}{2}$) of a group of objects or a number, you divide by 2. This will give you two equal parts.

What is a half of this group?

There are 8 balls altogether.
Divide 8 by 2 = 4
A half of 8 = 4

What is a half of these groups?
Circle the correct answer.

①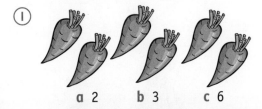

   a 2   b 3   c 6

②

   a 12   b 8   c 6

What is a half of these numbers?
Circle the correct answer.

③ $\frac{1}{2}$ of 10 =   a 2   b 5   c 10

④ $\frac{1}{2}$ of 16 =   a 8   b 10   c 16

⑤ $\frac{1}{2}$ of 20 =   a 5   b 10   c 20

Finding a quarter

To find a quarter ($\frac{1}{4}$) of a group of objects or a number, you divide by 4. This will give you four equal parts.

What is a quarter of these groups?
Circle the correct answer.

⑥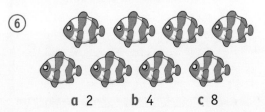

   a 2   b 4   c 8

⑦

   a 2   b 3   c 4

What is a quarter of these numbers?
Circle the correct answer.

⑧ $\frac{1}{4}$ of 16 =   a 4   b 6   c 10

⑨ $\frac{1}{4}$ of 20 =   a 4   b 5   c 6

⑩ $\frac{1}{4}$ of 40 =   a 10   b 12   c 8

Score 2 points for each correct answer!   **SCORE**   **/20**   (0-8)   (10-14)   (16-20)

Statistics & Probability

AC9M3ST03

Line graphs

This is a line graph. It shows the number of visitors to Redtown Museum last week.

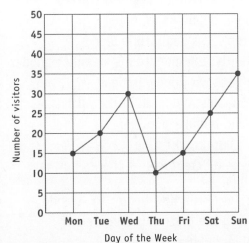

Each blue dot show the number of visitors to the museum that day.

On Monday, 15 people visited.

On Saturday, 35 people visited.

A red line joins up the red dots. It tells us that the information is connected to each other.

Use the line graph to answer the questions.

① How many people visited the museum on Tuesday? _____

② Which day of the week had the most visitors? _____

③ Which day of the week had the fewest visitors? _____

④ Wednesday had half-price entry. How many people visited on Wednesday?

_____

⑤ How many more people visited the museum on Wednesday than Thursday?

_____

⑥ 25 people visited the museum on Saturday. True or false?

_____

SCORE **/12** ⟨0-4⟩ ⟨6-8⟩ ⟨10-12⟩

Measurement & Space

AC9M3M02

Comparing masses

How many kilograms do you add to balance each scale? Circle the correct answer.

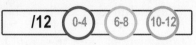

1 kg   2 kg   5 kg

①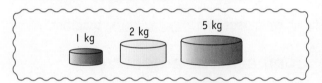

a 1   b 2   c 4

②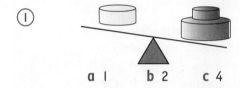

a 10   b 8   c 7

③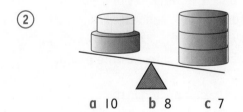

a 1   b 2   c 3

④ Number these items from 1 to 4 to order them from lightest (1) to heaviest (4).

a ☐   b ☐   d ☐

c ☐

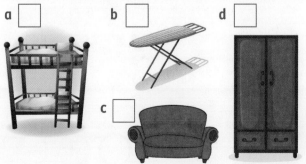

Estimate which object would have the greater mass. Circle the correct answer.

⑤ a a whale   b a starfish
⑥ a a bicycle   b a family car
⑦ a a laptop   b a mobile phone

True or false? Circle the correct answer.

⑧ There are 100 g in a kilogram.
   a true   b false

⑨ 40 kg is more than 40 g.
   a true   b false

⑩ $5\frac{1}{2}$ kilograms is equal to 5500 g.
   a true   b false

⑪ A cow is lighter than a dog.
   a true   b false

SCORE **/22** ⟨0-8⟩ ⟨10-16⟩ ⟨18-22⟩

Problem Solving

AC9M3M01

Problem solving using length

Solve these word problems about length. Show your working out.

① Ali is 124 cm tall. Imran is 12 cm shorter. How tall is Imran?

_____

② Sue walks 3 km every day to keep fit. How far does she walk in one week?

_____

③ A building has 100 floors. Each floor is 5 metres high. How high is the building?

_____

④ Jayne can run 2 km in 30 minutes. How long will it take her to run 6 km?

_____

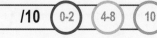

⑤ A ribbon was 65 cm long. After I cut off some, 37 cm was left. How much did I cut off?

_____

SCORE **/10** ⟨0-2⟩ ⟨4-8⟩ ⟨10⟩

TERM 3 MATHS

Grammar & Punctuation

AC9E3LE03

Comparative adjectives

> **Adjectives** can be used to show how people or things compare with each other.
>
> When *two things* are compared, you add the suffix **–er**.
>
> *Example*: My dog is **big**, but her dog is **bigger**.
>
> When *more than two things* are compared, you add the suffix **–est**.
>
> *Example*: His dog is the **biggest**.
>
> These **comparative adjectives** are tricky ones!
>
> | good | better | best |
> | bad | worse | worst |
> | many | more | most |
> | little | less | least |

Add the suffixes –er and –est to these adjectives.

	–er	–est
① wide	_____	_____
② small	_____	_____
③ loud	_____	_____
④ long	_____	_____
⑤ sweet	_____	_____

Circle the correct adjective for each sentence.

⑥ That is the _____ car I have ever seen.
(*smaller   smallest*)

⑦ An elephant is _____ than a flea.
(*larger   largest*)

⑧ Tom was the _____ person at the party.
(*older   oldest*)

⑨ It is _____ today than yesterday.
(*colder   coldest*)

Circle the correct adjective for each sentence.

⑩ That was the _____ cake I have ever eaten! (*better   best*)

⑪ He should be _____ careful on his bike.
(*more   most*)

⑫ I had a _____ toothache last week.
(*bad   worst*)

⑬ Cleaning is my _____ favourite chore. (*less   least*)

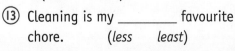

Phonic Knowledge & Spelling

AC9E3LY09, AC9E3LY10, AC9E3LY11

Letter team: ir

Say each word from the word bank. They all contain the letter team **ir**. The letters work together to make the one sound 'er'.

Word Bank

bird	third	shirt	skirt	dirt
girl	twirl	whirl	stir	firm
first	thirsty	circle	birthday	thirteen

Choose words from the word bank to complete these sentences.

① _____ is an unlucky number.

② I was _____, so I had a glass of water.

③ The _____ slipped on the hem of her long _____.

④ We all sat in a _____ together.

Comparative adjectives: spelling rules

> Remember to use these spelling rules when adding the suffixes **–er** or **–est**.
>
> When a word ends in a **short vowel followed by a single consonant**, double the last consonant before adding **–er** and **–est**.
>
> *Examples*: sad, sadd**er**, sadd**est**
>
> When a word ends in **y** and has a consonant before it, change the **y** to **i** before adding **–er** or **–est**.
>
> *Examples*: dirty, dirt**ier**, dirt**iest**

Add the suffixes –er and –est to these adjectives.

	–er	–est
⑤ hungry	_____	_____
⑥ big	_____	_____
⑦ pretty	_____	_____
⑧ wet	_____	_____
⑨ hot	_____	_____
⑩ early	_____	_____

Add bird to these words to make compound words.

⑪ _____bath   ⑬ _____song

⑫ _____seed   ⑭ _____cage

Imaginative text – Narrative
Author – Patricia Bernard, **Illustrator** – Mark Guthrie

Betty and Meow

Nyoman tucked a banana and a piece of fish, wrapped in a banana leaf, into his backpack. He tiptoed past his sleeping family and out of the house.

Weekends were always busy. In the mornings he sold herbs with his mother at the Ubud market. In the afternoons he helped his grandfather in the rice paddies. In the evenings he ran errands for his older brother, Wayan, and his sister, Kadek. They worked as dancers at the Water Palace.

If Nyoman wanted time to himself, he had to leave the house early. He ran between the paddies. He ran over the bridge where his father's taxi was parked, and through the laneway to Jalan Raya, the main road. He followed the road through Ubud to his destination: the Sacred Monkey Forest.

Nyoman loved the forest with its huge trees and wide-leafed ferns. He loved feeding the long-tailed macaques that lived there, especially the mothers with their tiny, black-haired babies.

His favourite monkey was a young female who'd adopted an unwanted kitten. The monkey keepers had named her Betty, and her kitten Meow.

Source: Sparklers, *The Sacred Monkey*, Blake Education.

Write or circle the correct answers.

1. **Nyoman's weekends were always busy. Number these tasks from 1–3 in the order Nyoman had to do them each day.**

   ☐ run errands for his sister and brother

   ☐ sell herbs at the market with his mother

   ☐ help his grandfather in the rice paddy fields

2. **What is another word for errands?**

   a shops   b chores   c games

3. **What does Nyoman's father do for a job?**

   a we are not told

   b rice farmer

   c taxi driver

4. **Why did Nyoman get up so early?**

   a He couldn't sleep.

   b He wanted to see the monkeys before he started his chores.

   c He had to go to the market.

5. **Nyoman lives in Bali, an island in Indonesia. What do you think Ubud is?**

   a the nearest town to where Nyoman lives

   b a taxi company

   c the name of the main road

6. **A macaque is a type of monkey. What was the name of the monkey that Nyoman was going to visit that day?**

   _____

7. **What was unusual about this monkey's baby?**

   a It had black hair.

   b It was a kitten.

   c It was lost.

TERM 3 ENGLISH

Score 2 points for each correct answer!   SCORE /14   0-4   6-10   12-14

My Book Review

Title _____

Author _____

Rating ☆☆☆☆☆

Comment _____

_____

Number & Algebra

AC9M3N01

Counting in 10s

The number **239** has

2 hundreds = 200
3 tens = 30
9 ones = 9

To count in 10s starting from **239**, we count like this:

239, 249, 259, 269, 279, 289, 299, 309

Can you see the pattern? The number in the tens place goes up by **1 ten** each time.

Complete these number patterns by counting in 10s.

① 126, 136, _____, _____, _____, _____

② 394, 404, 414, _____, _____, _____, _____

③ 5436, 5446, _____, _____, _____, _____, 5496

④ 12 388, 12 398, 12 408, _____, _____, _____

Counting in 100s

The number **239** has

2 hundreds = 200
3 tens = 30
9 ones = 9

To count in 100s starting from **239**, we count like this:

239, 339, 439, 539, 639, 739, 839, 939, 1039

Can you see the pattern? The number in the hundreds place goes up by **1 hundred** each time.

Complete these number patterns by counting in 100s.

⑤ 124, 224, 324, _____, _____, _____, _____

⑥ 638, _____, _____, _____, _____, 1138, 1238

⑦ 409, 509, 609, _____, _____, _____, _____

⑧ 5023, 5123, 5223, _____, _____, _____, _____

⑨ 23 338, 23 438, 23 538, _____, _____, _____

Counting in 1000s

The number **4239** has

4 thousands = 4000
2 hundreds = 200
3 tens = 30
9 ones = 9

To count in 1000s starting from **4239**, we count like this:

4239, 5239, 6239, 7239, 8239, 9239, 10 239

Can you see the pattern? The number in the thousands place goes up by **1 thousand** each time.

Complete these number patterns by counting in 1000s.

⑩ 1430, 2430, 3430, _____, _____, _____,

_____

⑪ 7788, 8788, _____, 10 788, _____,

_____, _____

⑫ 25 600, 26 600, _____, _____, _____,

_____, 31 600

Score 2 points for each correct answer! **SCORE** | **/24** (0-10) (12-18) (20-24)

Statistics & Probability

There are no statistics & probability activities in this unit.

Measurement & Space

AC9M3SP01

Prisms and pyramids

A **prism** is a 3D object with flat sides (faces). It has two ends that are the **same shape and size**. If you sliced through a prism, each slice would have the same size and shape as the ends.

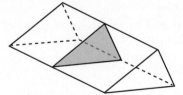

Note: a cylinder has the same shape at both ends but it is **not a prism** because it has curved sides, not flat.

TARGETING HOMEWORK 3 © PASCAL PRESS ISBN 9781925726459

A **pyramid** is a 3D object. It has a polygon **base** and flat, triangular **sides** (faces). The sides join at one point which is called the **apex**. If you sliced through a pyramid, the slices would have the same shape as the base but they would not be the same size.

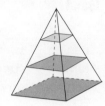

Note: a **polygon** is a shape with 3 or more sides.

Are these objects prisms or pyramids?

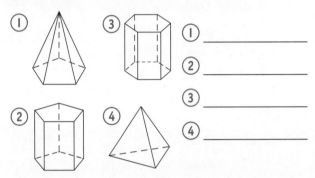

① _____

② _____

③ _____

④ _____

A **prism** is named after the shape of each **end**.

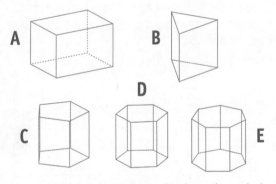

Prism **A** has a **rectangle** at both ends so it is called a **rectangular prism**.

Prism **B** has a **triangle** at both ends so it is called a **triangular prism**.

Look at the shapes at the ends of the other prisms. Circle the correct name for each one.

⑤ **Prism C**
   a triangular prism   b pentagonal prism

⑥ **Prism D**
   a pentagonal prism   b hexagonal prism

⑦ **Prism E**
   a octagonal prism   b heptagonal prism

Tree diagrams

Read this problem.
A tree diagram has been used to solve it.

Tom always wears either black shorts or white shorts. He wears his shorts with a red, blue or green T-shirt. How many different outfits does Tom have to choose from?

black shorts

white shorts

Tom has **6** choices of outfits.

Use a tree diagram like the one above to solve this problem.

Jackie likes to eat vanilla or lime ice-cream. For toppings, she chooses from chocolate, raspberry or strawberry.

How many different combinations of ice-cream and topping does Jackie have to choose from?

Score 2 points for each correct answer!

SCORE **/14** 0-4 6-10 12-14

TERM 3 MATHS

Grammar & Punctuation

AC9E3LA02, AC9E3LA11

Modal verbs

> **Modal verbs** are helper verbs. They give us more information about the verbs that follow them.
> *Examples:* can could will would
> may might should must
>
> Modal verbs can be used to show:
> - how likely something is to happen (I **might** play football)
> - someone's ability to do something (I **can** play football)
> - if something must be done (I **must** play football)
> - if permission is given to do something (I **can** play football)
> - if something is planned to be done (I **will** play football)

Write modal verbs to complete these sentences.

① We _____ go swimming if it were warmer.

② You _____ wear a helmet when you ride your bike.

③ Tim _____ ride a horse, but I can't.

④ I _____ remember to put my alarm clock on.

Modal verbs: contractions

> A **modal verb** + **not** presents a negative idea.
> *Example:* I **must not** go tomorrow.
>
> Sometimes a **contraction** is used, especially in speech. *Example:* I **mustn't** go tomorrow.

Write contractions for these negative modal verbs.

⑤ could not = _____

⑥ must not = _____

⑦ should not = _____

⑧ will not = _____

⑨ can not = _____

⑩ might not = _____

Circle the correct negative modal verb for each sentence.

⑪ I _____ see clearly because it was too dark. (*couldn't won't*)

⑫ The dog _____ sit on the sofa — or else! (*won't mustn't*)

⑬ I _____ give up, no matter what. (*shouldn't won't*)

⑭ I _____ agree more! (*won't couldn't*)

Phonic Knowledge & Spelling

AC9E3LY10, AC9E3LY11, AC9E3LY12

Letter team: er

Say each word from the word bank. They all contain the letter team **er**. The letters work together to make the one sound 'er'.

Word Bank

her	herd	serve	nerve	swerve
perch	jerk	kerb	fern	stern
term	germ	person	nervous	servant

Choose words from the word bank to complete these sentences.

① She picked pretty flowers from _____ garden.

② The picture was painted by a famous _____.

③ The _____ had to wear a purple uniform.

④ The car started to _____ then hit the _____.

Homophones

> **Remember! Homophones** are words that sound the same but have different spellings and meanings.
> *Examples:* **herd** (a group of cattle)
> **heard** (listened to a sound)

Circle the correct homophones for these sentences

⑤ The _____ postal worker delivered the _____. (*mail male*)

⑥ We made a cake using self-raising _____. (*flour flower*)

⑦ Mum went to the sale to get a _____ dress. (*cheap cheep*)

⑧ He _____ like to chop the _____ for you. (*wood would*)

Add endings to the words to complete the sentences. Choose from **–ed**, **–ing** or **–ly**.

⑨ (serve) Li asked for another _____ of cake.

⑩ (nervous) She was _____ biting her fingernails.

⑪ (jerk) The man quickly _____ his head around.

Informative text – Report
Author – Frances Mackay and Neil Johnson

Emblems of Australia

Each state and territory of Australia has special symbols to represent it. These are called emblems. Usually they are plants and animals that are native to that part of Australia. Not all states and territories have official flowers, animals and birds. However, there are some that many people feel are representative of a particular place, such as the Tasmanian Devil. These are known as 'unofficial' emblems.

Here are the animal emblems of the different Australian states and territories.

Queensland
Koala

Victoria
Leadbeater's Possum

Australian Capital Territory
(no animal emblem)

Western Australia
Numbat

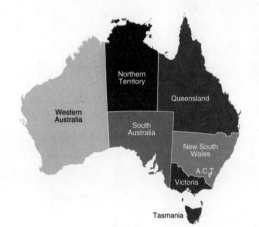

New South Wales
Platypus

Tasmania
Tasmanian Devil (unofficial)

South Australia
Southern Hairy-nosed Wombat

Northern Territory
Red Kangaroo

Source: *Australian History Centres*, Blake's Learning Centres, Blake Education.

TERM 3 ENGLISH

Write or circle the correct answers.

① **What is an emblem?**

a a flower

b a special symbol

c an animal

② **What are native plants and animals?**

a plants and animals that live in the same place they originally came from

b plants and animals that are new to an area

③ **What is the unofficial animal emblem of Tasmania?**

a Platypus   b Tasmanian Devil

④ **Which state of Australia has the koala as its animal emblem?**

a Western Australia

b New South Wales

c Queensland

⑤ **Which one of these is the odd word out?**

a special   c unimportant

b important   d unique

⑥ **Which state or territory does not have an animal emblem?**

_____

⑦ **Which word in the text means 'to stand for'?**

a particular

b represent

c official

Score 2 points for each correct answer! SCORE /14 (0-4) (6-10) (12-14)

My Book Review

Title _____

Author _____

Rating ☆☆☆☆☆

Comment _____

_____

Number & Algebra

AC9M3M06

Money – finding the total

When we add numbers, the answer is called the **total** or **sum**. Look at the toys in this shop.

If you bought a rocket and a teddy, it would cost $2.99 (rounded up to $3.00) + $3.00 = $6.00 in total.

Find the totals if you bought these toys from the shop.

① a rocket and a duck
total = _____

② two teddies
total = _____

③ a motorbike and a rocket
total = _____

④ a robot and a plane
total = _____

If you had $10, how much change would you get? Use your answers to questions 1 to 4 to help.

⑤ rocket and duck
change from $10 = _____

⑥ two teddies
change from $10 = _____

⑦ motorbike and rocket
change from $10 = _____

⑧ robot and plane
change from $10 = _____

If you subtract or take away one number from another, the answer is called the **difference**.

The difference in cost between a rocket ($2.99, rounded up to $3.00) and a plane ($2.50) is 50 cents. **$3.00 – $2.50 = $0.50**

What is the difference in cost between these items?

⑨ a train and a duck
difference = _____

⑩ a rocket and a duck
difference = _____

⑪ two teddies and a motorbike
difference = _____

⑫ a robot and a plane
difference = _____

Score 2 points for each correct answer! | SCORE **/24** (0-10) (12-18) (20-24)

Statistics & Probability

AC9M3ST02

Comparing results

These tables show the results of a survey that Jan and Michael carried out in school.

Jan's Results	Year 1	Year 2	Year 3
Ice-cream	17	20	12
Cake	10	10	6
Fruit	5	3	8
Doughnuts	0	0	2

Michael's Results	Year 4	Year 5	Year 6
Ice-cream	15	15	10
Cake	5	10	5
Fruit	5	3	9
Doughnuts	2	1	8

Answer the questions about their results.

① What would be the best title for their tables?
   a Favourite foods in our school
   b Number of boys and girls in each class
   c Favourite desserts in our school

② Which dessert is the most popular in the whole school? _____

③ Which dessert is the least popular in the whole school? _____

④ Do more older children like doughnuts than younger children?
   a yes   **b** no

⑤ Which class had the most students on the day of the survey?
   a Year 1   **b** Year 2   **c** Year 6

⑥ How many more students in Year 2 prefer ice-cream than those in Year 6? _____

Score 2 points for each correct answer! | SCORE **/12** (0-4) (6-8) (10-12)

Answer the questions or tick the box.

1. Who sits closest to the door?
   a Sue   b Ryan   c Lee

2. Who sits closest to the sink?
   a Georgia   b Lee   c Jayne

3. Who sits in front of Jayne?
   a Ben   b Sue   c Eli

4. Who sits next to Lee?
   a Nat   b Jack   c Jayne

5. Does Jo have to go past Will's desk to get to the sink?
   a yes   b no

6. Who sits nearest to the whiteboard?

   _____

7. What would be the quicker way for Jack to get to the sink?
   a walk past Mia's desk
   b walk past Tina's desk

8. What would be the quicker way for Sue to get to the door?
   a walk past Lee's desk
   b walk past David's desk

Problem Solving

AC9M3A01

Working backwards

Sometimes it helps to work backwards in order to work out the answer to a problem.

Example:

There were lots of people at Sam's party when Rae arrived. 5 more people arrived after Rae, then another 2. Finally, 6 more people arrived, making 25 people altogether.

How many people were at the party before Rae arrived?

We can work backwards from the total of 25 people. We take away the numbers of people who arrived to find out how many were already there.

$$25 - 1 - 5 - 2 - 6 = 11$$

Solve this problem using the working backwards method.

Before 10 o'clock, the baker had baked some cookies.

He baked 6 more cookies at 11 o'clock and 10 more before lunch.

After lunch he baked another 6 cookies, making a total of 30 cookies altogether.

How many cookies did he cook before 10 o'clock?

Grammar & Punctuation

AC9E3LA10

Adverbs

> **Adverbs** tell us more about <u>verbs</u>. They add extra information about what people and things are doing.
>
> They tell us:
>
> **HOW** things are being done
>   She <u>sang</u> **loudly**.
>
> **WHEN** things are happening
>   We <u>played</u> football **yesterday**.
>
> **WHERE** things are happening
>   I <u>will put</u> my hat **there**.

Underline the verb and circle the adverb in these sentences.

① She spoke loudly at the meeting.

② He crossed the road quickly.

③ Mum rode a horse today.

④ We will meet you at the restaurant tomorrow.

⑤ I have looked everywhere for you.

⑥ The dog ran away.

Circle a suitable adverb to complete each sentence.

⑦ The dog stretched _____.
  (*angrily*   *lazily*)

⑧ The three mice ran _____.
  (*away*   *neatly*)

⑨ We ate fish and chips _____.
  (*tomorrow*   *yesterday*)

⑩ The fire blazed _____ in the gloom.
  (*loudly*   *brightly*)

⑪ Look, she's hiding _____ the sofa!
  (*behind*   *nearby*)

⑫ Dry those glasses _____.
  (*easily*   *carefully*)

Write the adverbs from the box next to their matching verbs.

bravely	loudly	angrily	fast	high

⑬ laughed _____

⑭ ran _____

⑮ flying _____

⑯ fought _____

⑰ stomped _____

Phonic Knowledge & Spelling

AC9E3LY09, AC9E3LY10, AC9E3LY11

Letter team: ur

Say each word from the word bank. They all contain the letter team **ur**. The letters work together to make the one sound 'er'.

Word Bank

burn	turn	church	hurt	spurt
burst	turf	nurse	purse	curve
turkey	further	surfer	nursery	purple

Choose words from the word bank to complete these sentences.

① The family went to _____ every Sunday.

② My cousin is training to become a _____.

③ I didn't have enough money in my _____.

④ The eggplant was a dark _____ colour.

Adverbs of manner

> Adverbs that tell us *how* things are being done are called **adverbs of manner**. Many adverbs of manner are built from adjectives by adding the suffix **–ly**.
>
> When an **adjective** ends in **y**, you usually change the **y** to **i** before adding **–ly**.
>
> *Examples:*
> quick, quick**ly**   soft, soft**ly**   angry, angr**ily**

Add the suffix –ly to these adjectives to make adverbs.

⑤ rough _____

⑥ lazy _____

⑦ careful _____

⑧ easy _____

Write these words in dictionary order.

surf	spurt	purse	turn

⑨ _____

Circle the number of syllables these words have.

⑩ church (1 2 3)

⑪ further (1 2 3)

⑫ burning (1 2 3)

⑬ furniture (1 2 3)

TARGETING HOMEWORK 3 © PASCAL PRESS ISBN 9781925726459

Informative text – Report
Author – Frances Mackay

Climate zones of the world

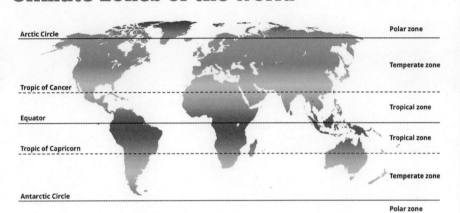

The weather in one place changes from day to day and can change very quickly. Climate, however, tells us what the weather has generally been like over many years.

There are several climate zones around the world, but the three main ones are polar, temperate and tropical.

Polar zone
The polar zones are very cold and dry all year. The polar zones include the Arctic, the Antarctic, Alaska, northern Canada and northern Russia.

Temperate zone
The temperate zones have cold winters and mild summers. The countries in this zone have distinct seasons of summer, autumn, winter and spring. The temperate zones include the United Kingdom, northern Europe, New Zealand, South Africa, the United States of America and parts of Australia.

Tropical zone
The tropical zones are hot and wet all year. The tropics are found in rainforest areas such as the Amazon, central Africa, South-East Asia and northern Australia.

Write or circle the correct answers.

① **What is the difference between weather and climate?**
  a There is no difference; they are the same.
  b We are not told.
  c Weather changes daily; climate is weather over a long period of time.

② **On the map, the tropical zone is represented by which colour?**
  a yellow/green
  b red/yellow
  c blue/green

③ **In which climate zone is New Zealand?**
  a temperate
  b polar
  c tropical

List the four seasons of the temperate zone.

④ _____

⑤ _____

⑥ _____

⑦ _____

⑧ **Which one of these is the odd word out?**
  a hot   c glacial
  b freezing   d cold

⑨ **Which word in the text means clear-cut or definite?**
  a region   b distinct   c found

Which two climate zones does Australia have?

⑩ _____

⑪ _____

Score 2 points for each correct answer! **SCORE** **/22** 0-8 10-16 18-22

My Book Review

Title _____

Author _____

Rating ☆ ☆ ☆ ☆ ☆

Comment _____

_____

Number & Algebra

AC9M3N01

Place value

Circle the largest number in each group.

① 51, 27, 15, 38

② 309, 447, 40 tens, 300 and 15 tens

③ 1640, 10 064, 16 350, 9999

④ 24 500, 36 789, 124 567, 89 202

True or false? Circle the correct answer.

⑤ There are 15 tens and 1 hundred in 250.
   a true   b false

⑥ There are 12 hundreds in 130.
   a true   b false

⑦ 1069 is 200 greater than 869.
   a true   b false

⑧ 100 000 is 1 more than 9999.
   a true   b false

⑨ There are 120 tens in 1200.
   a true   b false

⑩ There are 13 tens in 6130.
   a true   b false

Write these numbers as numerals.

⑪ nine hundreds and seven tens

_____

⑫ seven thousands, eight hundreds, nine tens and five ones

_____

⑬ fourteen tens and nine ones

_____

⑭ eight thousands, nineteen tens and six ones

_____

⑮ four thousands, five hundreds, twelve tens and four ones

_____

Score 2 points for each correct answer!

SCORE /30   (0-12) (14-24) (26-30)

Statistics & Probability

There are no statistics & probability activities in this unit.

TARGETING HOMEWORK 3 © PASCAL PRESS ISBN 9781925726459

Measurement & Space

AC9M3M04

Telling the exact time

Sometimes we need to know the exact time. For example, you might want to catch a bus or train.

Examples:

This clock shows 12:14 or 14 minutes past 12.

This clock shows 5:56 or 4 minutes to 6.

What is the exact time on these clocks? Circle the correct answer.

①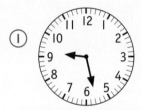
   a 9:30
   b 9:28
   c 20 past 9

②
   a 10 to 2
   b 10:09
   c 10:10

③
   a 1:44
   b 1:45
   c 1:46

④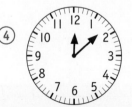
   a 2 o'clock
   b 12:10
   c 12:08

Circle the correct answer.

5. If it is 4:25 now, what time will it be in 26 minutes?
   a 4:50   b 4:51

6. The bus was due at 5:29 but it was 12 minutes late. What time did it arrive?
   a 5:41   b 5:40

7. It is 2:48 now. How many minutes until 3:00?
   a 13   b 12

8. May's favourite TV program starts at 4:30 and is 15 minutes long. What time does it finish?
   a 4:45   b 4:35

9. At 12:36, Mum said we would eat lunch in 10 minutes. What time did we eat lunch?
   a 12:46   b 12:26

Problem Solving

AC9M3ST02

Using a matrix

A matrix can help you work out the answer to a problem.

Example:

Three friends all play different sports.

Jon is 9 years old and plays football.

Crystal does not play netball and is 1 year older than Jon.

The person who plays netball is 10 years old.

Mandy does not play football.

Who goes swimming?

How to work it out

- We know Jon's age and sport, so put that in the matrix first.
- We know that Crystal is 10 years old, but we do not know her sport. Put in her name and age.
- We know that the other person is 10 years old and plays netball so put that in the matrix.
- We know that Crystal does not play netball, so it must be Mandy who plays netball. Put Mandy's name in the matrix.
- The only sport left is swimming, so Crystal must go swimming.

Name	Age	Sport
Jon	9	football
Crystal	10	swimming
Mandy	10	netball

TERM 3 MATHS

Use the matrix to solve this problem.

A modelling agency wants to know the hair and eye colour of some new models but the information has been mixed up.
Can you sort it out?

Maddy, **Fiona** and **James** all have different coloured eyes – blue, brown and green.

They each have different coloured hair – blonde, black and brown.

Maddy has the same eye colour as her hair.

Fiona has green eyes and doesn't have blonde hair.

The blue-eyed **boy** does not have black or brown hair.

What coloured eyes and hair do they each have?

Name	Eyes	Hair
Maddy		
Fiona		
James		

Grammar & Punctuation

AC9E3LA10

Adverbs

Remember! Adverbs tell us:
- *how* things are being done
- *when* things are happening
- *where* things are happening.

Some adverbs can also be used to ask questions.

How often do you go swimming?
When is your party?
Where are you going on Sunday?
Why were you late for dinner?

Write a question adverb to complete these sentences.

① _____ many toy cars do you have?

② _____ did you paint your door yellow?

③ _____ is your birthday?

④ _____ did you put your shoes?

⑤ _____ do you make a kite?

Write the questions for these answers.

Answer: I am nine years old.
Question: How old are you?

⑥ A: I live at 42 Redpath Street.
   Q: _____

⑦ A: I am crying because I fell over.
   Q: _____

⑧ A: There are three fish in the bowl.
   Q: _____

⑨ A: The party starts at 11 am.
   Q: _____

Circle the correct question adverbs for these sentences.

⑩ _____ aren't you ready yet?
   (*Where*   *Why*)

⑪ _____ many chocolates can you eat?
   (*How*   *Why*)

⑫ _____ do you turn 10 years old?
   (*When*   *Where*)

⑬ _____ is the dog?
   (*Why*   *Where*)

Phonic Knowledge & Spelling

AC9E3LY09, AC9E3LY10, AC9E3LY11, AC9E3LY12

Letter teams: or, ore and oar

Say each word from the word bank. They all contain letter teams **or**, **ore** or **oar**. The letters work together to make one sound 'or'.

Word Bank

storm	form	horn	sword	port
more	sore	wore	score	pore
oar	roar	soar	boar	board

Choose words from the word bank to complete these sentences.

① The violent _____ hit the coast.

② Is your knee feeling very _____?

③ The lion's _____ was quite loud.

Homophones

Some of the words in the word bank are **homophones**. They have the same sound as other words, but have different spellings and meanings.

Circle the correct words to complete these sentences.

④ Please _____ the milk carefully.
   (*paw   pore   pour   poor*)

⑤ We _____ Tom last week.
   (*soar   saw   sore*)

⑥ I _____ my red T-shirt yesterday.
   (*war   wore*)

Tricky words

Some words are tricky! At first sight they look almost the same, but they do not sound the same and they have different spellings and meanings.

Examples:
quiet, quite   dairy, diary
desert, dessert   bought, brought

Write the tricky words from the box next to their meanings.

dairy	brought	desert	quiet

⑦ a dry place: _____

⑧ little or no noise: _____

⑨ where milk is produced: _____

⑩ past tense of 'bring': _____

Informative text – Interview
Author – Frances Mackay

Dr Johnson

This is an interview with my doctor, Dr Johnson.

Question (Q): How long did it take for you to train as a doctor?

Answer (A): It took about nine years of studying and training.

Q: What is different about being a doctor now than when you first started?

A: Today we have a lot more information and treatments available to us. We can find out things on the internet, and our patient files can be easily accessed on the computer.

Q: How do you keep up with all the latest treatments?

A: I read medical journals and reports. These tell me about the latest scientific research that has been carried out and how useful it is in helping patients.

Q: How does science help in finding out what is wrong with your patients?

A: There are many ways science can help. Sometimes we take blood samples. The technician at the lab can test the blood for diseases. Sometimes patients have X-rays or scans to find out if anything is wrong. Sometimes a new drug is invented that helps the patient.

Q: What do you think is the best scientific invention ever made for making people better?

A: Now, that is a tricky question as there are so many of them, but I think one of the most important ones was the invention of antibiotics. These help people with lots of different infections. Penicillin was discovered by Alexander Fleming in 1928.

Write or circle the correct answers.

① **Where are Dr Johnson's patient files kept?**

   a on index cards

   b we are not told

   c on the computer

② **How do medical journals and reports help Dr Johnson to treat her patients?**

   a They give her the latest information on research and treatments.

   b They tell her how her patients like their treatments.

③ **What does the phrase 'patient files can be easily accessed' mean?**

   a It is difficult to get information about patients.

   b It is quick and easy to find information about patients.

④ **Which one of these is the odd word out?**

   a invention   c destruction

   b discovery   d creation

⑤ **Which word in the text means 'a person who does practical work in a laboratory'?**

   a antibiotics   b patient   c technician

Are these statements facts or opinions?

⑥ I think one of the most important ones was the invention of antibiotics. (fact   opinion)

⑦ Penicillin was discovered by Alexander Fleming in 1928. (fact   opinion)

⑧ **Why do doctors take blood samples?**

   _____

⑨ **Which word best describes Dr Johnson?**

   a young   b caring   c unhelpful

⑩ **What do you think was the purpose of the interview with Dr Johnson?**

   a to advertise Dr Johnson's surgery

   b to inform readers about the role of doctors today and how science can help patients

   c to persuade people to become doctors

Score 2 points for each correct answer!

SCORE /20   0-8   10-14   16-20

My Book Review

Title _____

Author _____

Rating ☆ ☆ ☆ ☆ ☆

Comment _____

_____

TERM 3 ENGLISH

Number & Algebra

AC9M3A01

Equivalent number sentences

Number sentences (equations) can be **equivalent**. 'Equivalent' means equal or balanced. So one side of the number sentence is equal to the other side.

Example:

$$3 + 5 = 10 - 2$$

3 + 5 is 8 and 10 − 2 is 8. So both sides of the equal sign have the same answer. They are equivalent or equal.

It's like a balance scale, where both sides must be the same for the scale to balance.

| 3 + 5 | | 10 − 2 |

Example:

$$20 - 4 = 10 + \underline{}$$

How to work it out

- Work out the answer to 20 − 4 first.
  Answer = 16.
- Then ask: What do I need to add to 10 to make 16?
  Answer = 6.
- The completed number sentence is:
  $$20 - 4 = 10 + 6$$

Complete these number sentences.

① $10 + 5 \quad = \quad 18 - \underline{}$

② $20 - \underline{} \quad = \quad 6 + 7$

③ $15 + 6 \quad = \quad 18 + \underline{}$

④ $20 + \underline{} \quad = \quad 30 - 6$

⑤ $14 - 9 \quad = \quad 15 - \underline{}$

⑥ $31 - 10 \quad = \quad 6 + 8 + \underline{}$

Are these number sentences true or false? Circle the correct answer.

⑦ $6 + 9 + 5 = 30 - 7$
   a true   b false

⑧ $20 - 7 = 15 + 8$
   a true   b false

⑨ $15 + 7 = 30 - 8$
   a true   b false

⑩ $30 - 12 = 6 + 6 + 6$
   a true   b false

⑪ $35 - 9 = 14 + 14$
   a true   b false

Statistics & Probability

AC9M3ST01, AC9M3ST02

Comparing bar graphs

Class 3T and class 3S went pond-dipping on different days. The graphs show the creatures they found.

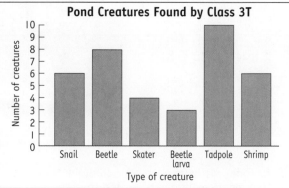

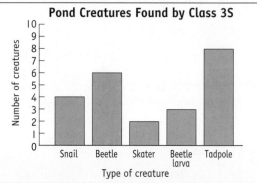

Use the graphs to answer the questions. Write or circle the correct answer.

① How many tadpoles did Class 3T find?
   a 8   b 10   c 5   d 6

② How many tadpoles did Class 3S find?
   a 8   b 10   c 5   d 6

③ Which class found more creatures? _____

④ How many more beetles did Class 3T find than Class 3S did?
   a 0   b 2   c 4   d 6

⑤ What is similar about the results from the two classes?

   a They both found exactly the same type of creatures.

   b They both found snails, beetles, skaters, larvae and tadpoles.

   c They both found fewer than two of each type of creature.

⑥ What is different about the results from the two classes?

   a Only one class found shrimps.

   b Tadpoles were the most common creatures found.

   c Only one class found three beetle larvae.

Pathways

This is a map showing where Will lives and the journey he takes to school.

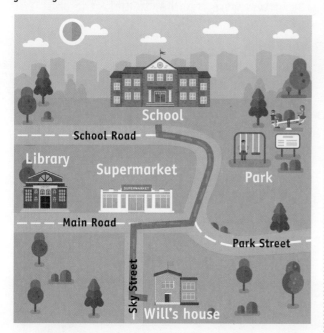

**Use the map to answer the questions.
Circle the correct answer.**

1. What is the name of the street that Will lives in?

   a Park Street   b Sky Street

2. What is the name of the road that the supermarket is on?

   a Main Road   b School Road

3. Which building is on Main Road?

   a school   b library

4. Which building does Will pass on his way to school?

   a library   b supermarket

5. Is the park near the school?

   a yes   b no

6. Does Will pass the park on his way to school?

   a yes   b no

Score 2 points for each correct answer!

SCORE: /12   0-4   6-8   10-12

Number crossword

This crossword has number clues instead of word clues. Complete the puzzle.

1	2		3	4	
	5	6		7	8
9		10	11		
12	13		14	15	
	16	17		18	19
	20				

Across

1. The next even number after 56
3. 40 – 4
5. 8 lots of 3
7. The even number between 22 and 26
10. 10 + 10 + 6
12. Half of 72
14. 3 lots of 5
16. 80 – 12
18. 1 less than 60
20. Double 15

Down

2. 90 – 8
4. 10 + 10 + 10 + 10 + 10 + 10 + 2
6. 50 – 8
8. Half of 90
9. 80 – 7
11. Double 30 plus 1
13. Double 33
15. Half of 110
17. 90 – 7
19. 100 – 5

Grammar & Punctuation

AC9E3LY06

Punctuation

Rewrite these sentences. Add the missing capital letters and punctuation marks at the end (. ! or ?).

① did chloe, lily and tom get home safely

_____

② mrs jones lives at 49 west street in sandy bay

_____

③ look out max, there's a train coming

_____

Underline the words the characters speak. Then add the speech marks (" ") where they belong.

④ You're a great goalie! yelled Ben, punching his hands in the air.

⑤ Why are we going there? moaned Jen.

⑥ We are going on holiday next week, announced Dad.

⑦ I'm tired, wailed Peter. can't we go back now?

Rewrite each sentence below as two sentences. Add the missing full stops and capital letters.

⑧ The car crashed into a tree luckily, the driver was not hurt

_____

_____

⑨ The furniture is stored in a warehouse vans deliver it to customers

_____

_____

⑩ My cousin has a Golden Retriever its name is Ginger

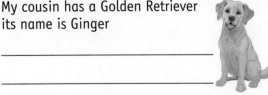

_____

_____

⑪ The storms caused a lot of damage thankfully, our house was not damaged

_____

_____

Phonic Knowledge & Spelling

AC9E3LY09, AC9E3LY10, AC9E3LY11

Letter team: ou

Say each word from the word bank.
They all contain the letter team **ou**.
The letters work together to make the one sound 'ow' (as in 'cow').

Word Bank

out	shout	loud	cloud	noun
south	mouth	pouch	crouch	pronoun
sound	round	count	doubt	mountain

Choose words from the word bank to complete these sentences.

① Only the summit of the _____ was covered in snow.

② The past tense of _____ is shouted.

③ The first _____ I hear each morning is Mum telling me to get up!

④ Last week we saw a kangaroo with a joey in its _____.

Compound words

Write words from the box to make compound words.

wash	about	side	less

⑤ cloud_____

⑥ out_____

⑦ round_____

⑧ mouth_____

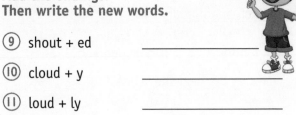

**Add the endings.
Then write the new words.**

⑨ shout + ed   _____

⑩ cloud + y   _____

⑪ loud + ly   _____

⑫ pouch + es   _____

⑬ round + er   _____

⑭ doubt + ing   _____

⑮ south + er + ly   _____

Persuasive text – Discussion
Author – Frances Mackay and Neil Johnson

Rabbits in Australia

Stacey: Rabbits have been here for a very long time, Brad. They were introduced to Australia with the First Fleet in 1788. It's too late now to say they shouldn't be here.

Brad: The problem with rabbits, Stacey, is that there are too many of them. Did you know that when they were introduced into Australia they spread very quickly to nearly every part of the country? It was the fastest spread ever recorded of any mammal anywhere in the world!

Stacey: What harm do they really do? During the 1930s when times were very hard, lots of people ate rabbits. They were a free source of food. Perhaps we should encourage more people to eat them today and that might solve a few problems.

Brad: They are not a native species and they cause huge problems. They eat vast areas of grass and plants, which causes the soil to wear away. They also eat large amounts of farmers' crops.

Stacey: Rabbits are so cute and they've been here such a long time. Surely, we can find ways to make them fit in with our environment?

Brad: We need to get rid of all the rabbits in Australia. I know they are cuddly and cute, but we need to look after our native animals and plants.

Source: *Australian History Centres*, Blake's Learning Centres, Blake Education.

Write or circle the correct answers.

1. **What do you think the purpose of this text is?**
   a to provide information about keeping rabbits
   b to present two different points of view about rabbits in Australia
   c to explain why rabbits were introduced into Australia

2. **What is Brad's point of view about rabbits in Australia?**
   a He thinks they are cute and cuddly.
   b He thinks rabbits are good for the Australian environment.
   c He thinks all rabbits should be removed from Australia.

3. **What does the phrase 'they were introduced into Australia' mean?**
   a They were brought into Australia from another country.
   b They already lived in Australia.

4. **What harm do rabbits do to the Australian environment?**
   a They eat native animals.
   b They don't do any harm.
   c They eat native plants and farmers' crops.

Are these statements facts or opinions?

5. They were introduced to Australia with the First Fleet in 1788.　(fact　opinion)

6. We need to get rid of all rabbits in Australia.　(fact　opinion)

7. **What is a native species?**
   a an animal or plant that has always lived in a place
   b an animal or plant that has been introduced to a place

8. **Which word in the text means 'the surroundings where people, plants and animals live'?**
   a native
   b environment
   c species

9. **What did people do in the 1930s that Stacey thinks we should do today?**

   _____

   _____

Score 2 points for each correct answer! **SCORE** /18 　0-6　8-14　16-18

My Book Review

Title _____

Author _____

Rating ☆☆☆☆☆

Comment _____

_____

Problem solving using multiplication

> How many chocolates do I have if I have five times as many as my brother, who has nine chocolates?
>
> How to work it out as a number sentence:
>
> $$5 \times 9 = 45$$
>
> I have 5 times his amount.   My brother has 9.

Write these problems as number sentences and work them out.

① How many pencils does Alex have if she has three times as many pencils as Maddy, who has nine pencils?

② Ian started with eight football cards and he tripled this number. How many football cards does he have now?

③ How many books does Sally-Anne have if she has five times as many books as Mike, who has seven?

④ How many computer games does Bryce have if he has three times as many as Ben, who has seven games?

⑤ Miles doubled his collection of toy cars when he went to the garage sale. He started with nine cars. How many did he end up with?

Write the correct number sentence after each word problem.

$5 \times 8 = 40$	$9 \times 2 = 18$
$3 \times 10 = 30$	$5 \times 7 = 35$

⑥ Tracy had nine stamps and she doubled them. How many stamps does she have now?

⑦ Deb had five times as many biscuits as Cam, who had seven. How many biscuits did Deb have?

⑧ Aled has ten fish in his pond. Kate has three times as many in her pond. How many fish does Kate have?

⑨ Ahmed has five times as many T-shirts as his brother, who has eight. How many T-shirts does Ahmed have?

Making estimates

> An **estimate** is an approximate answer that makes calculations easier but is close enough to the real answer. For example, 5×19 is difficult to work out quickly. $5 \times 20 = 100$ is easier. So 100 is an estimate for 5×19.

Choose the best estimation from the box for each multiplication below. Some numbers will be left over.

50	100	200	400
75	120	250	500
90	160	300	1000

⑩ 19×5 Estimate: _____

⑪ 3×28 Estimate: _____

⑫ 97×4 Estimate: _____

⑬ 26×2 Estimate: _____

⑭ 3×24 Estimate: _____

⑮ 147×2 Estimate: _____

⑯ 42×4 Estimate: _____

⑰ 99×2 Estimate: _____

⑱ 5×199 Estimate: _____

Score 2 points for each correct answer!

SCORE **/36**   (0-16) (18-30) (32-36)

Statistics & Probability

There are no statistics & probability activities in this unit.

Measurement & Space

AC9M3N02

Fractions of a shape

These diagrams show **halves**. True or false?
Circle the correct answer.

①
     a true   b false

②
     a true   b false

③
     a true   b false

These diagrams show **quarters**. True or false?
Circle the correct answer.

④
     a true   b false

⑤
     a true   b false

⑥
     a true   b false

These diagrams show **eighths**. True or false?
Circle the correct answer.

⑦
     a true   b false

⑧
     a true   b false

⑨
     a true   b false

These diagrams show **thirds**. True or false?
Circle the correct answer.

⑩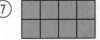
     a true   b false

⑪
     a true   b false

⑫
     a true   b false

What fractions are shown by the shapes?

⑬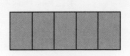
_____

⑭
_____

⑮
_____

⑯
_____

Score 2 points for each correct answer!
SCORE **/32** (0-14) (16-26) (28-32)

Problem Solving

AC9M3A02

3	17	11	9
5	15	7	13
12	8	1	19
2	10	16	4

① Which two numbers in this square do not fit the pattern?

_____, _____

② Why?

_____

_____

_____

_____

Grammar & Punctuation

AC9E3LA07

Sensing verbs

A **sensing verb** describes one of the five senses — seeing, hearing, smelling, tasting and touching. Sensing verbs help us to know what a person is thinking and feeling.

Five senses

touch   smell   taste

hearing   sight

Examples:
(seeing)	She **watched** television.
(hearing)	He **heard** the front door open.
(smelling)	The dog **sniffed** the grass.
(tasting)	The chef **tasted** the stew.
(touching)	The stone **felt** cold.

Circle the word that shows how the character is feeling.

① The man **glared** at the boy.
　　(*angry*　*sad*　*happy*)

② I **sipped** the hot soup.
　　(*afraid*　*cautious*　*tired*)

③ He could **feel** the hot drink warming him up.
　　(*unhappy*　*surprised*　*relieved*)

④ She **breathed** in the scent of the flowers.
　　(*angry*　*pleased*　*sad*)

⑤ He **concentrated** on the strange noise.
　　(*unsure*　*sad*　*happy*)

There are many verbs that mean 'look'. Choose seeing verbs from the box to complete these sentences.

watched peered stared glimpsed noticed

⑥ The children ＿＿＿＿＿＿＿ over the fence.

⑦ We just ＿＿＿＿＿＿＿ the parade as we drove past.

⑧ The policeman ＿＿＿＿＿＿＿ at the suspicious man.

⑨ Mum carefully ＿＿＿＿＿＿＿ the boiling pot.

⑩ I suddenly ＿＿＿＿＿＿＿ the approaching storm.

Score 2 points for each correct answer! **SCORE** **/20** (0-8) (10-14) (16-20)

Phonic Knowledge & Spelling

AC9E3LY09, AC9E3LY10, AC9E3LY11

Letter team: ow

Say each word from the word bank.
They all contain the letter team **ow**.
The letters work together to make the one sound 'ow' (as in 'cow').

Word Bank

cow	bow	how	fowl	growl
town	drown	shower	flower	tower
coward	township	downwards		

Choose words from the word bank to complete these sentences.

① The pretty ＿＿＿＿＿＿＿ smelled as sweet as sugar.

② We had to travel into ＿＿＿＿＿＿＿ to buy some salt.

③ We decided to leave before the next rain ＿＿＿＿＿＿＿.

Tricky words

Some words have the same spelling but are pronounced differently and have different meanings.

wind　(a current of air)
Example: The **wind** blew all day long.

wind　(to move in circles)
Example: He tried to **wind** up the rope.

Circle the correct meanings for the words in bold.

④ The girls had to **row** the boat ashore.
　a　to have a noisy quarrel
　b　to use oars to move a boat

⑤ They tied a **bow** in the dog's fur.
　a　a knot made with loops
　b　to bend your body forwards

Word shapes

Choose words from the word bank to write in these shapes. The first one has been done for you.

⑦ ＿＿＿＿＿

⑥ ＿＿＿＿＿

⑧ ＿＿＿＿＿

Compound words

Add **cow** to these words to make compound words.

⑨ ＿＿＿＿＿hide

⑪ ＿＿＿＿＿girl

⑩ ＿＿＿＿＿bell

⑫ ＿＿＿＿＿shed

Score 2 points for each correct answer! **SCORE** **/24** (0-10) (12-18) (20-24)

Informative text – Comparing illustrations
Author – Frances Mackay
Illustrator – Paul Lennon

Changes over time

Look at these illustrations of Meadowtown. The first illustration shows the town during the 1880s. The second illustration shows the town today.

Write or circle the correct answers.

① **Which building is the only one to remain unchanged between the 1880s and today?**

a the supermarket

b the inn

c none – they have all changed

② **What used to be behind the inn?**

a trees and a park

b houses

c a road

③ **What has the house next to the inn been replaced by?**

a a park

b a petrol station

④ **What is different about the transport in the 1880s compared with today?**

a Today there are more horse-drawn vehicles.

b There are no differences.

c Today there are cars, trucks and buses.

Are these statements facts or opinions?

⑤ A lot has changed in Redtown between the 1880s and today.　　(fact　opinion)

⑥ Redtown is not a pleasant place to live today.　　(fact　opinion)

⑦ **Which one of these is the odd word out?**

a change　　　　c alter

b remain　　　　d modify

⑧ **What could be a reason for the inn remaining the same?**

a The building is still in use as an inn (hotel) today.

b The main road is a long way away.

c The inn needs a lot of land.

Score 2 points for each correct answer! **SCORE** /16　0-6　8-12　14-16

My Book Review

Title _____

Author _____

Rating ☆☆☆☆☆

Comment _____

_____

Number & Algebra

AC9M3N02

Finding a third

To find a **third** ($\frac{1}{3}$), divide by **3**.
This gives you three **equal** parts.

Example:
What is a third of this group?

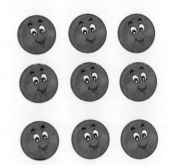

There are 9 circle faces altogether.

Divide 9 by 3 = 3
A third of 9 = 3

What is a third of these groups?
Circle the correct answer.

①

　a 1　　　b 2　　　c 3

②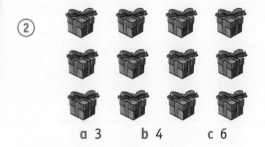

　a 3　　　b 4　　　c 6

What is a third of these numbers?
Circle the correct answer.

③　$\frac{1}{3}$ of 15 = 　　a 3　　b 5　　c 10

④　$\frac{1}{3}$ of 21 = 　　a 8　　b 10　　c 7

⑤　$\frac{1}{3}$ of 18 = 　　a 5　　b 6　　c 7

Finding a fifth

To find a **fifth** ($\frac{1}{5}$), divide by **5**.
This will give you five **equal** parts.

What is a fifth of these groups?
Circle the correct answer.

⑥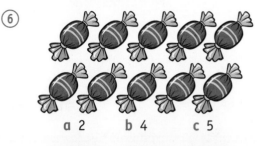

　a 2　　　b 4　　　c 5

⑦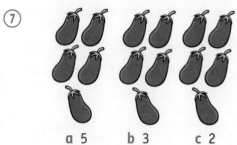

　a 5　　　b 3　　　c 2

What is a fifth of these numbers?
Circle the correct answer.

⑧　$\frac{1}{5}$ of 20 = 　　a 4　　b 5　　c 6

⑨　$\frac{1}{5}$ of 25 = 　　a 4　　b 5　　c 6

⑩　$\frac{1}{5}$ of 40 = 　　a 10　　b 12　　c 8

Score 2 points for each correct answer!　SCORE　**/20**　(0-8)　(10-14)　(16-20)

Statistics & Probability

AC9M3ST01, AC9M3ST02, AC9M3ST03

Tossing a coin

Ben tossed a coin 20 times. Here are his results.

Toss	Head	Tail		Toss	Head	Tail
1		✔		11		✔
2		✔		12		✔
3		✔		13	✔	
4		✔		14		✔
5	✔			15	✔	
6	✔			16		✔
7		✔		17	✔	
8	✔			18	✔	
9	✔			19		✔
10	✔			20		✔

① **Use Ben's results to complete the tally chart.**

Head	
Tail	

TERM 3 MATHS

② Use Ben's results to complete the bar graph.

Ben's results

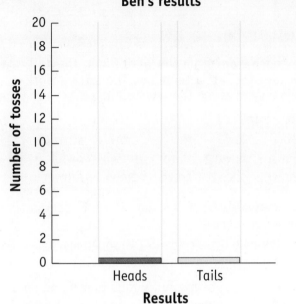

Write or circle the correct answers.

③ Were Ben's results as you expected?
a yes   b no

④ Why or why not? _____

_____

⑤ Ben had an equal chance (1 in 2) of tossing a head or a tail.
a true   b false

⑥ How likely was it that Ben would toss a tail?
a certain   b likely
c unlikely   d impossible

⑦ How likely was it that Ben would toss a 6?
a certain   b likely
c unlikely   d impossible

⑧ If Ben repeats his experiment, how likely is it that he will get similar results?
a certain   b likely
c unlikely   d impossible

Score 2 points for each correct answer!   SCORE **/16** (0-6) (8-12) (14-16)

Measurement & Space

Using a cm ruler

Look at the ruler.
It is divided into 8 **centimetres** (cm). Each centimetre is divided into 10 **millimetres** (mm), shown by the smaller marks on the ruler.

Use a ruler to measure the length of each object as close to the nearest cm as you can.

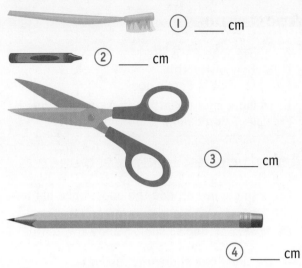

① _____ cm

② _____ cm

③ _____ cm

④ _____ cm

⑤ How long is the nail in millimetres?

_____ mm

Score 2 points for each correct answer!   SCORE **/10** (0-2) (4-8) (10)

Problem Solving

Square puzzle

A square can be divided into smaller squares. This square can be divided into 6 squares.

The squares do not have to be the same size, but the sides of each individual square must be equal.

Solve these square puzzles by dividing them into smaller squares.

① 7 Squares

② 10 Squares

Grammar & Punctuation

AC9E3LA11

Apostrophes

An apostrophe (') is used for two purposes.
i. To show **ownership**.
Example: That is **Pam's** book.
ii. To mark missing letters in a **contraction**.
Example: I **don't** want to go there.

Apostrophes – single owner

For a single owner, add the apostrophe before
the **s** ('s).
Examples: The **dog's** collar; **Mandy's** watch

Rewrite these the short way, using an
apostrophe.
Example: the kennel that belongs to the dog
the **dog's** kennel

① the toy belonging to the baby

_____

② the heat of the sun

_____

③ the tent belonging to Adam

_____

Apostrophes – more than one owner

For more than one owner, add the apostrophe
after the owners (s').
Examples: The **boys'** scooters; my **friends'** houses

Circle the correct use of the apostrophe for
each sentence.

④ Those _____ bicycles are brand new.

    (*girls'*   *girl's*)

⑤ Are you going to _____ party?

    (*Frankies'*   *Frankie's*)

⑥ The _____ classroom was a mess.

    (*students'*   *student's*)

WATCH OUT! An apostrophe
is **never** used to show the
plural of a word.
Examples: Two **cats** were cuddling.
Two **cat's** were cuddling.

TERM 3 ENGLISH

Phonic Knowledge & Spelling

AC9E3LY09, AC9E3LY10, AC9E3LY11

Letter team: aw

Say each word from the word bank. They all
contain the letter team **aw**. The letters work
together to make the one sound 'or'.

Word Bank

saw	jaw	raw	draw	strawberry
lawn	dawn	fawn	prawn	awful
hawk	shawl	crawl	drawl	drawer

Choose words from the word bank to complete
these sentences.

① It was a little cold, so I wrapped my
_____ around my shoulders.

② I _____ twelve fluffy rabbits jumping on
my front lawn.

③ I have to wiggle the top _____ in
my desk before it will open.

④ After dinner, we had a _____
cheesecake for dessert.

Adding endings

Add endings to the words to
complete the sentences.

⑤ (crawl)   The baby _____ along
the floor to my dad.

⑥ (prawn)   We ate some barbecued
_____ for lunch.

⑦ (dawn)   As day was _____, we
walked along the beach.

⑧ (strawberry)   I picked twenty
_____ and ate them all!

Plurals

Remember! Plural means 'more than
one'. To make the plural of a word,
you usually just add **s**.
Examples: drawer, drawer**s**   hawk, hawk**s**
shawl, shawl**s**

Some words have **irregular plurals**.
Examples: child, children   mouse, mice

Write the plural words from the box next to
their singular forms.

women	oxen	geese	teeth

⑨ ox _____   ⑪ goose _____

⑩ tooth _____   ⑫ woman _____

Persuasive text – Book review
Author – Frances Mackay

The Mysterious Stranger by I C U First

The Mysterious Stranger is one of the most exciting books I have ever read. It's not only a mystery story, as the title suggests, but it's also very funny. It will make you laugh out loud!

The story is set in New York, and it's all about a man called Harry who meets a stranger one day while eating his lunch in the park. The stranger, Mervin, manages to change Harry's life forever. I won't tell you how — you will have to read the story yourself to find out! Mervin has special powers, but he only uses these powers when Harry gets himself into trouble, which he often does!

It's an easy read and not too difficult. It moves at a fast pace and lots of things happen on every page, so you won't get bored reading it. You might get a bit fed up with Harry, though, as he seems to never learn his lesson and keeps on making the same mistakes. I won't spoil the ending for you, but if you enjoy a good mystery — and a good laugh — you will thoroughly enjoy this book.

First has written two other books called *The Lonely Child* and *Whispering Mountain*. In my opinion, this book is his best.

I highly recommend *The Mysterious Stranger* to readers over the age of 8.
I rate it 9 out of 10.
Steve Clark, book reviewer, *Blake Young Times*

Write or circle the correct answers.

① Who wrote *The Mysterious Stranger*?

_____

② Name another book written by this author.

_____

③ What age is this book suitable for?

  a any age

  b readers over the age of 8

Are these statements facts or opinions?

④ It's an easy read and not too difficult.
   (fact   opinion)

⑤ The story is set in New York.
   (fact   opinion)

⑥ Where does Harry meet the stranger?

  a in a restaurant

  b in the park

⑦ Why does the reviewer say,
  'You might get a bit fed up with Harry'?

_____

_____

⑧ Which one of these is the odd word out?

  a exciting   c gripping

  b thrilling   d dull

⑨ Which word from the text means
  completely or **absolutely**?

  a though   b bored   c thoroughly

⑩ Which statement does the reviewer use to try and persuade his readers to read this book?

  a You might get a bit fed up with Harry.

  b You will thoroughly enjoy this book.

  c I won't spoil the ending for you.

Score 2 points for each correct answer!   SCORE   **/20**   (0-8) (10-14) (16-20)

My Book Review

Title _____

Author _____

Rating ☆ ☆ ☆ ☆ ☆

Comment _____

_____

Splitting numbers to multiply

When you multiply larger numbers, you can split the larger number.

Example:

$$5 \times 18$$

10   8

Split the 18 into 10 and 8.

Then multiply each number by 5.

$$5 \times 10 = 50 \qquad 5 \times 8 = 40$$

Add 50 and 40.

$$5 \times 18 = 90$$

Use the splitting method to work out the answer. Show your working out.

① 5 × 16

_____
_____
_____

② 3 × 19

_____
_____
_____

③ 2 × 18

_____
_____
_____

④ 9 × 17

_____
_____
_____

Use the splitting method to work out the answers to these number problems. Show your working out.

⑤ Tim's mother buys $5 cinema tickets for Tim and his 14 friends. How much does she spend?

_____
_____
_____
_____

⑥ Melanie, Tabitha and Sarah have 18 chocolate buttons each. How many chocolate buttons altogether?

_____
_____
_____
_____

⑦ Dan worked 5 hours a day for 14 days. How many hours did he work in total?

_____
_____
_____

⑧ Sam has lunch with his two friends. They each buy the $16 special meal. What is the total cost of their lunch?

_____
_____
_____
_____

⑨ Max was at the beach for 3 days. He found 14 shells every day. How many shells did he find altogether?

_____
_____
_____

Score 2 points for each correct answer!

SCORE /18   0-6   8-14   16-18

Statistics & Probability

There are no statistics & probability activities in this unit.

TARGETING HOMEWORK 3 © PASCAL PRESS ISBN 9781925726459

Measurement & Space

AC9M3M05

Right angles

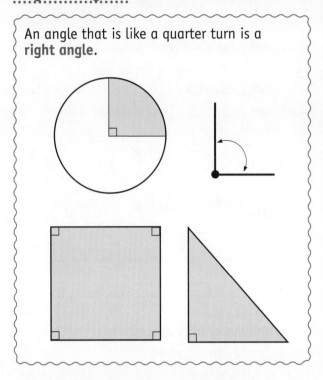

An angle that is like a quarter turn is a right angle.

Which picture shows a right angle?
Circle the correct answer.

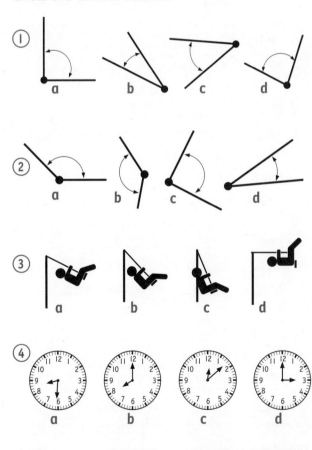

① a b c d

② a b c d

③ a b c d

④ a b c d

⑤ a b c d

Put a red dot in the corner of every right angle in this picture. One has been done for you.

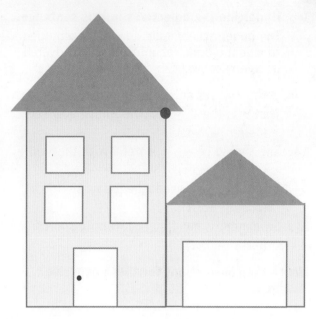

⑥ **How many right angles did you find altogether?**

_____

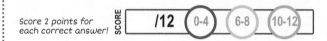

Score 2 points for each correct answer!

SCORE /12   0-4   6-8   10-12

Problem Solving

AC9M3M05

Knight's move puzzle

In the game of chess, a knight can move two squares in one direction and then one square at a right angle.

How many different squares can the knight reach from its starting point?

Put an '**X**' in each square the knight can reach.

Grammar & Punctuation

① **Underline the adjectives in this sentence.**
The huge, rickety door slowly creaked open to reveal a dark, rat-infested room covered in creepy cobwebs.

Circle the correct adjective for each sentence.

② That was the _____ movie I have ever seen.
  (*better   best*)

③ She should be _____ careful with that knife.
  (*more   most*)

④ I had a _____ headache today.
  (*bad   worst*)

⑤ Swimming is my _____ favourite sport.
  (*less   least*)

Write the contractions for these negative modal verbs.

⑥ could not = _____   ⑧ must not = _____

⑦ will not = _____   ⑨ can not = _____

Underline the verbs and circle the adverbs in these sentences.

⑩ She spoke quietly at the meeting.

⑪ Liam crossed the street carefully.

⑫ Dad ate a whole cake today.

Circle the correct question adverbs for these sentences.

⑬ _____ aren't you going to the party?
  (*Where   Why*)

⑭ _____ many cards do you have?
  (*How   Why*)

⑮ **Rewrite this sentence. Add the missing capital letters and punctuation marks.**
did max ali and tim come to your party

_____

_____

Underline the words that the character speaks. Then add the speech marks (" ") where they belong.

⑯ Come on, you lot, said Maddie.

⑰ When will we get there? asked Jai.

⑱ **Rewrite the sentences, adding the missing capital letters and full stops.**
a mouse ran into our kitchen thankfully, I did not see it

_____

_____

Underline the sensing verbs in these sentences.

⑲ She watched a movie.

⑳ He heard a strange noise

㉑ The dog sniffed the bone.

Circle then write the correct use of the apostrophe for each sentence.

㉒ _____ house is brand new.
  (*Lees'   Lee's*)

㉓ Those _____ T-shirts look cool.
  (*boys'   boy's*)

Score 2 points for each correct answer! **SCORE** **/46** (0-20) (22-40) (42-46)

Phonic Knowledge & Spelling

① **Circle the correct meaning for the word in bold.**
We had a **row** about who was doing the washing up.

  a to have a noisy quarrel

  b to use oars to move a boat

Add the suffixes –er and –est to these adjectives.

		–er	–est
②	dirty	_____	_____
③	big	_____	_____
④	pretty	_____	_____
⑤	wet	_____	_____

Write the homophones of these words.

⑥ herd _____   ⑦ flower _____

Add the suffix –ly to these adjectives to make adverbs.

⑧ quick _____

⑨ angry _____

⑩ noisy _____

⑪ helpful _____

Write the plurals of these words.

⑫ life _____   ⑭ child _____

⑬ roof _____   ⑮ man _____

Write words from the box to make compound words.

wash	about	proof	side

⑯ sound_____   ⑱ mouth_____

⑰ out_____   ⑲ round_____

Circle the number of syllables these words have.

⑳ strawberry   (1   2   3)

㉑ powder   (1   2   3)

㉒ nervously   (1   2   3)

TARGETING HOMEWORK 3 © PASCAL PRESS ISBN 9781925726459

㉓ Write these words in dictionary order.

down	growl	drown	coward	cow

_____

_____

Add endings to the words to complete these sentences. Choose from –ed, –ing and –ly.

㉔ The tennis player was _____ the ball. (serve)

㉕ The cowman _____ the cows into the shed. (herd)

㉖ She was chewing her nails _____. (nervous)

Write the words from the box next to their meanings.

diary	quiet	dairy	quite

㉗ a daily account: _____

㉘ littlet or no noise: _____

㉙ slightly, a little: _____

㉚ where milk is produced:

_____

Score 2 points for each correct answer! **SCORE** /60 (0-28) (30-54) (56-60)

Reading & Comprehension

Information text
Author – Frances Mackay

Anyone can take up painting. You don't need to spend a lot of money to get started, but you do need to have some tools to help you. First of all, you need paint. It's best to buy just the primary colours first (red, yellow and blue), and then you can mix nearly any colour you need. You will need a palette to mix the colours on. You will also need a range of brushes — from a wide brush for larger areas, down to a small brush for detail work. Always clean your brushes well after use. An easel is a good idea, especially if you want to paint pictures outside. Almost any kind of paper can be used. Experiment to find out which type of paper you like best.

Write or circle the correct answers.

① What are the three primary colours?

_____

② What is a **palette**?

  a a paintbrush

  b a board an artist uses to mix colours

  c a type of easel

③ What is the meaning of **experiment** in this text?

  a a scientific study

  b to try out something to see what happens

④ Which one of these is the odd word out?

  a range   c few

  b assortment   d variety

⑤ What are small brushes used for?

_____

⑥ What should you always do after using paintbrushes?

  a clean them well

  b put them away

  c buy new ones

List the five kinds of equipment that you would need to take up painting.

⑦ _____

⑧ _____

⑨ _____

⑩ _____

⑪ _____

Score 2 points for each correct answer! **SCORE** /22 (0-8) (10-16) (18-22)

Number & Algebra

What is a half of these numbers?
Circle the correct answer.

① $\frac{1}{2}$ of 14　　a 6　　b 7　　c 8

② $\frac{1}{2}$ of 20　　a 8　　b 9　　c 10

③ What is a quarter of this group?
Circle the correct answer.

a 2　　　b 4　　　c 8

Complete these number patterns by counting in 10s.

④ 145, 155, _____, _____, _____, _____

⑤ 1302, 1312, 1322, _____, _____, _____, _____

Find the totals if you bought these toys.
What change would you get from $10.00?

A rocket for $2.99 and a plane for $2.50

⑥ total = _____　　⑦ change = _____

A duck for $1.99 and a train for $4.99

⑧ total = _____　　⑨ change = _____

Circle **true** or **false**.

⑩ There are ten odd numbers between 60 and 70.
　　a true　　　　　　b false

⑪ 2375 is an even number that is written as two thousand, three hundred and seventy-five
　　a true　　　　　　b false

⑫ The smallest even number you can make from the digits 8, 6 and 4 is 468
　　a true　　　　　　b false

Complete these number sentences.

⑬ 10 + 6 = 19 − ____　⑮ 7 + 5 = 19 − ____

⑭ 20 − ____ = 7 + 7　⑯ 14 + 6 = 17 + ____

⑰ Write this problem as a number sentence and work it out.
How many books does Ria have if she has five times as many books as Emma, who has nine books?

_____

Circle the correct answer.

⑱ $\frac{1}{3}$ of 18　　a 3　　b 6　　c 10

⑲ $\frac{1}{3}$ of 21　　a 8　　b 10　　c 7

⑳ $\frac{1}{5}$ of 15　　a 3　　b 4　　c 5

㉑ $\frac{1}{5}$ of 25　　a 4　　b 5　　c 6

Use the splitting method to work out the answers. Show your working out.

㉒ 7 × 13　　　　　　　㉓ 5 × 19

Score 2 points for each correct answer! **SCORE**  **/46** ⓪-20　22-40　42-46

Statistics & Probability

Favourite ice-cream topping flavour for Class 3S

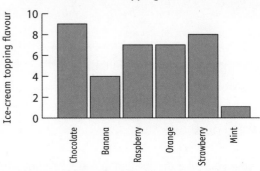

Favourite ice-cream topping flavour for Class 3T

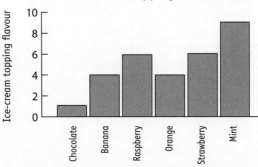

Use the graphs to answer the questions.
Write or circle the correct answers.

① Which flavour was most popular in Class 3S?

_____

② Which flavour was most popular in Class 3T?

_____

③ Which flavour was the favourite for 4 children in both classes?
　　a chocolate　　b banana　　c raspberry

④ How many more children in Class 3T preferred mint to those in Class 3S? _____

⑤ Fewer than 4 children preferred orange in both classes.
　　a true　　b false

⑥ What are the two **main differences** in the graphs for the two classes?
　　a the raspberry and orange results
　　b the chocolate and mint results
　　c the banana and orange results

Score 2 points for each correct answer! **SCORE** **/12** 0-4　6-8　10–12

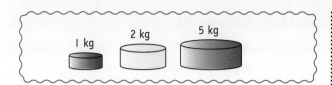

Circle the correct answers.

① **How many kilograms need to be added to balance the scale?**

a 1   b 2   c 4

② **There are 1000 g in a kilogram.**
a true   b false

③ **40 kg is less than 40 g.**
a true   b false

④ **What is the name of this prism?**

a pentagonal prism
b hexagonal prism
c triangular prism

⑤ **What is the name of this pyramid?**
a triangular pyramid
b pentagonal pyramid
c square pyramid

This is a map of Clever School.
Use the map to answer the questions.

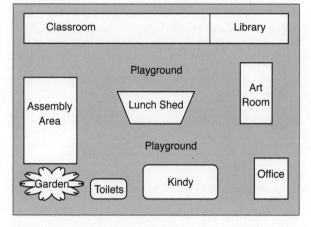

⑥ **Which building is closest to the library?**
a office   b art room   c toilets

⑦ **You are at the office. Do you pass the library on your way to the garden?**
a yes   b no

What is the exact time showing on these clocks? Circle the correct answer.

⑧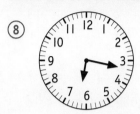
a 6:15
b 6:17
c $\frac{1}{4}$ past 6

⑨
a 11:34
b 20 to 12
c 11:30

⑩ **At 12:26, Mum told me to wait for 10 minutes before we ate lunch. What time did we eat lunch?**
a 12:46   b 12:36

Are these shapes cut into quarters?

⑪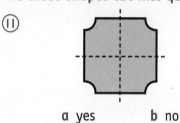
a yes   b no

⑫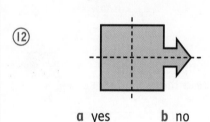
a yes   b no

⑬ **What does the arrow point to? Round to the nearest cm.**
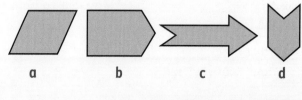
a 5 cm   b 6 cm   c 7 cm   d 8 cm

⑭ **Circle the shape that has right angles.**

a   b   c   d

Score 2 points for each correct answer!   SCORE   /28   0-12   14-22   24-28

TERM 3 MATHS

Grammar & Punctuation

AC9E3LA10, AC9E3LY06

Collective nouns

Collective nouns are names given to groups of people, animals and things.
Examples: a **team** of players
a **bunch** of flowers
a **pack** of cards

There are some amazing collective nouns for groups of animals.
Examples:
a **murder** of crows   a **smack** of jellyfish
a **wisdom** of wombats   a **tower** of giraffes
a **parliament** of owls   a **bloat** of hippos
a **flamboyance** of flamingos

Match the collective nouns in the box to the groups of animals.

swarm	litter	pack	herd
colony	mob	flock	pod

① bees _____   ⑤ cows _____
② whales _____   ⑥ sheep _____
③ kittens _____ ⑦ kangaroos _____
④ dogs _____   ⑧ ants _____

Choose the best collective noun phrases to complete these sentences.

stack of wood	block of flats
set of clubs	fleet of ships
bunch of keys	army of soldiers

⑨ I gave my dad a new _____ and a golf bag.

⑩ A _____ set sail at dawn today.

⑪ We have a huge _____ ready for our fireplace.

⑫ My nan lives in a tall _____.

⑬ An _____ was sent to fight the battle.

⑭ I lost a big _____ with my front door key on it.

Phonic Knowledge & Spelling

AC9E3LY09, AC9E3LY10, AC9E3LY11, AC9E3LY12

Letter team: au

Say each word from the word bank. They all contain the letter team **au**. The letters work together to make one sound 'or'.

Word Bank

Paul	haunt	sauce	cause
autumn	August	caught	daughter
auburn	naughty	automatic	audience

Choose words from the word bank to complete these sentences.

① My _____ always says she has nothing new to wear!

② The actor waited until the _____ had stopped clapping.

③ None of my friends have a birthday in the month of _____.

④ I have two brothers. One is good, but the other is _____.

Homophones

Remember! Homophones are words that sound the same but have different spellings and meanings. Circle the correct homophone in the brackets for each sentence.

⑤ We had to (haul hall) our suitcases upstairs.

⑥ My dad (court caught) a big fish.

⑦ I like tomato (sauce source) on my chips.

⑧ Our dog has huge (paws pause).

Tricky words

Some words are tricky to spell. You can make up ways to remember how to spell them.
Examples:
• Think of a word for every letter of the tricky word.
sigh = she is going home
• Group words that go together.
You hear with your ears.
• Break the word up into smaller parts.
on–i–on
• Find little words in the word.
together = to get her
• Make up a silly saying or rhyme.
There's a rat in separate.

⑨ **Find five small words in the word automatic and list them.**

TERM 4 ENGLISH

Informative text – Factual recount
Author – Claire Craig

Hooping It Up

As long ago as 1000 BCE, children in ancient Greece and Rome played with hoops made from vines. In colonial days in America, children rolled hoops along the streets, guiding them with sticks. Australian children used bamboo hoops in sports classes at school. But in 1957 the idea was taken one step further. That was the year the Hula Hoop, a hollow plastic hoop, appeared in stores.

This hoopy toy became a huge success. People held contests to see who could twirl the most hoops around their waists, arms, wrists, legs, feet — even around their heads and necks. But the company that made them was not able to get a patent for such an ancient idea. Soon, others were making Spin-a-Hoops and Hoop-d-dos. It is estimated that between 60 and 100 million hoops were sold in two years!

Hula Hoops were made in all colours and patterns. At the peak of the craze, one company manufactured 20 000 a day.

Source: *Whose Crazy Idea was That?*, Brainwaves, Blake Education.

Write or circle the correct answers.

① **What were the very first hoops made from?**

a plastic

b vines

c bamboo

② **When did Hula Hoops first appear in stores?**

a 1957

b in ancient Greece and Rome

c we are not told

③ **What does colonial mean?**

a old

b early times in a settlement

c new

④ **Which one of these is the odd word out?**

a success   c failure

b victory   d triumph

⑤ **What is a patent?**

a a person in hospital

b a right given by the government to an inventor, allowing them to be the only person to make or sell an invention

⑥ **What was the Hula Hoop made from?**

_____

Name two other brands of hoops manufactured after the Hula Hoop was introduced.

⑦ _____

⑧ _____

⑨ **Which word in the text means 'guessed'?**

a estimated

b manufactured

c appeared

Score 2 points for each correct answer!   **SCORE** /18

My Book Review

Title _____

Author _____

Rating ☆ ☆ ☆ ☆ ☆

Comment _____

_____

TERM 4 ENGLISH

Number & Algebra

AC9M3N01

Numbers to 10 000s

The value of each digit
in the number **24 769** is:
  2 ten thousands
  4 thousands
  7 hundreds
  6 tens
  9 ones
Written in words, it is: **twenty-four
thousand, seven hundred and sixty-nine.**

Write these numbers in words.

① 643

_____

② 1792

_____

③ 2050

_____

④ 12 568

_____

_____

⑤ 56 705

_____

_____

Write these numbers in digits.

⑥ six hundred and fifty-six _____

⑦ four hundred and five _____

⑧ two thousand, seven hundred and ninety-
  three _____

⑨ thirteen thousand, four hundred and eighty-
  one _____

⑩ eighty-two thousand, nine hundred and sixty
  _____

**What is the value of the bold digit?
Circle the correct answer.**

⑪ **4**89   a 800   b 80   c 8

⑫ 7**0**2   a 200   b 20   c 2

⑬ **5**609   a 5000   b 500   c 50

⑭ 12 **4**87   a 2000   b 200   c 20

⑮ 5**7** 489   a 50 000   b 5000   c 500

What numbers do these make?
Hint: Write the highest value first.

⑯ 5 ones, 4 tens, 7 hundreds and 3 thousands

_____

⑰ 6 hundreds, 7 ones and 5 thousands

_____

⑱ 5 ones, 6 tens, 5 hundreds and 6 thousands

_____

⑲ 7 hundreds, 9 thousands, 8 tens and 2 ones

_____

Score 2 points for
each correct answer!   SCORE   **/38**   (0-16)   (18-32)   (34-38)

Statistics & Probability

AC9M3ST02

Line graphs

Class 3S held an art exhibition last week.
They charged 50 cents entry to raise money
for art supplies.

The line graph shows the number of visitors
to their exhibition.

Visitors to our Exhibition

(Line graph: y-axis "Number of visitors" from 0 to 36, x-axis "Day of the week" Mon–Sat. Points: Mon 12, Tue 6, Wed 9, Thu 18, Fri 25, Sat 34.)

**Use the graph to answer the questions.
Write or circle the correct answers.**

① How many people visited the exhibition on
  Tuesday? _____

② How many visitors on Saturday? _____

TERM 4 MATHS

③ What is the difference in visitor numbers between Tuesday and Saturday? _____

④ The entry fee to the exhibition was 50 cents. How much money did they raise on Tuesday? _____

⑤ How many visitors did they have altogether?
   a 94   **b** 104   **c** 114

⑥ How much money did they raise altogether?
   a $50.50   **b** $51   **c** $52.00

⑦ **Use the information in the line graph to complete this bar graph with the same information.**

Visitors to our Exhibition

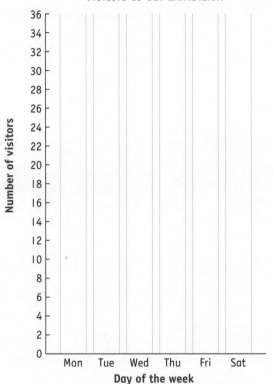

Measurement & Space

AC9M3M02

Mass

1 kg = 1000 g
$\frac{1}{2}$ kg = 500 g
$\frac{1}{4}$ kg = 250 g

Circle the correct answers.

① 2 kg = 2000 g   **a** true **b** false
② $\frac{1}{2}$ kg + $\frac{1}{2}$ kg = 1000 g   **a** true **b** false
③ 1$\frac{1}{2}$ kg = 1250 g   **a** true **b** false
④ $\frac{1}{4}$ kg + $\frac{1}{4}$ kg = 500 g   **a** true **b** false
⑤ 3$\frac{1}{2}$ kg = 3250 g   **a** true **b** false

Write < , > or = to make these statements true.

Hint: < means 'less than', > means 'greater than'. The point of the arrow always points to the smaller number.

⑥ 1000 g ____ 1 kg
⑦ 500 g + 500 g ____ 2 kg
⑧ $\frac{1}{4}$ kg + $\frac{1}{4}$ kg ____ $\frac{1}{2}$ kg
⑨ 1$\frac{1}{2}$ kg ____ 1$\frac{1}{4}$ kg
⑩ 1000 g – 500 g ____ 500 g
⑪ 1 kg – $\frac{1}{4}$ kg ____ 500 g

Read the scales and write the weight.

⑫ 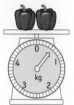   ⑬

_____   _____

Problem Solving

AC9M3N01

The Ancient Romans used a different number system to ours. They used capital letters to represent numbers.

Roman numerals
I   II   III   IV   V   VI   VII   VIII   IX   X

Our numerals
1   2   3   4   5   6   7   8   9   10

To convert Roman Numerals, you add.

Example: XII = 10 + 1 + 1 = 12

If there is a 4 or a 9, you subtract.

Examples: IV = 5 – 1 = 4   IX = 10 – 1 = 9

Look at these:
XX = 20, XXIV = 24, XXXII = 32

Write our numbers.   **Write Roman numerals.**

① XI = ____   ⑨ 6 = _____
② VII = ____   ⑩ 10 = _____
③ XX = ____   ⑪ 4 = _____
④ III = ____   ⑫ 19 = _____
⑤ IX = ____   ⑬ 12 = _____
⑥ XXII = ____   ⑭ 25 = _____
⑦ XXIV = ____   ⑮ 21 = _____
⑧ XXXV = ____   ⑯ 34 = _____

Grammar & Punctuation

AC9E3LA07

Relating verbs

> **Relating verbs** show what things *are* and what things *have*. There is no action taking place.
> *Examples*: A horse **is** a mammal.
> A frog **has** four legs.
> These verbs in these sentences are **action** or **doing verbs**.
> *Examples*: The horse **ran** down the road.
> The frog **jumped** into the pond.

Use relating verbs to complete these sentences. Choose from are, have, am, has and was.

① She _____ a very careful girl.

② Butterflies _____ wings.

③ Flies _____ insects.

④ A frog _____ two eyes.

⑤ I _____ fond of spiders.

For each sentence, write whether the bold verb is an action verb or a relating verb.

⑥ My dog **chased** my neighbour's cat up a tree.

_____

⑦ A snake **is** a reptile.

_____

⑧ I **am** taller than you.

_____

⑨ The river **flowed** into the sea.

_____

⑩ Cars **are** made from metal and plastic.

_____

⑪ The frog **swam** across the pond.

_____

⑫ **Circle the four relating verbs in this paragraph.**

Insects are small animals with six legs. Insects have a hard shell or an exoskeleton. Most insects have wings and antennae. One of the largest insects in the world is the Rhinoceros Beetle.

Score 2 points for each correct answer! **SCORE** /24 (0-10) (12-18) (20-24)

Phonic Knowledge & Spelling

AC9E3LY09, AC9E3LY10, AC9E3LY11

Letter teams: oy and oi

Say each word from the word bank. They each contain the letter teams oy or oi. The letters work together to make the same sound.

Word Bank

boy	toy	enjoy	employ	royal
oil	boil	coil	spoil	coin
joint	point	voice	choice	noise

Choose words from the word bank above to complete these sentences.

① We _____ going to the movies.

② The singer had an amazing _____.

③ What is that loud _____?

④ The baby _____ dropped his _____.

Rhyming words

> **Rhyming words** have the same sound at the end, but not necessarily the same spelling.
> *Examples*: shoe, two, too, chew, do, who, blue, flu, true, ewe, knew, view

Write the words from the box next to their rhyming words.

tower	toe	hurt	sleigh

⑤ day _____ ⑦ dirt _____

⑥ flour _____ ⑧ grow _____

Compound words

Make compound words by writing a word from the box on each line.

mail	less	shop	hood

⑨ boy_____ ⑪ point_____

⑩ toy_____ ⑫ voice_____

Join the syllables then write the words.

⑬ em + ploy + ee _____

⑭ poi + son _____

⑮ loy + al + ty _____

⑯ hoi + sting _____

Score 2 points for each correct answer! **SCORE** /32 (0-14) (16-26) (28-32)

TARGETING HOMEWORK 3 © PASCAL PRESS ISBN 9781925726459

Narrative text – Description
Author – Frances Mackay

Leon's Bedroom

I live in a new house on River View Lane. My bedroom is upstairs and has a large window that looks out over the river. I can see the river, a farmhouse and some mountains in the distance. The window has blue curtains. My bed is right in front of the window, so I can look out when I wake up. It's a single bed, made from wood. At the moment, I have white sheets and pillowcase with a green bedcover.

Next to my bed is a bedside table. It has two drawers. The top drawer is painted blue and the bottom one is green. I have a red reading lamp on top of the drawers. In front of the drawers is a yellow rug.

Above my bed, I have two wooden shelves. I keep a few books here and some of my treasures.

Adjacent to the window is a tall bookcase. It has four shelves at the top and three drawers at the bottom. The top and bottom drawers are painted green and the middle drawer is blue. I keep books on the shelves, and some small boxes with some of my bits and pieces in them.

In the middle of the room is a large round rug. It has rings of yellow and orange on it. The carpet in the room is dark blue and the walls are turquoise.

Write or circle the correct answers.

① **Where does Leon live?**

_____

② **Why is Leon's bed in front of the window?**
   a so he can get fresh air
   b so he can look out when he wakes up
   c so he can hear the river

③ **What does adjacent to mean?**
   a above
   b behind
   c next to

④ **Which one of these is the odd word out?**
   a sole   c double
   b single   d one

⑤ **Which object in Leon's bedroom is red?**

_____

What colours are the following objects in Leon's bedroom?

⑥ walls

_____

⑦ large round rug

_____

⑧ curtains

_____

⑨ bedcover

_____

⑩ bedside table drawers

_____

Score 2 points for each correct answer!

SCORE **/20**

My Book Review

Title _____

Author _____

Rating ☆☆☆☆☆

Comment _____

_____

TERM 4 ENGLISH

Number & Algebra

AC9M3N02

Fractions

These shapes are all divided in **half**.

For each shape, the number of parts coloured is equal to the number of parts not coloured.

The total number of parts has been **divided by two**.

$\frac{1}{2}$ is equal to $\frac{2}{4}$ and is also equal to $\frac{4}{8}$.

Complete the fractions. Use the diagrams to help you.

① $\frac{1}{2} = \frac{\square}{4}$

② $\frac{1}{2} = \frac{\square}{6}$

③ $\frac{1}{2} = \frac{\square}{10}$

④ $\frac{1}{2} = \frac{\square}{8}$

Colour one half of each shape and complete the fraction.

⑤ $\frac{1}{2} = \frac{\square}{10}$

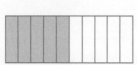

⑥ $\frac{1}{2} = \frac{\square}{12}$

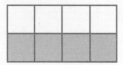

⑦ $\frac{1}{2} = \frac{\square}{20}$

Complete the number lines.

⑧
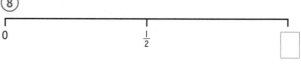
0    $\frac{1}{2}$ $\square$

⑨
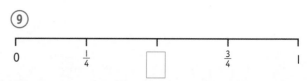
0   $\frac{1}{4}$ $\square$ $\frac{3}{4}$ 1

⑩

0   $\frac{1}{8}$ $\frac{2}{8}$ $\square$ $\square$ $\frac{6}{8}$ $\frac{7}{8}$ 1

⑪
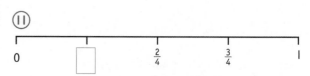
0   $\square$ $\frac{2}{4}$ $\frac{3}{4}$ 1

Score 2 points for each correct answer!   **SCORE**   **/22**   (0-8) (10-16) (18-22)

Statistics & Probability

There are no statistics & probability activities in this unit.

Measurement & Space

AC9M3M01

Capacity

We use the word **capacity** when we are measuring **liquids**. Liquids are measured in millilitres and litres.

1000 millilitres (mL) = 1 litre (L)

Circle the correct answer.

① If a jug holds exactly 2 litres of water and it takes 4 jugs to fill a bucket, what is the capacity of the bucket?

   a 4 litres   **b** 6 litres
   c 8 litres   **d** 10 litres

② A bath holds 12 litres of water. If a bucket holds 3 litres, how many bucketsful do you need to fill the bath?

   a 4   **b** 6   **c** 8   **d** 12

③ A bottle holds 1 L of water. It takes 7 bottles to fill a watering can. What is the capacity of the watering can?

   a 1000 mL   **b** 4000 mL
   c 7 L   **d** 8000 mL

TERM 4 MATHS

④ A hot tub holds 400 L of water when it is full. It is only half full at the moment. How much water is in the hot tub?

a 100 L   b 200 L

c 300 L   d 400 L

⑤ It will take five 2 litre jugs of water to fill up a 12 litre water container.

a true   b false

Measuring jug scales

The water in this jug measures 800 mL.

How do we work this out? Each mark on the scale equals 50 mL. The water level is one mark above the 750 mL mark, so we add 50 mL to 750 mL to get 800 mL.

How many millilitres of water are in these jugs? Read the scales and write the answer.

Hint: some scales are marked in 50 mL, some are marked in 100 mL.

⑥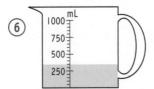

_____

⑨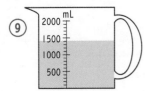

_____

⑦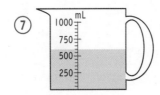

_____

⑩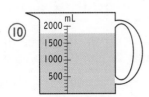

_____

⑧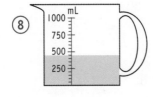

_____

⑪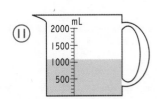

_____

Problem Solving

AC9M3M03

TV Guide

Here is part of a TV guide for Channel 48.

Star Vet	5.05 pm
Quick Quiz	5.40 pm
Young News	6.00 pm
Tim & Tanya	6.35 pm
Cartoon	7.05 pm

Write the correct answer. How long is each program?

① Star Vet _____

② Young News _____

③ Quick Quiz _____

④ If you watched Star Vet and Quick Quiz, how long have you been watching TV?

_____

⑤ The cartoon goes for 35 minutes. What time does it end?

_____

⑥ If you watched Quick Quiz five nights a week, how long is this each week?

_____

⑦ If you watched TV from the beginning of Star Vet to the end of the cartoon, how long is this?

_____

Score 2 points for each correct answer!

SCORE **/22**   0-8   10-16   18-22

Grammar & Punctuation

AC9E3LA04

Paragraphs

Longer texts are organised into **paragraphs**. A paragraph is a group of sentences used to introduce new parts of a story, characters or pieces of information.

Paragraphs break up the text into easy-to-read sections. They show the reader when one set of ideas has ended and another has begun.

The first sentence of a paragraph usually tells us the main idea — what the paragraph is about. The **main idea** of the following paragraph is to describe the bedside table to the reader.

Example:

Next to my bed is a bedside table. It has two drawers. The top drawer is painted blue and the bottom one is green. In front of the drawers is a yellow rug.

Underline the main idea in each of the paragraphs.

① He ran and ran until his sides started to ache. He dropped down, exhausted, against an old tree. "Phew, I made it," he thought.

② Mal knocked on the door. When no answer came, he cautiously turned the handle and peered inside. The room was empty.

③ Mal quickly turned around. What was it? The sound made his blood run cold. "Run," he thought. "I've got to run."

④ He stepped further into the room and called Becky's name. No-one replied. Suddenly, he became aware of a strange shuffling sound in the corner.

⑤ **The paragraphs above are in the wrong order. Number the small boxes beside the paragraphs from 1–4 to tell the story in the correct order.**

Score 2 points for each correct answer! **SCORE** **/10** (0-2) (4-8) (10)

Phonic Knowledge & Spelling

AC9E3LY09, AC9E3LY10, AC9E3LY11

Letter teams: are and air

Say each word from the word bank. They each contain the letter team **are** or **air**. The letters work together to make the same sound 'air', like the air we breathe.

Word Bank

care	mare	dare	rare
stare	spare	share	square
hair	chair	fair	stairs

Choose words from the word bank to complete these sentences.

① We crept slowly down the dark _____.

② Mum says I should _____ with my brother.

③ My friend has long _____ down to her waist.

④ Uncle Ted fixes old cars in his _____ time.

Adding –ed and –ing

Add **–ed** and **–ing** to these words. Remember the spelling rules!

	–ed	–ing
⑤ scare	_____	_____
⑥ glare	_____	_____
⑦ share	_____	_____
⑧ blare	_____	_____
⑨ prepare	_____	_____

Compound words
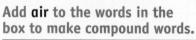

Add **air** to the words in the box to make compound words.

way	bag	port	fare	line
ship	craft	tight	waves	borne

⑩ _____   ⑮ _____

⑪ _____   ⑯ _____

⑫ _____   ⑰ _____

⑬ _____   ⑱ _____

⑭ _____   ⑲ _____

Score 2 points for each correct answer! **SCORE** **/38** (0-16) (18-32) (34-38)

TARGETING HOMEWORK 3 © PASCAL PRESS ISBN 9781925726459

Information text – Report
Author – Frances Mackay

Day and Night

The Earth is a sphere that travels around the Sun. The Earth is tilted and spins round and round on an imaginary line called its **axis**. The axis runs through the centre of the Earth from the North Pole to the South Pole. The Earth's axis is always tilted at the same angle.

As the Earth spins, one side of the Earth faces the Sun and we call this **day**. The side facing away from the Sun is dark and we call this **night**.

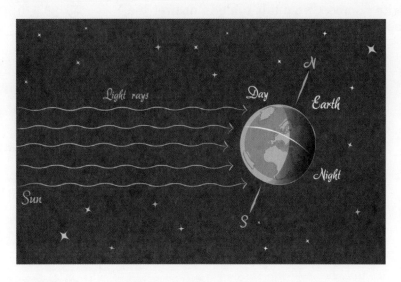

Because the Earth is always spinning, the line between day and night is always moving around the planet. It takes 24 hours for the Earth to spin once, and we call this a **day**.

The Sun appears to rise in the East and set in the West. The time when the Sun appears is called **sunrise**, and the time when it disappears is called **sunset**.

Write or circle the correct answers.

① **What does tilted mean?**
a straight
b on an angle
c bent

② **What is the imaginary line that runs through the centre of the Earth from the North Pole to the South Pole?**

_____

③ **Which one of these is the odd word out?**
a pretend   c real
b imaginary   d make-believe

④ **Why does only half of the Earth have day and the other half night?**
a not sure
b because we have always had night and day
c because the Earth spins around and only one side faces the Sun at any one time

⑤ **Which word in the text means 'the time when the Sun appears in the East'?**

_____

⑥ **In this text, the word angle means:**
a a point of view
b a space where two lines meet, measured in degrees

⑦ **Why is the line between day and night always moving around the planet?**

_____

Score 2 points for each correct answer! **SCORE** **/14** ⟨0-4⟩ ⟨6-10⟩ ⟨12-14⟩

My Book Review

Title _____

Author _____

Rating ☆ ☆ ☆ ☆ ☆

Comment _____

_____

TERM 4 ENGLISH

Number & Algebra

AC9M3N01

Comparing numbers

Write numbers from this table to answer the questions.

578	603	790	488	915
1248	2030	6190	4002	5706
24 500	38 609	75 432	85 620	99 258

① An even number between 688 and 792

_____

② A number that is 100 more than 503

_____

③ A number with 8 tens

_____

④ An odd number between 600 and 700

_____

⑤ The first even number after 2028

_____

⑥ A number that is 10 more than 3992

_____

⑦ A number that is 100 less than 1348

_____

⑧ A number that is double 12 250

_____

⑨ A number that is half of 8004

_____

⑩ A number with 9 thousands

_____

⑪ Write the numbers in the second row of the table in order from smallest to largest.

_____

_____

Write <, > or = to make these statements true.
Hint: < means 'less than', > means 'greater than'. The point of the arrow always points to the smaller number.

⑫ 488 _____ 915

⑬ 75 432 _____ 38 609

⑭ 5706 _____ 5806 − 100

⑮ 244 × 2 _____ 488

⑯ 4002 + 10 _____ 4022

⑰ 578 ÷ 2 _____ 290

Write **true** or **false**.

⑱ The next odd number after 915 is 917.

_____

⑲ 6290 is 100 more than 6190.

_____

⑳ 85 620 is a larger number than 99 258.

_____

㉑ The value of 5 in 24 500 is 5000.

_____

㉒ 38 609 is an odd number.

_____

㉓ 488 ÷ 2 = 244.

_____

Score 2 points for each correct answer!

SCORE **/46**

Statistics & Probability

AC9M3ST03

When you carry out a survey, the most important thing to do is to **ask the right questions.**

Task: Find out how many children in Year 3 have a dog for a pet.

Question 1: Do you like dogs?

Question 2: Do you have a pet?

The answer to these questions will not tell you if the person has a dog for a pet.

Question 3: Do you have a dog for a pet?

This is the right question to ask children in Year 3.

Which question will gather the information needed? Circle the correct answer.

① **Tabitha wants to find out the favourite colour of teachers in her school.**
   a Do you like the colour blue?
   b What is your favourite colour?
   c Do you prefer red to green?

② **Jake wants to find out how many children in his class prefer football to basketball.**
   a Do you like football and basketball?
   b Do you like football best?
   c Which do you like better, football or basketball?

③ **May wants to find out how many children in her class walk to school.**
   a Do you come to school by car?
   b How do you get to school?
   c Do you like walking to school?

Once they have the right question, who should they ask? Circle the correct answer.

④ **Who should Tabitha ask?**
  a her friends
  b her family
  c the teachers in her school

⑤ **Who should Jake ask?**
  a the boys in his class
  b the girls in his class
  c the boys and girls in his class

⑥ **Who should May ask?**
  a the children in her school
  b the children in her class
  c her teacher

Score 2 points for each correct answer! **SCORE** /12 0-4 6-8 10-12

Measurement & Space

AC9M3M03

Time –
seconds, minutes and hours

> 60 seconds = 1 minute
> 60 minutes = 1 hour
>
>
>
> The **red** hand on this clock is the second hand. It counts the **seconds**.
>
> If there is no second hand, you can count seconds approximately by saying at a steady rate: 'ONE thousand, TWO thousand, THREE thousand' and so on. This gives you an idea of how long one second is.

Write or circle the correct answers.

① Which activity would take approximately one second?
  a count to four
  b eat an apple
  c make a cup of tea

② How many seconds are there in 2 minutes?
  a 60   b 2   c 120

③ If the second hand has moved from the 3 to the 6 on a clock, how many seconds have gone by?
  a 5   b 10   c 15

④ If the second hand has gone around the clock twice, how many minutes have gone by?
  a 1   b 2   c 0

---

⑤ It took Ben two minutes to write an email. How many seconds is that?
  a 60   b 120   c 180

⑥ Alice took 1 minute and 40 seconds to run to the shop. It took Jayne 98 seconds. Who was faster?
  a Alice   b Jayne

⑦ It takes Reece half an hour to get to school by car. It takes Melanie takes 40 minutes. Who has the shorter journey? _____

⑧ The football match started 30 minutes late. It was due to begin at 4:15 pm. What time did the match start? _____

⑨ The man arrived 1 minute and 15 seconds late for his train. By how many seconds was he late? _____

Score 2 points for each correct answer! **SCORE** /18 0-6 8-14 16-18

Problem Solving

AC9M3N01

Number card puzzles

> Here are 3 number cards.
>
>

① Write all the different three-digit numbers you can make with the cards.
_____

② What is the largest number you made?
_____

③ What is the smallest number you made?
_____

④ Write the numbers in order, from smallest to largest.
_____

⑤ Write your numbers in the table. Multiply each one by 10 and then by 100.

Number	×10	×100

TERM 4 MATHS

Grammar & Punctuation

AC9E3LA08

Irregular verbs

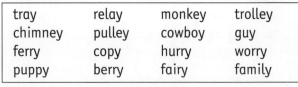

> Most **verbs** use the same endings to show the **present** and **past tense**.
> *Examples:*
> **Present tense** (happening now)
> add **–s** or **–es**   He **plays** a tune.
>   She **mixes** the cake.
> add **–ing**   He **is playing** a tune.
> **Past tense** (happened in the past)
> add **–ed**   He **played** a tune.
> add **–ing**   He **was playing** a tune.
>
> Some verbs are called **irregular verbs**. These have **special past tense** forms.
> *Examples:*
> **Present tense**   She **runs** to the shop.
> **Past tense**   She **ran** to the shop.
> **Present tense**   I **am writing** a story.
> **Past tense**   I **wrote** a story.

Circle the correct past tense verb in each sentence.

1. The man slipped and (falled   fell).
2. We (ate   eated) roast lamb for dinner.
3. The plane (flew   flied) overhead.
4. The fielder (catched   caught) the ball.
5. The cleaner (swept   sweeped) the floor.
6. The actor (speaked   spoke) very clearly.
7. The lady (gived   gave) me my change.
8. I (cleant   cleaned) my bedroom.

Write the past tense verbs from the box next to their matching present tense verbs.

grew	bit	rang	stood
drank	sang	told	hid

9. hides _____
10. sings _____
11. bites _____
12. tells _____
13. rings _____
14. drinks _____
15. stands _____
16. grows _____

Score 2 points for each correct answer!   **SCORE** /32 (0-14) (16-26) (28-32)

Phonic Knowledge & Spelling

AC9E3LY09, AC9E3LY10

More words that end in y

Say each word from the word bank. They all end in the letter **y**.

Word Bank

tray	relay	monkey	trolley
chimney	pulley	cowboy	guy
ferry	copy	hurry	worry
puppy	berry	fairy	family

Choose words from the word bank to complete these sentences.

1. We went across the river in a _____.
2. The _____ had smoke coming out of it.
3. Dad bought me a _____ of my favourite book.
4. Everyone in my _____ came to the party.

Plurals: y after a vowel

> **Remember!** When a word ends in a **y** after a vowel (**ay, ey, oy** or **uy**), just add **–s** to make it plural (more than one).
> *Examples*: ray, ra**ys**   monk**ey**, monk**eys**
>   t**oy**, t**oys**   g**uy**, g**uys**

Write these words as plurals.

5. essay _____
6. boy _____
7. cowboy _____
8. kidney _____
9. pulley _____
10. day _____

Plurals: y after a consonant

> **Remember!** When a word ends in a **y** after a consonant, change the **y** into **i** and add **–es** to make it plural.
> *Examples*: lady, lad**ies**   party, part**ies**
>   family, famil**ies**

Write these words as plurals.

11. puppy _____
12. trophy _____
13. diary _____
14. baby _____
15. city _____
16. gully _____

Score 2 points for each correct answer!   **SCORE** /32 (0-14) (16-26) (28-32)

Information text – Report
Author – Lisa Nicol

May Day

May Day is a celebration of spring in the northern hemisphere. Such celebrations began in ancient Greece and Rome. The Romans celebrated Flora, the goddess of flowers and plants. The Greeks celebrated Chloris, a spirit of springtime, flowers and new growth.

May Day celebrations feature flowers and dancing. In England, children dance around a maypole decorated with flowers or ribbons. Morris dancers perform folk dances. A May Queen wears a crown of flowers.

In Germany, Sweden, Finland and the Czech Republic, they celebrate on the night before May Day. Walpurgis Night includes singing, dancing, bonfires and street parties.

In many countries, including Australia, May Day has become Labour Day. It's a day to celebrate the achievements of workers. It also remembers the campaign for shorter working hours. In the 1800s, most Australians worked 12–14 hours a day, six days a week. Workers wanted more time to be with their families. They fought for and won an eight-hour work day — eight hours for work, eight hours for sleep and eight hours for leisure.

Source: *World Celebrations*, Go Facts, Blake Education.

Write or circle the correct answers.

1. In the northern hemisphere, what is May Day is a celebration of?
   a shorter working days
   b flowers and plants
   c spring

List three things that happen on May Day in England.

2. _____

3. _____

4. _____

5. What is May Day called in Finland?
   a not sure
   b Walpurgis Night
   c Labour Day

6. Which word in the text means 'marked' or 'honoured'?
   a fought
   b decorated
   c celebrated

7. Who was Flora?
   a a Greek spirit
   b a Roman goddess
   c an English queen

8. What does the word **campaign** mean in this text?
   a a series of activities done to achieve something
   b a battle in war time

Score 2 points for each correct answer!

SCORE /16   0-6   8-12   14-16

TERM 4 ENGLISH

My Book Review

Title _____

Author _____

Rating ☆☆☆☆☆

Comment _____
_____

Number patterns

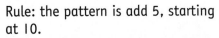

Look at these number patterns.
10, 15, 20, 25, 30, 35
Rule: the pattern is add 5, starting at 10.

300, 290, 280, 270, 260
Rule: the pattern is subtract 10, starting at 300.

Write the rules for these number patterns.

① 15, 18, 21, 24, 27

_____

② 60, 55, 50, 45, 40

_____

③ 45, 55, 65, 75, 85

_____

④ 133, 130, 127, 124

_____

⑤ 254, 259, 264, 269

_____

⑥ 578, 588, 598, 608

_____

⑦ 1345, 1335, 1325, 1315

_____

Use the rule to complete these number patterns.

⑧ add 5, starting at 60
60, _____, _____, _____, _____

⑨ subtract 3, starting at 28
28, _____, _____, _____, _____

⑩ add 10, starting at 62
62, _____, _____, _____, _____

⑪ subtract 5, starting at 160
160, _____, _____, _____, _____

⑫ add 2, starting at 583
583, _____, _____, _____, _____

⑬ add 10, starting at 346
346, _____, _____, _____, _____

⑭ add 100, starting at 193
193, _____, _____, _____, _____

⑮ subtract 100, starting at 1640
1640, _____, _____, _____, _____

When adding 10, what numbers come before and after these?

⑯ _____, 56, _____

⑰ _____, 72, _____

⑱ _____, 139, _____

⑲ _____, 4368, _____

⑳ _____, 24 523, _____

When subtracting 10, what numbers come before and after these?

㉑ _____, 24, _____

㉒ _____, 89, _____

㉓ _____, 540, _____

㉔ _____, 5670, _____

㉕ _____, 56 341, _____

Score 2 points for each correct answer! SCORE /50 (0-22) (24-44) (46-50)

Statistics & Probability

There are no statistics & probability activities in this unit.

Measurement & Space

AC9M3SP01

3D objects

3D objects have **faces**, **edges** and **vertices**.

face: the flat part of the surface
edge: the line where two faces meet
vertex: the corner (plural is **vertices**)

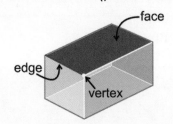

TARGETING HOMEWORK 3 © PASCAL PRESS ISBN 9781925726459

Write the missing numbers for each 3D object

① A square-based pyramid has _____ faces.

② It has _____ face shaped like a square.

③ A square-based pyramid has _____ vertices.

④ A square-based pyramid has _____ edges.

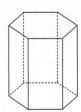

⑤ A triangular prism has _____ faces.

⑥ It has _____ faces shaped like a triangle.

⑦ A triangular prism has _____ vertices.

⑧ A triangular prism has _____ edges.

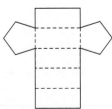

⑨ A hexagonal prism has _____ faces.

⑩ It has _____ faces shapes like a hexagon.

⑪ A hexagonal prism has _____ vertices.

⑫ A hexagonal prism has _____ edges.

⑬ **Which 3D object can be made with this net?**

a square-based pyramid
b pentagonal prism
c triangular prism
d hexagonal prism

Fraction puzzles

Solve these word problems.

① Suzie had 4 oranges and cut them all into quarters. How many quarters does this make?

_____

② Will, Jack, Georgia and Mia share this chocolate bar equally. Draw on the diagram to show how you would divide the chocolate bar.

③ Lee had $10. He spent half of it on a book and then he gave $3 to his brother to buy some toffee. How much money does Lee have left?

_____

④ Fran had a bag of lollies. She gave $\frac{1}{4}$ of them to her brother. She started with 28 lollies. How many did she have left?

_____

⑤ Mum, Dad and I shared a pizza. Mum had $\frac{1}{4}$, Dad had $\frac{1}{2}$ and I had the rest. How much of the pizza did I eat?

_____

TERM 4 MATHS

Score 2 points for each correct answer!

SCORE /26 (0-10) (12-20) (22-26)

Grammar & Punctuation

AC9E3LA02

Adverbial phrases

> A **phrase** is a group of words without a verb. It often begins with a **preposition**.
>
> Here are some prepositions:
>
> | | | | | |
> |---|---|---|---|---|
> | above | across | after | around | at |
> | below | beneath | between | by | down |
> | during | except | for | from | into |
> | near | of | on | over | past |
> | through | to | under | upon | with |
>
> An **adverbial phrase** tells us *how*, *when*, *where* and *why* things happen.
>
> *Examples*:
> **(how)**   Jenny replied <u>with a nod</u>.
> **(when)**   Mum went shopping <u>after lunch</u>.
> **(where)**   Mike ran <u>along the street</u>.
> **(why)**   Jayne bought a cake <u>for her mother</u>.

Choose a preposition from the list above to complete each underlined adverbial phrase.

① I like riding horses _____ <u>the forest</u>.

② The frightened dog hid _____ <u>our sofa</u>.

③ _____ <u>home</u>, we eat dinner at 6 o'clock.

④ Zac received an award _____ <u>his painting</u>.

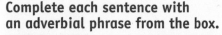

Complete each sentence with an adverbial phrase from the box.

after school	with a smile
in the bowl	across the road

⑤ The dog ran _____.

⑥ We went to the park _____.

⑦ Our teacher greeted us _____.

⑧ I mixed the cake batter _____.

Score 2 points for each correct answer!   SCORE   **/16**   (0-6) (8-12) (14-16)

Phonic Knowledge & Spelling

AC9E3LY09, AC9E3LY10

Prefixes: un– and dis–

Say each word from the word bank.
They all begin with the prefixes un– or dis–.

> **Remember!** A **prefix** is a letter or group of letters that is added to the beginning of a word. The prefixes **un–** and **dis–** mean 'not' or 'the opposite of'.

Word Bank

undo	unfair	unhappy	unfold
unopened	untidy	untie	unclean
dishonest	dislike	disbelieve	discontinue
disobey	distrust	disappear	disconnect

Choose words from the word bank to complete these sentences.

① The native bush looked very _____, so we pruned it.

② I _____ having to push my baby brother in his pram when he's crying.

③ I put my clean socks in my drawer and my _____ ones in the laundry basket.

④ If you pull on the electric cord, you will _____ the television.

Antonyms

> **Antonyms** are words opposite in meaning to another word.

Choose antonyms for these words from the word bank.

⑤ tie   _____

⑥ believe   _____

⑦ fold   _____

⑧ appear   _____

⑨ honest   _____

⑩ obey   _____

Write the antonyms of these words by adding the prefixes un– or dis–.

⑪ _____afraid   ⑰ _____plug

⑫ _____respect   ⑱ _____obedient

⑬ _____agree

⑭ _____safe

⑮ _____continue

⑯ _____well

Score 2 points for each correct answer!   SCORE   **/36**   (0-16) (18-30) (32-36)

TARGETING HOMEWORK 3 © PASCAL PRESS ISBN 9781925726459

Information text – Exposition
Author – Ann Harth

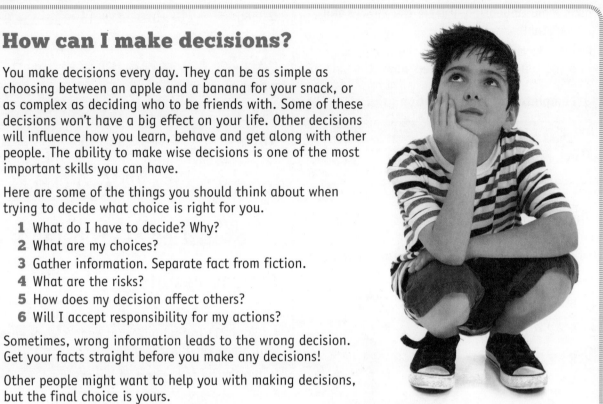

How can I make decisions?

You make decisions every day. They can be as simple as choosing between an apple and a banana for your snack, or as complex as deciding who to be friends with. Some of these decisions won't have a big effect on your life. Other decisions will influence how you learn, behave and get along with other people. The ability to make wise decisions is one of the most important skills you can have.

Here are some of the things you should think about when trying to decide what choice is right for you.

1 What do I have to decide? Why?
2 What are my choices?
3 Gather information. Separate fact from fiction.
4 What are the risks?
5 How does my decision affect others?
6 Will I accept responsibility for my actions?

Sometimes, wrong information leads to the wrong decision. Get your facts straight before you make any decisions!

Other people might want to help you with making decisions, but the final choice is yours.

Source: *Who am I?*, Health & Understanding, Blake Education

Write or circle the correct answers.

① **Which one of these is the odd word out?**

a decision   c indecision

b outcome   d choice

② **Which word in the text means 'difficult' or 'made up of many different parts'?**

a influence

b complex

c information

③ **What is a wise decision?**

a a decision made after asking others

b a decision made in a hurry

c a decision made after considering all the options

List three things you should think about when trying to decide what choice is best for you.

④ _____

⑤ _____

⑥ _____

What example does the text give for each of the following?

⑦ a simple decision _____

⑧ a complex decision _____

⑨ **Which word is an antonym of important?**

a significant   b chief   c unimportant

⑩ **What does the author say is 'one of the most important skills you can have'?**

_____

Score 2 points for each correct answer! SCORE **/20** (0-8) (10-14) (16-20)

My Book Review

Title _____

Author _____

Rating ☆☆☆☆☆

Comment _____

_____

TERM 4 ENGLISH

Number & Algebra

AC9M3A03

Multiplication grid

This is a multiplication grid for the 2, 3, 5 and 10 times tables.

To complete the grid, multiply the numbers along the top with the numbers down the side.

① Complete the multiplication grid.

×	2	3	4	5	6	7	8	9	10
2	→4	6							
3						21			
5				25					
10									100

Use the grid to complete these number facts.

② 3 × 4 = _____

③ 5 × 10 = _____

④ 6 × 2 = _____

⑤ 5 × 9 = _____

⑥ 8 × 2 = _____

⑦ 3 × 8 = _____

⑧ 10 × 7 = _____

⑨ 3 × 9 = _____

⑩ 5 × 6 = _____

> You can use the multiplication grid to work out divisions too.
>
> *Example:*
>
> To find the answer to 21 ÷ 3, go down the side to the 3 and follow along the row until you get to 21. The number at the top of that column is the answer (7).

Use the multiplication grid to solve these divisions.

⑪ 70 ÷ 10 = _____

⑫ 30 ÷ 5 = _____

⑬ 18 ÷ 2 = _____

⑭ 40 ÷ 10 = _____

⑮ 50 ÷ 5 = _____

⑯ 27 ÷ 3 = _____

⑰ 14 ÷ 2 = _____

⑱ 12 ÷ 3 = _____

⑲ 20 ÷ 2 = _____

Complete each fact family.
Use the multiplication grid if you need to.

⑳ 5 × _____ = 50

㉑ _____ × 10 = 50

㉒ 50 ÷ _____ = 10

㉓ 50 ÷ _____ = 5

㉔ 3 × _____ = 18

㉕ _____ × 6 = 18

㉖ 18 ÷ _____ = 6

㉗ 18 ÷ _____ = 3

㉘ 2 × _____ = 16

㉙ _____ × 8 = 16

㉚ 16 ÷ _____ = 8

㉛ 16 ÷ _____ = 2

㉜ 10 × _____ = 70

㉝ _____ × 7 = 70

㉞ 70 ÷ _____ = 7

㉟ 70 ÷ _____ = 10

Score 2 points for each correct answer! SCORE /70 (0-32) (34-64) (66-70)

Statistics & Probability

AC9M3ST01

Survey results

Tasha carried out a survey in her class (Class 3T) to find out what snacks were eaten at break time last Monday.

Here is the tally chart of her results.

Food	Tally
Fruit	ЖЖ IIII
Cake	II
Biscuits	IIII
Chips	II
Chocolate	ЖЖ III
Health Bar	ЖЖ
Nothing	III

Circle the correct answer.

① What would be the best title for Tasha's table?

  a Food students like to eat at break time

  b Snacks eaten by the students in Class 3T last Monday

  c Class 3T's favourite snacks

TARGETING HOMEWORK 3 © PASCAL PRESS ISBN 9781925726459

② If Tasha made a bar graph to show her results, how many columns would she need?

a 2   **b** 4   **c** 7

③ On Tasha's bar graph, which snack would have the longest column?

a chips   **b** chocolate   **c** fruit

Does Tasha's tally chart show this information? Answer yes or no.

④ Some students in the class did not eat a snack at break time that day. _____

⑤ More students preferred chips to biscuits. _____

⑥ Tasha ate fruit for her snack. _____

⑦ The most popular snack that day was fruit. _____

Think about how you would carry out the same survey in your class. Circle the correct answer.

⑧ What would be the best way to collect the data?

a Go around the playground at break time to see what the students are eating.

b Ask the students in your class what they ate when they return to class after break time.

c Take a photo of what the students are eating.

Score 2 points for each correct answer! SCORE **/16** (0-6) (8-12) (14-16)

Measurement & Space

AC9M3M02

Drawing lengths

Sometimes you need to measure and draw lengths accurately.

To draw a line exactly the correct length, you need to use a ruler.

Example:

To draw a line that is 5 cm long, first place the zero on the ruler at the beginning of the line. Then draw along the ruler until you reach the 5 cm mark.

Use a ruler to draw these lines and shapes.

① A line 4 cm long

② A line 5½ cm long

③ A square with sides of 1.5 cm

④ A rectangle 6 cm long and 1 cm wide.

Score 2 points for each correct answer! SCORE **/8** (0-2) (4-6) (8)

Problem Solving

AC9M3N06

World's tallest mountains

Here are some of the world's tallest mountains.

NAME	REGION	HEIGHT (m)	Order of height
Aconcagua	South America	6961	
Mount Vinson	Antarctica		
Mount Kosciuszko	Australia		
Mount Everest	Asia	8848	
Puncak Jaya	Asia	4884	
Mount Elbrus	Europe		
Denali	North America	6144	
Kilimanjaro	Africa	5885	

Look at the data in the table. Fill out the table with the answers to these questions.

How tall is:

① Mount Kosciuszko if it is 6620 m shorter than Mount Everest?

② Mount Elbrus if it is 3107 m shorter than Mount Everest?

③ Mount Vinson if it is 8 m higher than Puncak Jaya?

④ **In the last column of the table above, number the mountains in order of height with number 1 as the highest.**

Answer these questions.

⑤ How much taller is Mount Everest than Aconcagua? _____

⑥ What is the difference in height between the tallest and shortest mountain?

_____

Grammar & Punctuation

AC9E3LA11, AC9E3LY06

Apostrophes

> **Remember!** An **apostrophe (')** is used for two purposes.
> i. To show **ownership**.
> *Example*: **Michael's** keys were lost.
> ii. To mark missing letters in a **contraction**.
> *Example*: We **aren't** allowed there.

The apostrophes are missing or have been used incorrectly on these signs.
Rewrite the signs correctly.

①

> Apple's, pear's
> and orange's
> **ON SALE**

②

> **Come to Bobs Café!
> Its the BEST COFFEE
> in town!**

③

> Sorry!
> **Were CLOSED.**
> Please come back tomorrow.

Phonic Knowledge & Spelling

AC9E3LY09, AC9E3LY10

Suffix: –ful

Say each word from the word bank.
They all end with the suffix **–ful**.

Word Bank

helpful	joyful	doubtful	cheerful
colourful	tearful	playful	hurtful
plentiful	beautiful	peaceful	wonderful

Choose words from the word bank to complete these sentences.

① Even though it was a _____ day, we played indoors.

② Beneath the table, we found some _____ crayons.

③ "You have both been very _____," said the smiling lady.

④ "This tiny kitten is very happy and _____," he said.

Adding –ful

> A **suffix** is added to the end of a word.
> The suffix **–ful** means 'full of'. When **'full'** is added to words, one **'l'** is dropped.
> Adding **–ful** to a word can turn it into an **adjective**.
> *Examples*: harm, harm**ful**   colour, colour**ful**

Add **–ful** to these words.

⑤ care_____   ⑨ wonder_____

⑥ cheer_____   ⑩ hope_____

⑦ help_____   ⑪ pain_____

⑧ power_____   ⑫ peace_____

Adding –ful: words ending in y

> If a word ends in **y** and has a consonant before it, change the **y** to **i** before adding **–ful**. If the word has a vowel before the **y**, just add **–ful**.
> *Example*: beau**t**y, beaut**iful**

Add **–ful** to these words.

⑬ pity   _____

⑭ joy   _____

⑮ play   _____

⑯ plenty   _____

Score 2 points for each correct answer! SCORE /6 0 2-4 6

Score 2 points for each correct answer! SCORE /32 0-14 16-26 28-32

Persuasive text – Formal letter
Author – Frances Mackay

Letter to the Council

Ms N Charge
Council Offices
Decision Street, Banksiaville

10 May 2018

Dear Ms Charge

The parents of Banksiaville Primary greatly appreciate that you have responded to previous requests for safety improvements to the local playground. I am now writing to ask you to consider the installation of new equipment in the playground.

The two swings are better than nothing, but most playgrounds have a merry-go-round, a slide and climbing frames. In fact, nearby Daisydale also has a skateboard park, a fitness circuit and a basketball court. And yet Banksiaville has none of these things. We all know what happens when children have nothing to do — boredom seems to encourage littering and vandalism. Do you want this to happen in beautiful Banksiaville?

On behalf of the parents of Banksiaville Primary, and indeed all of the parents in this district, I am urging you to investigate the possibility of upgrading our local playground to match, or preferably surpass, the standards and facilities of our neighbouring council playgrounds.

I know the children would find these extra facilities extremely useful and enjoyable, and I hope this suggestion will be acted upon in the very near future.

I look forward to receiving a positive reply.

Yours sincerely

Mrs V Concerned
Chairperson
Banksiaville Primary Parents' Association

Write or circle the correct answers.

1. **Has Mrs Concerned written to Ms Charge in the past?**

   a yes

   b no

   c don't know

2. **What is Mrs Concerned asking Ms Charge to do?**

   a install extra facilities

   b investigate the possibility of upgrading Banksiaville playground

   c visit the school to talk to parents

3. **What does the word circuit mean in this text?**

   a the path of an electric current

   b a circular course

   c a horse racing track

List three things the Daisydale playground has that Banksiaville does not.

4. _____

5. _____

6. _____

7. **What is Mrs Concerned worried about if the local children get bored because they have nothing to do?**

   a They will carry out littering and vandalism.

   b They will become unfit.

   c They will move out of the area.

8. **Which word is an antonym of ugly?**

   a unattractive   b beautiful   c unsightly

9. **Which word in the text means 'to be better than'?**

   a facilities   b positive   c surpass

10. **What does 'a positive reply' mean?**

    a a reply that says Ms Charge is going to agree to investigate improving the playground

    b a friendly reply

Score 2 points for each correct answer!

SCORE /20 (0-8) (10-14) (16-20)

TERM 4 ENGLISH

My Book Review

Title _____

Author _____

Rating ☆ ☆ ☆ ☆ ☆

Comment _____

_____

Number & Algebra

AC9M3N03

Adding three numbers – look for 20

When you add more than two numbers, use number facts to help you.

Example:

12 + 13 + 8

Look for the numbers that add to make 20.

Add the 12 and 8 first to make 20.

Then add 20 and 13.

Answer = 33

Look for 20 to help you add these numbers.

1. 14 + 12 + 6 = _____
2. 15 + 17 + 5 = _____
3. 13 + 7 + 19 = _____
4. 11 + 15 + 9 = _____
5. 16 + 18 + 4 = _____
6. 10 + 10 + 23 = _____

Adding three numbers – look for 100

You can use the same method to add larger numbers.

Example:

60 + 18 + 40

Look for the numbers that add to make 100.

Add the 60 and 40 first to make 100.

Then add 100 and 18.

Answer = 118

Look for 100 to help you add these numbers.

7. 50 + 50 + 45 = _____
8. 30 + 23 + 70 = _____
9. 80 + 20 + 62 = _____
10. 90 + 39 + 10 = _____
11. 45 + 55 + 20 = _____
12. 65 + 48 + 35 = _____

How quickly can you solve these? Circle the correct answer.

13. Which one equals 29?
    a 14 + 8 + 6
    b 12 + 8 + 5
    c 18 + 9 + 2

14. Which one equals 34?
    a 10 + 14 + 10
    b 19 + 1 + 9
    c 15 + 3 + 5

15. Which one equals 56?
    a 13 + 36 + 7
    b 6 + 14 + 33
    c 12 + 26 + 8

16. Which one equals 152?
    a 70 + 30 + 42
    b 20 + 52 + 80
    c 60 + 50 + 40

17. Which one equals 198?
    a 35 + 43 + 65
    b 45 + 55 + 98
    c 35 + 65 + 89

Score 2 points for each correct answer! **SCORE** /34 0-14 16-28 30-34

Statistics & Probability

There are no statistics & probability activities in this unit.

Measurement & Space

AC9M3SP02

Pathways

This map shows how Tanya got from the church to her school. The path she took is marked in red.

TARGETING HOMEWORK 3 © PASCAL PRESS ISBN 9781925726459

Use the map to answer the questions.
Write or circle the correct answer.

① What street is the church in?

_____

② In which direction did Tanya walk when she walked up High Street?

a north   b south
c east   d west

③ At the corner, Tanya turned right into Hill Street. What were the numbers of the houses that she walked past? _____

④ At house number 5, Tanya turned south into which street? _____

⑤ Follow these directions to draw a new path on the map.

- Max started at the shop at 2 Hill Street.
- He walked past the post office and 6 Hill Street before crossing at the pedestrian crossing to 5 Hill Street.
- Max walked a little way down Park Street where he used the pedestrian crossing to cross over the road near his school.
- Then Max walked up Park Street and turned right, walking past his school to get to the pedestrian crossing in front of the garage.
- He crossed over at this crossing and turned right to walk to his house at 12 Hill Street.

Cub conundrum

Help the zookeeper solve this problem.

The weight of three lion cubs has to be recorded. Each cub is a different weight. No cub weighs less than 6 kg.

- The 1st and 2nd cubs weigh 15 kg altogether.
- The 2nd and 3rd cubs weigh 17 kg altogether.
- The 1st and 3rd cubs weigh 18 kg altogether.

What is the weight of each cub?

① Cub 1 weighs _____.

② Cub 2 weighs _____.

③ Cub 3 weighs _____.

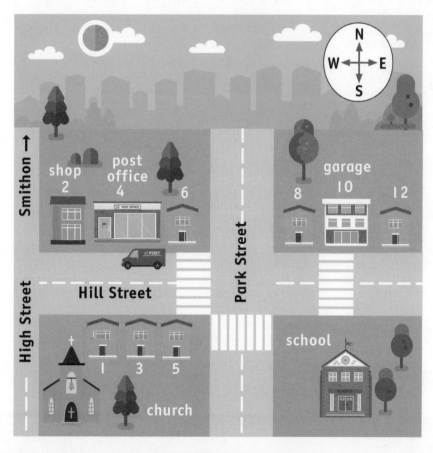

TERM 4 MATHS

Grammar & Punctuation

AC9E3LA03

Adjectival phrases

An **adjectival phrase** is a group of words that does the work of an adjective. It tells you *which* person, place or thing is being spoken about. It usually follows the noun and often begins with a preposition.
Example: The **man** <u>with purple hair</u> sang a song.
noun   adjectival phrase

Underline the adjectival phrases that describe the nouns in bold.

① A **boy** with his arm in a sling sat down next to me.

② The **painting** on the wall was stunning.

③ The **cat** with long, shaggy fur was stalking a bird.

④ The **newspaper** on the table is Dad's.

⑤ We played a **game** of backyard cricket.

⑥ The **mouse** under the bed squeaked loudly.

Write adjectival phrases from the box next to their sentence beginnings.

with hot fudge	in a blue dress
from small twigs	of chocolates
beside you	with floppy ears

⑦ We bought a huge **box** _____

_____.

⑧ We met a **lady** _____

_____.

⑨ Pass me the **book** _____

_____.

⑩ I ate an **ice cream** _____

_____.

⑪ The bird built a **nest** _____

_____.

⑫ I saw a cute **rabbit** _____

_____.

Score 2 points for each correct answer! SCORE **/24** (0-10) (12-18) (20-24)

Phonic Knowledge & Spelling

AC9E3LY09, AC9E3LY10

Suffix: –less

Say each word from the word bank. They all end with the suffix –less.

Word Bank

useless	friendless	cloudless	pointless
harmless	restless	fearless	careless
hopeless	painless	breathless	endless

Choose words from the word bank to complete these sentences.

① We started to feel _____, so we decided to go outside.

② Yesterday the beautiful blue sky was _____.

③ Huntsman spiders are big but quite _____.

④ There was nothing he could do and he felt _____.

Adding –less

A **suffix** is added to the end of a word. The suffix **–less** means 'without'. When **–less** is added to a word, it changes it to an **adjective**.
Examples:
hope + **less** = hope**less**   (without hope)
pain + **less** = pain**less**   (without pain)

Add –less to these words. Write the new word and its meaning.

⑤ taste + less = _____

without _____

⑥ life + less = _____

without _____

⑦ home + less = _____

without _____

Adding –ly

When you add **–ly** to an adjective, it changes it to an **adverb**.

Add –ly to these adjectives to make adverbs.

⑧ endless + ly = _____

⑨ helpless + ly = _____

⑩ senseless + ly = _____

Score 2 points for each correct answer! SCORE **/20** (0-8) (10-14) (16-20)

Information text – Report
Author – Ally Chumley

The Pacific Islands

The Pacific Islands are what we call the islands found in the Pacific Ocean. Some of these are very close to Australia, such as New Zealand, Indonesia and Papua New Guinea. Although they are close, they are very different to Australia in many ways.

New Zealand has many beautiful and natural wonders that attract visitors from all over the world. These include snow-capped mountains, glaciers, green pastures and blue waterways.

Papua New Guinea is a very mountainous country. It has a monsoonal climate — this means that it has a hot and dry season, followed by a time of flooding rains and violent storms.

Indonesia has extreme weather events and natural disasters like many countries in the South Pacific. This includes volcano eruptions, earthquakes, tsunamis, floods and cyclones.

Country	Australia	New Zealand	Papua New Guinea	Indonesia
Capital city	Canberra	Wellington	Port Moresby	Jakarta
Population	24 million	4.6 million	7.9 million	264 million

Source: *Australian Geography Centres*, Blake's Learning Centres, Blake Education

Write or circle the correct answers.

List four natural wonders that attract visitors to New Zealand.

① _____

② _____

③ _____

④ _____

⑤ **What is a monsoonal climate?**

a very hot and dry

b a hot and dry season followed by a wet season

c violent storms

List two natural disasters that occur in Indonesia.

⑥ _____

⑦ _____

⑧ **Does Australia have a larger population than New Zealand?**

(yes   no)

Which words in the text have these meanings?

⑨ areas of land surrounded by water

i _ _ _ _ _ _ _

⑩ large masses of ice that slowly move through a valley

g _ _ _ _ _ _ _

⑪ having lots of mountains

m _ _ _ _ _ _ _ _ _ _ _

⑫ **Which of these statements are true?**

a Jakarta is the capital city of Indonesia.

b New Zealand is north of Australia.

c Indonesia has more than ten times the population of Australia.

⑬ **What is the capital city of Papua New Guinea?**

_____

Score 2 points for each correct answer! **SCORE** **/26**

My Book Review

Title _____

Author _____

Rating ☆☆☆☆☆

Comment _____

_____

TERM 4 ENGLISH

Number & Algebra

AC9M3N0I

Money in other countries

In Australia, the currency is called the Australian dollar. But other countries use different kinds of money. Here are the currencies used in some other countries.

Indonesia: rupiah

Japan: Yen

Papua New Guinea: kina

China: yuan renminbi

New Zealand: dollar

United Kingdom: British pound

Solomon Islands: dollar

When you travel to another country, you need to use money that can be spent in that country. When you travel from Australia to Japan, for example, you need to change Australian dollars into Japanese yen.

The table shows approximately how much one Australian dollar is worth in other currencies. This is called an exchange rate and it can change from one day to the next.

Currency	Approximate value of one Australian dollar
Indonesian rupiah	9924 rupiah
Papua New Guinean kina	2 kina
New Zealand dollar	I dollar
Solomon Islands dollar	6 dollars
Japanese yen	83 yen
Chinese yuan renminbi	`5 yuan
British pound	½ pound

Use the table to answer the questions.

① 2 Australian dollars = _____ kina

② 5 Australian dollars = _____ New Zealand dollars

③ 2 Australian dollars = _____ pound

④ 2 Australian dollars = _____ rupiah

⑤ 5 Australian dollars = _____ yuan

⑥ 2 Australian dollars = _____ Solomon Islands dollars

Score 2 points for each correct answer! SCORE /12   0-4 6-8 10-12

Statistics & Probability

AC9M3P0I

What are the chances?

There is a rabbit under one of these hats. What are your chances of guessing which hat it is?

There is I rabbit and 5 hats, so the chances are I in 5.

If there were 2 rabbits and 5 hats, the chances would be 2 in 5.

Circle the correct answer.

① There is a rabbit under one of these hats. What are your chances of guessing which hat it is?

a I in 5   b I in 6
c 2 in 6   d 2 in 5

② Two of these hats have rabbits under them. What is the chance of choosing a hat that has a rabbit?

a I in 8   b 2 in 6
c 2 in 8   d 7 in 8

TARGETING HOMEWORK 3 © PASCAL PRESS ISBN 9781925726459

TERM 4 MATHS

③ Without looking, what chance is there of pulling a black marble from the box?

a 1 in 10   **b** 2 in 10
c 5 in 10   **d** 8 in 10

Use the spinner to answer the questions. Circle the correct answer.

④ What are the chances of spinning a 5?

a 1 in 6   **b** 1 in 5
c 2 in 5   **d** 5 in 6

⑤ What are the chances of spinning yellow?

a 2 in 6   **b** 3 in 6
c 1 in 6   **d** 1 in 4

⑥ What are the chances of spinning yellow or a 5 on the spinner?

a 2 in 6   **b** 3 in 6
c 1 in 6   **d** 1 in 5

Score 2 points for each correct answer! SCORE **/12** (0-4) (6-8) (10-12)

Measurement & Space

AC9M3SP02

Plan a classroom

You are going to plan a classroom using the grid.

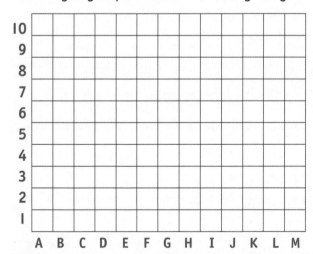

KEY
- desk
- cupboard
- sink
- art & craft tables
- class library
- teacher's desk

Use the key to draw and colour the objects on your plan.

① Draw a class library to cover the grid squares A8, A9, A10, B8, B9, B10, C8, C9 and C10.

② Draw a teacher's desk to cover B4 and B5.

③ Draw a sink to cover M8 and M9.

④ Draw a cupboard at M7 and G1.

⑤ Draw the art & craft tables to cover J7, J8 and J9.

Draw the students' desks at:

⑥ C1, C2, D1, D2

⑦ D5, D6, E5, E6

⑧ E8, E9, F8, F9

⑨ G4, G5, H4, H5

⑩ H8

⑪ H10

⑫ J1, J2, K1, K2

⑬ L4, L5, M4, M5

Score 2 points for each correct answer! SCORE **/26** (0-10) (12-20) (22-26)

Problem Solving

AC9M3A03

Making patterns

Follow the instructions to make a coloured pattern in this number square.

1	2	3	4	5
6	7	8	9	10
11	12	13	14	15
16	17	18	19	20
21	22	23	24	25
26	27	28	29	30
31	32	33	34	35

① Colour all the multiples of 5 blue.

② Colour all the multiples of 4 red.

③ Colour all the odd numbers green.

④ What numbers have not been coloured in?

_____

TERM 4 MATHS

Grammar & Punctuation

AC9E3LA02, AC9E3LA03

Comparing adjectives

> **Adjectives** can be used to show how people or things compare with each other.
>
> To compare *two* things, add **–er** to the adjective.
> *Examples*: A **big** dog. A **bigger** dog.
> A **soft** bed. A **softer** bed.
>
> To compare *more than two* things, add **–est** to the adjective.
> *Examples*:
> A **hot** drink. A **hotter** drink. The **hottest** drink.
> An **old** house. An **older** house. The **oldest** house.

Add –er and –est to these adjectives.

		–er	–est
①	sad	_____	_____
②	loud	_____	_____
③	tall	_____	_____
④	long	_____	_____
⑤	small	_____	_____
⑥	low	_____	_____

Adjectives ending in y

> **Remember!** If an **adjective** ends in **y**, change the **y** to **i** before adding **–er** or **–est**.

Add –er and –est to these adjectives.

		–er	–est
⑦	pretty	_____	_____
⑧	funny	_____	_____
⑨	noisy	_____	_____
⑩	busy	_____	_____
⑪	dry	_____	_____
⑫	juicy	_____	_____

Complete these sentences by writing suitable comparing adjectives.

⑬ My puppy is cute, but your puppy is _____.

⑭ Mum's curry is spicy, but Dad's curry is the _____ in our family.

⑮ I am quite brave, but my brother is _____.

⑯ The whale is the _____ mammal in the world today.

Phonic Knowledge & Spelling

AC9E3LY09, AC9E3LY10

Words ending in ic

Say each word from the word bank. They all end in ic.

Word Bank

comic	tragic	magic	music	basic
drastic	classic	frantic	clinic	artistic
elastic	fabric	atomic	garlic	attic
panic	tunic	toxic	picnic	logic

Choose words from the word bank to complete these sentences.

① The strange scratching sounds were coming from the _____.

② In a _____ act, a magician usually pulls a rabbit out of a hat.

③ We are having a _____ at the park for my birthday.

④ When Dad cooks spaghetti sauce, he uses lots of _____.

Adding –ly

> **Remember!** If a word ends in **y**, change the **y** to **i** before adding **–ly**.
> If a word ends in **ic**, add **–ally**.
> *Examples*: eas**y**, eas**ily**   happ**y**, happ**ily**
> bas**ic**, bas**ically**   trag**ic**, trag**ically**

Add –ly to these words to make adverbs.

⑤ comic _____

⑥ magic _____

⑦ sleepy _____

⑧ tragic _____

⑨ logic _____

⑩ angry _____

Join the syllables then write the new words.

⑪ au + to + mat + ic = _____

⑫ pho + to + gen + ic = _____

⑬ re + al + is + tic = _____

⑭ or + gan + ic = _____

⑮ At + lan + tic = _____

⑯ ath + let + ic = _____

Uncle Andy Arrives

Imaginative text – Narrative
Author – Helen Evans
Illustrator – John Yahyeh

Uncle Andy was loaded up like a Christmas tree. I grabbed an armful of his boxes and led the way to my bedroom. I felt a thrill in my stomach. What had he brought this time?

Uncle Andy was a collector. He collected anything from thimbles to giant stick insects. He'd brought a stick insect back for me on his last trip. Mum said it had to go after it fell into a cup of tea at one of her card parties.

Mum didn't approve of Uncle Andy.

"I know he loves the wild orang-utans in Borneo," she'd say, "but there's no need for him to look like one."

Where had Uncle Andy been this time? His shirt was stained and the leg of his jeans was ripped. He dragged a lumpy, orange sleeping-bag into the room. I helped him arrange the boxes into a crazy, leaning tower.

"Show me what you've collected this time, Uncle Andy." I was very excited.

"There are frogs for you. Run some cold water into the bath while I find them. Don't fill it right to the top, we don't want to drown them. And there's a surprise, too. But that had better wait till your mother goes out."

What a piece of luck! Frogs and a surprise, too. Uncle Andy was the best.

Source: *The Big Squeeze*, Gigglers, Blake Education.

Write or circle the correct answers.

① **Which one of these is the odd word out?**

a sadness   c joy

b excitement   d thrill

② **What does 'Mum didn't approve of Uncle Andy' mean?**

a Mum agreed with everything Uncle Andy did.

b Mum didn't agree with the things Uncle Andy did.

c Mum didn't like Uncle Andy's hair.

③ **The boy telling the story is called Tom. Why was Tom so excited at the arrival of his uncle?**

a His uncle always brought him interesting things to look at.

b His uncle brought him a stick insect.

c His uncle brought him a Christmas tree.

④ **What was Uncle Andy carrying when he arrived at Tom's house?**

a a Christmas tree

b some boxes and an orange sleeping-bag

c some thimbles

⑤ **Which word in the text means 'something you did not expect'?**

a excited   b approve   c surprise

⑥ **Why did Tom's mum say the stick insect had to go?**

_____

⑦ **What is an orang-utan?**

a an ape   b a frog   c don't know

⑧ **Uncle Andy often brought things that Tom's mother didn't approve of. What do you think the surprise could be?**

a a toy car   b a snake   c a hat

Score 2 points for each correct answer!

SCORE **/16** (0-6) (8-12) (14-16)

TERM 4 ENGLISH

My Book Review

Title _____

Author _____

Rating ☆ ☆ ☆ ☆ ☆

Comment _____

_____

Number & Algebra

AC9M3N03

Large numbers

Write these numbers.

① 1000 + 500 + 40 + 8

= _____

② 4000 + 600 + 70 + 3

= _____

③ 8000 + 200 + 30 + 9

= _____

④ 5000 + 300 + 80

= _____

⑤ 6000 + 500 + 6

= _____

⑥ 7000 + 60 + 9

= _____

⑦ 2000 + 456

= _____

⑧ 3000 + 19

= _____

⑨ 6500 + 54

= _____

⑩ 3500 + 5

= _____

Write the correct answer.

⑪ Which odd number is between 3457 and 3461? _____

⑫ Which even number is between 45 600 and 45 604? _____

⑬ What is the difference between 5489 and 5480? _____

⑭ What is 3580 add 2419? _____

⑮ Which number is 1000 more than 6786?

_____

⑯ Is 415 + 309 approximately 700 or 600?

_____

⑰ A man won $8600. He gave half to charity. How much did he have left?

_____

⑱ What is double 600? _____

⑲ Which number is 1000 less than 8740?

_____

⑳ What is 54 × 1000? _____

SCORE **/40** (0-18) (20-34) (36-40)

Statistics & Probability

There are no statistics & probability activities in this unit.

Measurement & Space

AC9M3M04

Digital time

> With digital time, we say the hour first and then the minutes past the hour.
> *Example:*
>
>
>
> **This clock shows 4:45.**

What is the exact time on these clocks? Write the correct answer in digital time.

①  ②

_____   _____

③  ④

_____   _____

⑤ 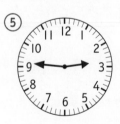 ⑥

_____   _____

⑦ 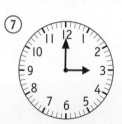 ⑧

_____   _____

Draw the digital time on these analogue clocks.

⑨ 5:50

⑩ 2:37

⑪ 3:56

⑫ 6:39

⑬ 4:08

⑭ 5:48

Magic squares

Fill in the missing numbers so that the totals across, down and diagonally are all the same.

① Total = 18

9	2	
4	6	8
	10	3

② Total = 21

10		8
	7	9
6	11	

③ Total = 15

4		2
	5	

TERM 4 MATHS

Grammar & Punctuation

Write the groups of animals from the box next to their collective nouns.

cards	flowers	lions	students

① class _____   ③ pride _____

② bouquet _____   ④ deck _____

Write whether the verbs in bold are action verbs or relating verbs.

⑤ The policeman **raced** after the thief._____

⑥ A whale **is** a mammal._____

⑦ I **am** shorter than you._____

Circle the correct past tense verbs in these sentences.

⑧ I slipped and (falled   fell) into the pool.

⑨ The concert (beginned   began) at eight o'clock.

⑩ My uncle (gived   gave) me his old computer.

Write prepositions to complete the underlined adverbial phrases.

⑪ Our neighbour greeted us _____ a frown.

⑫ _____ home, we eat breakfast at 8 o'clock.

⑬ Ryan received an award _____ his spelling.

Rewrite each sentence with the missing apostrophes.

⑭ Rileys dog chased after my eldest sisters cat.

_____

⑮ At Emmas salon, were open until 7 pm every night, except Sundays.

_____

Underline the adjectival phrases that describe the nouns in bold.

⑯ I saw a **man** with a gold walking stick.

⑰ Mum bought a **basket** of fresh fruit.

⑱ Who is that **boy** in your class?

Add –er and –est to these adjectives.

	–er	–est
⑲ hot	_____	_____
⑳ old	_____	_____
㉑ pretty	_____	_____
㉒ noisy	_____	_____

㉓ **What is a paragraph?**

   a a type of text

   b a group of sentences used to introduce new parts of a story, characters or pieces of information

   c a poem

Match the present tense verb to its past tense.

yelled	ran	climbed	dug

㉔ climbs _____

㉕ runs _____

㉖ digs _____

㉗ yells _____

Score 2 points for each correct answer! **SCORE** /54 (0-24) (26-48) (50-54)

Phonic Knowledge & Spelling

Circle the correct homophone in each sentence.

① The tennis (court   caught) had a new surface.

② Make sure to pull the rope (taut   taught).

③ There was a long (paws   pause) before he replied.

Write the words from the box next to their rhyming words.

neigh	tale	flour	noise

④ ray _____   ⑥ shower _____

⑤ nail _____   ⑦ boys _____

Add –ed and –ing to these words. Remember the spelling rules!

	–ed	–ing
⑧ scare	_____	_____
⑨ dare	_____	_____
⑩ share	_____	_____
⑪ blare	_____	_____

Write these words as plurals.

⑫ cowboy _____

⑬ story _____

⑭ journey _____

⑮ city _____

Write the antonyms of these words by adding the prefixes un– or dis–.

⑯ _____happy   ⑱ _____obey

⑰ _____like   ⑲ _____safe

Add –ful to these words.

⑳ play _____

㉑ power _____

㉒ pity _____

㉓ plenty _____

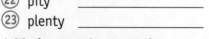

Add –less to these words. Write the new word and its meaning.

㉔ care + less = _____

   without _____

㉕ hope + less = _____

   without _____

TARGETING HOMEWORK 3 © PASCAL PRESS ISBN 9781925726459

Add **–ly** to these adjectives to make adverbs.

㉖ painless + ly = _____

㉗ helpless + ly = _____

Add **–ly** to these words to make adverbs.

㉘ easy _____

㉙ basic _____

㉚ magic _____

㉛ sleepy _____

Add **air** to these words to make compound words.

㉜ line _____

㉝ ship _____

㉞ port _____

㉟ fare _____

Score 2 points for each correct answer!   SCORE **/70** (0-32) (34-64) (66-70)

Reading & Comprehension

Imaginative text – Narrative
Author – Frances Mackay

The van stopped and the driver clambered out. He picked up a short ladder and tied it to the roof of the van. He loaded the van with some paint and brushes. Then he shouted up the stairs, "I took the long ladder up there yesterday."

"Okay," shouted the foreman, "better go now or it will be lunchtime before they can make a start. I'll follow on when I've completed the paperwork in the office."

Write or circle the correct answers.

① What were the people in the text going to do?

_____

② Was it morning or afternoon?

_____

③ What does **clambered** mean?
   a to shout
   b to move in an awkward way
   c to sing

④ Was the foreman upstairs or downstairs?

_____

⑤ Could the workmen start before the van got there? (yes   no)

⑥ What line in the text tells you that the van driver had been there before?

_____

_____

⑦ What was the foreman doing when the driver arrived?
   a stacking paint and brushes
   b getting a ladder
   c paperwork

⑧ Which one of these is the odd word out?
   a finished
   b completed
   c started
   d concluded

Score 2 points for each correct answer!   SCORE **/16** (0-6) (8-12) (14-16)

Number & Algebra

What is the value of the bold digit?
Circle the correct answer.

① 5**8**2   a 800   b 80   c 8

② 5**6**21   a 6000   b 600   c 60

③ 3**2**484   a 2000   b 200   c 20

Use the diagrams to answer the questions.

④ one half = _____ quarters

⑤ one half = _____ eighths

Write <, > or = to make these statements true.

⑥ 589 ____ 925

⑦ 72 482 ____ 39 829

⑧ 6506 ____ 6606 – 100

⑨ 144 × 2 ____ 288

Use the rule to complete these number patterns.

⑩ add 5, starting at 50

    50, ____, ____, ____, ____

⑪ subtract 3, starting at 21

    21, ____, ____, ____, ____

⑫ add 100, starting at 254

    254, ____, ____, ____, ____

Complete each fact family.

⑬ 6 × _____ = 60   ⑰ 3 × _____ = 21

⑭ _____ × 10 = 60   ⑱ _____ × 7 = 21

⑮ 60 ÷ _____ = 10   ⑲ 21 ÷ _____ = 7

⑯ 60 ÷ _____ = 6   ⑳ 21 ÷ _____ = 3

Look for number facts to 20 to help you add these numbers.

㉑ 13 + 12 + 7 = ____   ㉓ 11 + 9 + 14 = ____

㉒ 15 + 19 + 5 = ____   ㉔ 12 + 15 + 8 = ____

Look for number facts to 100 to help you add these numbers.

㉕ 50 + 50 + 75 = _____

㉖ 20 + 23 + 80 = _____

㉗ 90 + 46 + 10 = _____

Use the currency list to answer the questions.

> **Approximate value of 1 Australian dollar**
> 1 New Zealand dollar
> 6 Solomon Islands dollars
> 83 Japanese yen

㉘ 3 Australian dollars = _____ Solomon Islands dollars

㉙ 10 Australian dollars = _____ New Zealand dollars

㉚ 166 Japanese yen = _____ Australian dollars

Write the answer.

㉛ Which odd number is between 3421 and 3425? _____

㉜ Which even number is between 25 502 and 25 506? _____

㉝ What is the difference between 7459 and 7359? _____

Score 2 points for each correct answer!   SCORE   /66   (0-30)   (32-60)   (62-66)

Statistics & Probability

① Su wants to find out the favourite book of the students in her class. Which question should she ask? Circle the correct answer.
   a Do you like the Harry Potter books?
   b What is your favourite book?
   c What kind of books do you like to read?

Class 3T set up a cake stall to raise money for charity. They sold cupcakes for 50 cents each.

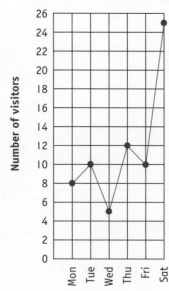

Visitors to our Cupcake Stall

The line graph shows the number of visitors to their stall.

Use the graph to answer the questions.

② How many people visited the stall on Monday? _____

③ How many people visited the stall on Saturday? _____

④ What is the difference in visitor numbers between Wednesday and Saturday? _____

TARGETING HOMEWORK 3 © PASCAL PRESS ISBN 9781925726459

(5) Everyone who visited the stall on Friday bought a cupcake. How much money did the stall make that day? _____

(6) How many visitors did the stall have for the entire week? _____

Use this spinner to answer the questions.
Circle the correct answer.

(7) What are the chances of spinning a 3?

   a 1 in 6   **b** 5 in 6

   c 2 in 5   **d** 1 in 6

(8) What are the chances of spinning red?

   a 1 in 6   **b** 3 in 6

   c 2 in 6   **d** 5 in 6

Score 2 points for each correct answer!   SCORE **/16**   0-6   8-12   14-16

Measurement & Space

Write true or false.

(1) 3 kg = 3000 g   _____

(2) $\frac{1}{2}$ kg + $\frac{1}{2}$ kg = 2000 g   _____

(3) $1\frac{1}{2}$ kg = 1500 g   _____

Circle the correct answer.

(4) If a jug holds exactly 3 litres of water and it takes 4 jugs to fill a bucket, what is the capacity of the bucket?

   a 3 litres **b** 4 litres **c** 7 litres **d** 12 litres

(5) A bath takes 12 litres of water to fill it. If a bucket holds 2 litres, how many bucketsful do you need to fill the bath?

   a 6   **b** 8   **c** 12

(6) It took Jack one minute to write an email. How many seconds is that?

   a 60   **b** 120   **c** 180

(7) Anna took 1 minute and 30 seconds to run to the shop. It took Jay 99 seconds. Who was faster?

   a Anna   **b** Jay

Look at this 3D object and write the missing numbers.

(8) A pentagonal pyramid has _____ faces.

(9) It has _____ face shaped like a pentagon.

(10) A pentagonal pyramid has _____ vertices.

(11) A pentagonal pyramid has _____ edges.

(12) Draw a line $7\frac{1}{2}$ cms long.

(13) Draw a square with sides of 2 cm.

Write the digital time.

(14)

(15)

_____   _____

Draw the digital time.

(16) 4:52

(17) 1:36

(18) How many millilitres of water are there in this jug?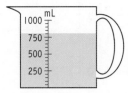

_____

Use the classroom map and key to answer the questions.

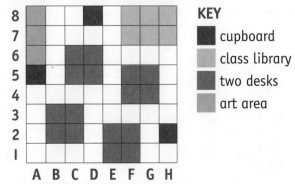

KEY
- cupboard
- class library
- two desks
- art area

(19) How many desks are in this classroom? _____

(20) What is located at F7, F8, G7, G8, H7 and H8? _____

(21) How many cupboards are in the classroom? What are their coordinates?

_____

(22) What are the coordinates of the art area?

_____

Score 2 points for each correct answer!   SCORE **/44**   0-20   22-38   40-44

MY READING LIST

TARGETING HOMEWORK 3 © PASCAL PRESS ISBN 9781925726459

Name: _____

_____

	Title	Author	Rating	Date
1			☆☆☆☆☆	
2			☆☆☆☆☆	
3			☆☆☆☆☆	
4			☆☆☆☆☆	
5			☆☆☆☆☆	
6			☆☆☆☆☆	
7			☆☆☆☆☆	
8			☆☆☆☆☆	
9			☆☆☆☆☆	
10			☆☆☆☆☆	
11			☆☆☆☆☆	
12			☆☆☆☆☆	
13			☆☆☆☆☆	
14			☆☆☆☆☆	
15			☆☆☆☆☆	
16			☆☆☆☆☆	
17			☆☆☆☆☆	
18			☆☆☆☆☆	
19			☆☆☆☆☆	
20			☆☆☆☆☆	
21			☆☆☆☆☆	
22			☆☆☆☆☆	
23			☆☆☆☆☆	
24			☆☆☆☆☆	
25			☆☆☆☆☆	
26			☆☆☆☆☆	
27			☆☆☆☆☆	
28			☆☆☆☆☆	
29			☆☆☆☆☆	
30			☆☆☆☆☆	
31			☆☆☆☆☆	
32			☆☆☆☆☆	

Unit 1 ENGLISH: Grammar & Punctuation

1. a, c
2. b, c
3. When will you be going on holiday? <The 'W' and the '?' should be circled>
4. ?
5. .
6. .
7. ?
8. Did ?
9. We .
10. Why ?
11. Today .
12. How ?

Unit 1 ENGLISH: Phonic Knowledge & Spelling

1. sad
2. men
3. gift
4. hot
5. tub
6. nest
7. think
8. drop
9. knit
10. flags
11. crumbs
12. rocks
13. gifts
14. nets
15. Possible words include:
    bump – lump, dump, hump, jump, pump, rump, sump
16. hill – pill, sill, dill, kill, mill, bill, rill, till, will
17. bent – cent, dent, gent, lent, pent, rent, sent, tent, vent, went
18. cot – knot, dot, got, hot, jot, lot, pot, rot, tot
19. bang – fang, gang, hang, pang, rang, sang, tang

Unit 1 ENGLISH: Reading & Comprehension

1. at the dam
2. a frog
3. He had just eaten 3 slugs so he may not have been very hungry.
   It would use up too much energy as he was feeling lazy and snoozy.
4. to look shiny or glossy
5. the eggs of a frog
6. what his life was like as a tadpole
7. wiggled
8. plants and small bugs
9. Answers will vary but a reason must be provided such as – not all tadpoles survive and turn into frogs, so he may be wishing them luck to survive; growing up can be difficult for any animal so he may be wishing them luck for growing up.

Unit 1 MATHS: Number & Algebra

1. 17, 18, 19
2. 37, 38, 39
3. 25, 24, 23
4. 96, 95, 94
5. 28
6. 99
7. 63
8. eighty-eight
9. sixty-seven
10. 18 36 45 60
11. 55 76 84 98
12. 5
13. 5
14. 20
15. 10

Unit 1 MATHS: Statistics & Probability

1. football
2. softball
3. 5
4. 2
5. soccer and netball
6. no
7. 29
8. 6
9. no

Unit 1 MATHS: Measurement & Space

1. 17 cm
2. 13 cm
3. 12 cm
4. 30 cm
5. 6 cm
6. 4 cm
7. 8 cm
8. 3 cm
9. 30 cm
10. 21 cm

Unit 1 MATHS: Problem Solving

1. 6
2. You add the first three numbers in each row to get the end number.
3. The highest possible number is 61. The strategy is to put the largest number in the centre brick, followed by the next largest in the adjacent bricks and so on.

Unit 2 ENGLISH: Grammar & Punctuation

1. b, d
2. a, d
3. C
4. E
5. E
6. C
7. .
8. ?
9. !
10. !

Unit 2 ENGLISH: Phonic Knowledge & Spelling

1. tap
2. jet
3. will
4. rock
5. truck
6. jam
7. flock
8. sing
9. hen
10. slammed, slamming
11. strapped, strapping
12. hopped, hopping
13. skipped, skipping
14. slipped, slipping
15. butterfly
16. seahorse
17. grasshopper
18. jellyfish
19. bulldog
20. earthworm

Unit 2 ENGLISH: Reading & Comprehension

1. b. bootees
2. b. He was talking on a mobile phone.
3. half-a-dozen colas and a couple of meat pies
4. outside the store on the corner of Pitt and Stuart Streets
5. c. He hated it.
6. b. revolting
7. A rucksack or backpack
8. The baby was in a pram.

Unit 2 MATHS: Number & Algebra

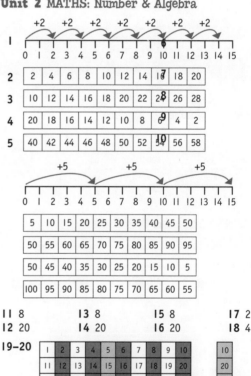

1. (number line with +2 jumps, 0 to 15)
2. 2 4 6 8 10 12 14 16 18 20
3. 10 12 14 16 18 20 22 24 26 28
4. 20 18 16 14 12 10 8 6 4 2
5. 40 42 44 46 48 50 52 54 56 58

(number line with +5 jumps, 0 to 15)

5 10 15 20 25 30 35 40 45 50
50 55 60 65 70 75 80 85 90 95
50 45 40 35 30 25 20 15 10 5
100 95 90 85 80 75 70 65 60 55

11. 8
12. 20
13. 8
14. 20
15. 8
16. 20
17. 2
18. 4

19–20. (100 square with coloured columns and +)

21. Both the two and five times patterns run in columns down the 100 square. In the last column, the squares are coloured red and blue – so the numbers 10, 20, 30, 40, 50, 60, 70, 80, 90 and 100 are in the two and five times tables.

Unit 2 MATHS: Measurement & Space

1. square, 4, 4
2. rectangle, 4, 4
3. pentagon, 5, 5
4. hexagon, 6, 6
5. circle, 0, 0
6. oval, 0, 0
7. triangle, 3, 3
8. decagon
9. heptagon
10. octagon
11. nonagon

ANSWERS

Unit 2 MATHS: Problem solving

1 5 + 5 = ☐   4 12   7 18 ÷ 2 = ☐
2 10   5 20 − 5 = ☐   8 9
3 6 × 2 = ☐   6 15

Unit 3 ENGLISH: Grammar & Punctuation

1 elephant, log, trunk
2 dog, cat, tree
3 shop, park, school
4 brother, sister, uncle
5 Jack, Georgia, Hobart
6 August, Singapore, Qantas
7 Coles, Saturday, Sunday
8 Tenzing Norgay, Edmund Hillary, Mount Everest

9 PN	13 PN	17 PN	21 PN
10 PN	14 CN	18 CN	22 CN
11 CN	15 CN	19 CN	23 PN
12 CN	16 PN	20 CN	24 PN

Unit 3 ENGLISH: Phonic Knowledge & Spelling

1 ant	7 went	13 wishes
2 tent	8 trunk	14 princesses
3 trick	9 list	15 brushes
4 across	10 buses	16 compasses
5 sun	11 watches	17 patches
6 lost	12 classes	18 brooches

Unit 3 ENGLISH: Reading & Comprehension

1 b. NSW
2 c. Canberra
3 Uluru (Ayers Rock) and Kata Tjuta (The Olgas)
4 Western Australia
5 Melbourne
6 b. about
7 Canberra
8 Sydney
9 Darwin
10 Brisbane
11 Adelaide
12 Hobart
13 Melbourne
14 Perth

Unit 3 MATHS: Number & Algebra

1 40
2 50, 3, 90
3 50, 30, 8, 80, 83
4 60, 70, 3, 130, 133
5 50, 50, 8, 100, 108
6 70, 90, 2, 160, 162

Unit 3 MATHS: Statistics & Probability

1 b. impossible
2 a. certain
3 a. very likely
4 a. very likely
5 b. very unlikely

6–10

impossible	very unlikely	likely	very likely	certain
6	10	9	8	7

11 a. red
12 c. green

Unit 3 MATHS: Measurement & Space

1 b. green square
2 c. orange rectangle
3 a. red pentagon

4–8
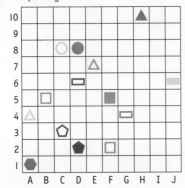

Unit 3 MATHS: Problem Solving

1 5, 8	3 4	5 3, 6
2 8, 9	4 10	6 5, 6

Unit 4 ENGLISH: Grammar & Punctuation

1 earrings, birthday
2 toolbox, workroom
3 sunflower, greenhouse
4 something, newspaper
5 bookcase
6 bookshop
7 bookkeeper
8 headlight
9 headlines
10 headband
11–16 Possible answers: watermelon, waterway, waterwheel, wheelchair, toothbrush, railway, basketball, snowman, snowball, armchair, armpit, eyelid, eyeball, raincoat, rainwater
17 We bought fruit, bread, milk and butter at the shop.
18 There were trees, flowers and statues in the park.

Unit 4 ENGLISH: Phonic Knowledge & Spelling

1 Any two from: ribbon, middle, dribble, sniffle, ripple, wriggle, bitter
2 pepper, better
3 soccer, bottle
4 Any two from: sudden, nugget, shuffle, huddle, bubble, struggle
5 Any two from: battle, happen, traffic

6 traffic	10 two	14 foxes	18 faxes
7 bottle	11 one	15 fizzes	19 lynxes
8 one	12 two	16 topazes	
9 two	13 one	17 annexes	

Unit 4 ENGLISH: Reading & Comprehension

1 b. respiration   2 oxygen
3 taste, sight, hearing, touch, smell
4 a. sunlight   5 a. True
6 Any one from: grow towards the light; open and close petals; move when you touch them
7 a. Green plants can make their own food.
c. All living things need food to stay alive.
8 Any one from: cars do not breathe; cars cannot respond to things; cars cannot grow and get bigger; cars cannot reproduce (make more of) by themselves; cars do not need food to grow and stay alive.
9 b. doing away with things that are not needed
10–16 (in any order) move, breathe, respond, grow, reproduce, get rid of waste, take in food

Unit 4 MATHS: Number & Algebra

1 5	9 3	17 5	25 12	33 11
2 6	10 16	18 8	26 14	34 29
3 8	11 20	19 4	27 11	35 23
4 9	12 17	20 3	28 8	36 28
5 7	13 25	21 6	29 6	37 27
6 4	14 20	22 8	30 9	38 27
7 2	15 40	23 6	31 12	39 24
8 1	16 1	24 9	32 14	

40 48 + 2 = 50, add 4 = 54   42 79 + 1 = 80, add 4 = 84
41 83 + 7 = 90, add 1 = 91   43 45 + 5 = 50, add 4 = 54

Unit 4 MATHS: Measurement & Space

1 b. 8 o'clock
2 a. $\frac{1}{4}$ past 6
3 b. $\frac{1}{2}$ past 9
4 c. $\frac{1}{4}$ to 8
5 60
6 30
7 15
8 b. 15 minutes past 6
9 a. 30 minutes past 5
10 a. 15 minutes to 7
11 a. 25 minutes past 7

TARGETING HOMEWORK 3 © PASCAL PRESS ISBN 9781925726459

Unit 4 MATHS: Problem Solving
Answers will vary. Check that each group of numbers adds up to 20

Unit 5 ENGLISH: Grammar & Punctuation
1 <u>The rubber ball</u> **rolled** down the road.
2 <u>Li</u> **sings** very loudly!
3 <u>Mum</u> **shut** the front door.
4 <u>Zac</u> **hates** computer games.

5 closed	8 wrote	11 announced
6 bites	9 saw	12 strike
7 shaped	10 shouted	13 reckon

Unit 5 ENGLISH: Phonic Knowledge & Spelling
1 Any two from: life, knife, bite, write, mice
2 Any two from: hose, close, phone, stone, smoke
3 Any two from: game, flame, tape, shape, face
4 Any two from: tube, cube, cute, flute, rule

5 mice	9 ruled, ruling	13 raced, racing
6 tube	10 voted, voting	14 moved, moving
7 bite	11 raised, raising	15 tasted, tasting
8 phone	12 hoped, hoping	

Unit 5 ENGLISH: Reading & Comprehension
1 two-syllable
2 The beat of the words sounds like a machine working. It gives rhythm to the poem.
3 verbs
4 b. gathering
5 b. smoothing
6–9 hit, bang, drill, chop

Unit 5 MATHS: Number & Algebra
1 b. $\frac{1}{2}$ 2 b. $\frac{2}{4}$ 3 c. $\frac{3}{4}$ 4 b. $\frac{2}{2}$

5   6   7

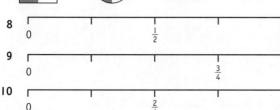

8   0 — $\frac{1}{2}$ — 1

9   0 — $\frac{3}{4}$ — 1

10   0 — $\frac{2}{4}$ — 1

Unit 5 MATHS: Statistics & Probability
1 3	5 impossible	9 a. red
2 2	6 20	10 a. impossible
3 3	7 b. orange	11 d. 5 in 20
4 1	8 c. blue	

Unit 5 MATHS: Measurement & Space
1 a. 2 kg	5 b. $\frac{1}{4}$ kg	9 6 kg	13 37 kg
2 b. $\frac{1}{2}$ kg	6 a. $1\frac{1}{4}$ kg	10 20 kg	14 64 kg
3 b. 4 kg	7 5 kg	11 40 kg	15 55 kg
4 a. $4\frac{1}{2}$ kg	8 12 kg	12 30 kg	

16
17
18

19 mouse – 19 g	22 cow – 720 kg
20 galah – 330 g	23 elephant – 5400 kg
21 cat – 4 kg	24 blue whale – 140 000 kg

Unit 5 MATHS: Problem Solving
1–6 These four ways are the most commonly found:

Other ways include:

Unit 6 ENGLISH: Grammar & Punctuation
1 <u>I</u> **bought** a new telescope.
2 <u>My uncle</u> **rides** a scooter.
3 Yesterday, <u>we</u> **went** to the zoo.
4 <u>A woman on a horse</u> **galloped** past my car.

5 barks	9 is watching	13 Those books
6 is	10 like	14 Emily and Dylan
7 knows	11 Jai	15 the cat
8 are playing	12 Chloe	

Unit 6 ENGLISH: Phonic Knowledge & Spelling
1 Any two words from: use, excuse, tune, dune, duke
2 Any two words from: hole, whole, joke, broke, rose
3 Any two words from: bake, shake, page, stage, late
4 Any two words from: ride, slide, dine, shine, twice

5 shine	11 dined	17 sliding	23 bony
6 hole	12 staged	18 riding	24 slimy
7 late	13 tuned	19 using	25 icy
8 bake	14 joked	20 shining	26 lazy
9 used	15 shaking	21 rosy	
10 excused	16 making	22 tasty	

Unit 6 ENGLISH: Reading & Comprehension
1 25 April
2 Australian and New Zealand Army Corps
3 Any three from:
People gather at dawn.
They wait in silence for two minutes to remember those who died.
A soldier plays the *Last Post* on a bugle.
Some people wear a red poppy or place poppies on memorials.
4 a. regard
5 b. a statue or structure built to remember an event
6 Turkey
7 The Anzac soldiers fought against Turkish soldiers. The battle lasted eight months and more than 8000 Anzacs died. Thousands more were injured.
8 b. commemorates

Unit 6 MATHS: Number & Algebra
1 105, 106, 107	13 99
2 524, 525, 527, 528, 529	14 15 126
3 596, 595, 594, 593	15 80
4 452, 450, 448	16 10
5 b. 564	17 40
6 a. 880	18 30
7 b. 199	19 80
8 349, 598, 682, 872	20 50
9 900, 980, 989, 990	21 105
10 258	22 107
11 574	23 109
12 258	24 104

25 487 + 3 = 490, 490 + 3 = 493
26 729 + 1 = 730, 730 + 7 = 737
27 60 + 30 = 90, 5 + 2 = 7, 90 + 7 = 97
28 50 + 30 = 80, 6 + 3 = 9, 80 + 9 = 89
29 8, 9
30 15, 15 – 9, 15 – 6
31 32, 32 – 8 = 24, 32 – 24 = 8
32 45, 45 – 9 = 36, 45 – 36 = 9
33 58, 58 – 11 = 47, 58 – 47 = 11
34 7 + 11
35 13 + 14
36 27 + 9
37 9 + 14
38 92 + 9

Unit 6 MATHS: Problem Solving
1 28 **2** 60 **3** 9 **4** 19

Unit 7 ENGLISH: Grammar & Punctuation
1 Mum had a bad cold **so** she could not go to work.
2 The man chased the dog **but** he did not catch it.
3 We went to the park **and** we walked around the lake.
4 I could go on the ride **if** I were taller.
5 Do you like tea **or** coffee?
6 I cannot fall asleep **unless** I'm in bed.
7 We stayed at the party **until** Dad picked us up.
8 Galahs, cockatoos **and** emus are birds.
9 We were late for school **because** we slept in.

Unit 7 ENGLISH: Phonic Knowledge & Spelling
1 awake, because, potion   5 spider
2 trifle, often, mobile   6 station
3 table, motion   7 secret
4 lotion

8 stories that are made up: fiction
9 someone who belongs to your family: relation
10 adding things together: addition
11 the answer to a problem: solution
12 sucking in liquid or air: suction
13 the place where something is: position

Unit 7 ENGLISH: Reading & Comprehension
1 opinion
2 fact
3 fact
4 opinion
5 b. certain
6 get into debt; lose their livestock and income
7 c. to owe money
8 b. The moisture in the soil will increase.
9 By creating creeks and channels similar to pre-European settlement

Unit 7 MATHS: Number & Algebra
1 70, 80, 90   8 90   15 700
2 30, 40, 50   9 20   16 900
3 80, 70, 60   10 500, 600, 700   17 700
4 60   11 600, 700, 800   18 300
5 40   12 500, 400, 300   19 900
6 90   13 400, 300, 200
7 70   14 500

	thousands	hundreds	tens	ones
20	2	3	9	7
21	8	4	1	9
22	6	0	4	1

23 5234   24 8408

Unit 7 MATHS: Statistics & Probability
1 b. 8
2 c. 7
3 b. car
4 32

5

Pets in class 3B

Unit 7 MATHS: Measurement & Space
1 6   8 1   15 6
2 12   9 1   16 5
3 8   10 3   17 8
4 6   11 2   18 5
5 12   12 0   19 1
6 8   13 5   20 0
7 2   14 9   21 0

Unit 7 MATHS: Problem Solving
	A	B	C	D
5 and 4	9	1	11	14
6 and 3	9	3	13	15
7 and 5	12	2	12	19
8 and 3	11	5	15	19
10 and 9	19	1	11	29
6 and 2	8	4	14	14
5 and 1	6	4	14	11

Unit 8 ENGLISH: Grammar & Punctuation
1 juicy   7 old, icy
2 fluffy, long   8 black, large
3 naughty, beautiful   9 shiny, gold
4 sad, quiet   10 sharp, pointy, silver
5 huge, rough   11 wooden, old, brown
6 noisy, little   12 red, fancy

Unit 8 ENGLISH: Phonic Knowledge & Spelling
1 bait   6 wait   11 to   16 break
2 train   7 pray   12 write   17 Our
3 afraid   8 mail   13 eight
4 stay   9 rain   14 blue
5 waist   10 main   15 new

Unit 8 ENGLISH: Reading & Comprehension
1 Tip Top   7 all tees (t-shirts)
2 b. 3 days   8 $30
3 no   9 all girls' & boys' singlets
4 b. to attract the attention of the reader   10 c. gigantic
5 b. parents of school-age children   11 SCHOOL18
6 up to 30%   12 Pretty party pinafores

Unit 8 MATHS: Number & Algebra
1 10c   7 a. true   13 $4.10
2 10c   8 b. false   14 $5.00 or $5
3 10c   9 a. true   15 $3.05
4 20c   10 a. true   16 $10.95
5 50c   11 $1.50
6 50c   12 $0.70 or 70c

Unit 8 MATHS: Measurement & Space
1 4   4 0   7 2   10 2   13 1
2 5   5 6   8 1   11 3
3 4   6 3   9 4   12 4

Unit 8 MATHS: Problem Solving
1 $12.00   5 $13.00
2 $8.00   6 Answers will vary. Total must add up to $20 or less.
3 $6.50
4 $2.00

TERM 1 REVIEW

Term 1 ENGLISH: Grammar & Punctuation
1 b. I am going to Jack's birthday party.
2 !
3 ?
4 .
5 Aidan, school, Monday
6 dog, cat, Perry Street
7–10 (in any order) rainbow, raincoat, buttercup, butterfly
11 We bought carrots, potatoes, beans, bread and milk at the shop.
12 The car **raced** down the road.
13 Josh and Mia
14 a. Ahmed is five years old.
15 because
16 green, muddy

Term 1 ENGLISH: Phonic Knowledge & Spelling
1 hot   8 boxes   14 2
2 truck   9 tables   15 1
3 bite   10 matches   16 2
4 stay   11 dropped, dropping   17 slimy
5 cats   12 jumped, jumping   18 hilly
6 glasses   13 raced, racing   19 shaky
7 dishes

TARGETING HOMEWORK 3 © PASCAL PRESS ISBN 9781925726459

20 part of a whole: fraction
21 movement: motion
22 flame
23 rule
24 phone
25 short
26 long
27 short
28 long
29 sniffle
30 soccer
31 pepper
32 ate
33 blew
34 hear
35 right

Term 1 ENGLISH: Reading & Comprehension
1 7
2 house
3 3
4 2
5 in the small bedroom
6 during the school holidays
7 the dog
8 c. troublesome
9 Max
10 a. having everything needed in a small space

Term 1 MATHS: Number & Algebra
1 16, 18, 20
2 75, 70, 65
3 600, 500, 400
4 58
5 129
6 406
7 2550
8 15
9 18
10 12
11 10
12 23, 75, 3, 11
13 25
14 21
15 8
16 5
17 20
18 70
19 4059
20 2937
21 $\frac{1}{4}$
22 $\frac{2}{4}$ or $\frac{1}{2}$
23 20c
24 20c
25 20c
26 50c

Term 1 MATHS: Statistics & Probability
1 d. certain
2 a. impossible
3 b. unlikely
4 c. likely
5 d. certain
6 b. 2
7 d. 1
8 d. house
9 31
10 12

Term 1 MATHS: Measurement & Space
1 8 m
2 20 m
3 6 cm
4 c. square
5 b. triangle
6 a. pentagon
7 4
8 4
9 3
10 5
11 c. red pentagon
12 b. D6
13 b. 5 o'clock
14 a. $\frac{1}{4}$ past 3
15 a. 1 kg
16 b. $\frac{1}{2}$ kg
17 c
18 cube
19 6
20 12
21 8
22 pyramid
23 4
24 3
25 1
26 2

Unit 9 ENGLISH: Grammar & Punctuation
1 I ate <u>a meat pie</u>.
2 The farmer planted <u>a wheat crop</u>.
3 After school, we baked <u>some cakes</u> for Mum.
4 In the story, there was a scary monster frightening <u>the people</u>.
5 Liam and Jake are playing <u>football</u> in the park.
6 the lily pad
7 porridge
8 the sky
9 a tiny ball
10 a new car

Unit 9 ENGLISH: Phonic Knowledge & Spelling
1 pony
2 tidy
3 baby / boy
4 city / busy
5 bays
6 keys
7 toys
8 guys
9 monkeys
10 delays
11 trolleys
12 convoys
13 parties
14 ladies
15 ferries
16 armies
17 families
18 enemies
19 fairies
20 factories

Unit 9 ENGLISH: Reading & Comprehension
1 hot, steamy, crowded
4 a. negotiated a lower price
5 b. Thailand
6–9 In any order: rambutans, mangosteens, pomelos, durian
10 c. disgusting
11–13 Any three from: motorbikes, tuk-tuks, shops with birds in cages, fortune tellers, Buddha shop, longboats
14 c. waterways
15 tuk-tuk

Unit 9 MATHS: Number & Algebra
1 1015
2 1016
3 1017
4 1018
5 1015 = one thousand and fifteen
6 1016 = one thousand and sixteen
7 1017 = one thousand and seventeen
8 1018 = one thousand and eighteen
9 1000, 1002, 1006, 1009
10 6002, 6012, 6022, 6023
11 9100, 9200, 9300, 9400
12 1004, 1005, 1006
13 4994, 4992, 4990
14 1012
15 6666
16 7046

Unit 9 MATHS: Statistics & Probability
1 b. no
2 green
3 red
4 b. no
5 b. likely
6 c. unlikely
7 d. impossible
8 b. likely

Unit 9 MATHS: Measurement & Space
1 2 litres
2 $\frac{1}{2}$ litres
3 $\frac{1}{4}$ litre
4 25 mL
5 135 mL
6 250 mL
7 550 mL
8 984 mL
9 b. 1 litre
10 c. $\frac{1}{2}$ litre
11
12
13

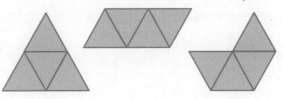

Unit 9 MATHS: Problem Solving
There are three possible solutions. If the joined shape can be rotated or turned over, it is counted as the same shape.

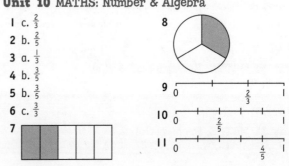

Unit 10 ENGLISH: Grammar & Punctuation
1 We <u>should</u> leave before dark.
2 If you try it, you <u>might</u> like it.
3 We <u>will</u> have pies for dinner.
4 We <u>could</u> go to the movies.
5 an
6 the, the
7 The, the
8 a, a
9 an, the
10 an, an

Unit 10 ENGLISH: Phonic Knowledge & Spelling
1 deer
2 need
3 steep
4 beef/deer
5 3
6 2
7 3
8 2
9 3
10 3
11 2
12 3
13 meet
14 steep
15 peer
16 cheer
17 wheel
18 queen
19 feet
20 keep

Unit 10 ENGLISH: Reading & Comprehension
1 Arnhem Land in the far north of Australia
2 b. a crumbly red rock used for painting
3 a. a blazing torch
4 b. West
5 descends
6 decorates
7 blazing
8 create
9 travels
10 c. destroying
11 stringy-bark tree
12 a. where the sky appears to meet the land or sea

Unit 10 MATHS: Number & Algebra
1 c. $\frac{2}{3}$
2 b. $\frac{2}{5}$
3 a. $\frac{1}{3}$
4 b. $\frac{3}{5}$
5 b. $\frac{3}{5}$
6 c. $\frac{3}{3}$
7
8
9
10
11

Unit 10 MATHS: Measurement & Space

1 1:15	4 2:45	7 a. true	10 a. true
2 4:30	5 3:00	8 b. false	11 a. true
3 8:30	6 a. true	9 b. false	

Unit 10 MATHS: Problem Solving

1 5 × 6 = 30 cupcakes
2 2 × 10 = 20 puppies
3 4 × 4 = 16 wheels
4 3 × 7 = 21 km
5 8 × 5 = 40 bars
6 5 × 4 = 20 elephant legs
7 5 × 2 = 10 elephant ears

Unit 11 ENGLISH: Grammar & Punctuation

1 He, them, her	7 me	13 him
2 You, us, he	8 They	14 her
3 they, us	9 us	15 they
4 She, me, her	10 it	16 she
5 I, I, it	11 she	17 her
6 He	12 her	18 it

Unit 11 ENGLISH: Phonic Knowledge & Spelling

1 speak, hear	7 dreamland	13 halves
2 fear	8 spearmint	14 calves
3 meal	9 teamwork	15 knives
4 gear	10 leaflet	16 lives
5 fearsome	11 leaves	
6 mealworm	12 sheaves	

Unit 11 ENGLISH: Reading & Comprehension

1 b. He wanted to create an exciting beginning so the reader would read on to find out more.
2 a. long body parts used for feeling or feeding
3 b. They live in very deep water and it's difficult for scientists to travel there.
4 b. 36 times heavier
5 enormous
6 roam
7 suckers
8 ashore
9 beak
10 a. a boat that can travel underwater

Unit 11 MATHS: Number & Algebra

1 3	10 10	19 20	28 3
2 18	11 3	20 6	29 3
3 6	12 30	21 5	30 18
4 6	13 8	22 40	31 5
5 20	14 6	23 6	32 5
6 4	15 2	24 10	33 20
7 4	16 12	25 5	34 5
8 20	17 5	26 2	35 10
9 30	18 3	27 16	36 30

37 15 ÷ 5 = 3
3 chocolate bars each
38 9 × 2 = 18
2 + 2 + 2 + 2 + 2 + 2 + 2 + 2 + 2 = 18
18 rabbit ears
39 3 × 3 = 9
$9
40 10 × 8 = 80
8 + 8 + 8 + 8 + 8 + 8 + 8 + 8 + 8 + 8 = 80
80 spider legs

Unit 11 MATHS: Statistics & Probability

1 8.30–9.00 am
2 b. People are travelling to work or school at that time.
3 38
4 23
5 4
6 2
7 9.30–10.00 am
8 8.30–9.00 am
9 a. to decide if a pedestrian crossing is needed outside the school

Unit 11 MATHS: Measurement & Space

1 6, 8, 12	4 2, 4, 8, 12
2 2, 1, 1	5 1, 4, 5, 8
3 3, 0, 2	

Unit 11 MATHS: Problem Solving

1 11, 22, 33, 44, 55, 66, 77, 88, 99

2 9, 18, 27, 36, 45, 54, 63, 72, 81, 90

3

1	2	3	4	5	6	7	8	9	10
11	12	13	14	15	16	17	18	19	20
21	22	23	24	25	26	27	28	29	30
31	32	33	34	35	36	37	38	39	40
41	42	43	44	45	46	47	48	49	50
51	52	53	54	55	56	57	58	59	60
61	62	63	64	65	66	67	68	69	70
71	72	73	74	75	76	77	78	79	80
81	82	83	84	85	86	87	88	89	90
91	92	93	94	95	96	97	98	99	100

Unit 12 ENGLISH: Grammar & Punctuation

1 Any word that has the same meaning as 'laughed'.
2 Any word that has the same meaning as 'cried'.
3 Any word that has the same meaning as 'laughed'.
4 Any word that has the same meaning as 'cried'.
5 laughed
6 yelled
7 giggled
8 "You're out!" yelled the umpire.
9 "I can't walk any further," wailed Ruby.
10 "Those monkeys are really funny," laughed Ahmed.

Unit 12 ENGLISH: Phonic Knowledge & Spelling

1 toast	10 mowed, mowing
2 mow	11 rowed, rowing
3 coach	12 followed, following
4 grow	13–20 Any eight from: boathouse, houseboat, boatshed, sailboat, paddleboat, boatyard, boatbuilder, speedboat, rowboat
5 loaded, loading	
6 coached, coaching	
7 poached, poaching	
8 moaned, moaning	
9 groaned, groaning	

Unit 12 ENGLISH: Reading & Comprehension

1 hockey   2 b. worried   3 c. climbing
4 a. He pretended he was happy about being goalie when he wasn't.
5 b. He was so worried that his stomach was hurting.
6 It wanted Ben to tell the Coach the truth — that he wasn't ready to be goalie for the game.
7 b. Ben plays the game and turns out to be a good goalie.

Unit 12 MATHS: Number & Algebra

1 10 × 2, 6 × 2 20, 12 32	5 20 ÷ 2, 6 ÷ 2 10, 3 13	9 40
2 20 × 2, 4 × 2 40, 8 48	6 30 ÷ 2, 4 ÷ 2 15, 2 17	10 400 11 120
3 30 × 2, 5 × 2 60, 10 70	7 40 ÷ 2, 8 ÷ 2 20, 4 24	12 1200 13 560 14 5600
4 70 × 2, 3 × 2 140, 6 146	8 80 ÷ 2, 6 ÷ 2 40, 3 43	15 1300 16 13 000

Unit 12 MATHS: Measurement & Space

1 metre, m
2 millilitre, mL
3 centimetre, cm
4 gram, g
5 millimetre, mm
6 litre, L
7 kilogram, kg

Unit 12 MATHS: Problem Solving

1 23
2 33
3 88
4 33

TARGETING HOMEWORK 3 © PASCAL PRESS ISBN 9781925726459

Unit 13 ENGLISH: Grammar & Punctuation

1 her	5 our	8 it's
2 your	6 yours/mine, his/	9 it's
3 their	hers, ours/theirs	10 its
4 his/its	7 its	11 its

Unit 13 ENGLISH: Phonic Knowledge & Spelling

1 I've, I'm	7 that's	14 your
2 it's	8 shouldn't	15 its
3 we're	9 we're	
4 I'm/She's/He's/	10 I'll	
You're	11 could've	
5 she's	12 you're	
6 you've	13 They're	

Unit 13 ENGLISH: Reading & Comprehension

1 a. an important event
2 c. established
3 to welcome others to the traditional lands of Aboriginal and Torres Strait Islander peoples
4 an Elder or recognised community spokesperson of the region
5 b. a person who is recognised as having special knowledge about customs and traditions
6 native plants are burned to produce smoke to cleanse the area and ward off evil spirits
7 c. pollute
8 b. refusal

Unit 13 MATHS: Number & Algebra

1 80c	5 $1.30	9 $1, 10c, 5c
2 $3.55	6 $0.50	10 $1, 10c, 5c, 5c
3 $2.05	7 $2.00	11 $1, $1, $1, 5c, 5c
4 $2.55	8 $0.60	

Unit 13 MATHS: Statistics & Probability

1 a. true	5 b. false	9 a. certain
2 a. true	6 a. yes	10 a. double the chance
3 a. true	7 b. likely	
4 b. false	8 d. impossible	

Unit 13 MATHS: Measurement & Space

1 b. 7:15
2 a. 8:30
3 b.
4 c.
5 a.
6 c.

Unit 13 MATHS: Problem Solving

1 Monday	3 17	5 4 February
2 4	4 21 January	6 11 January

Unit 14 ENGLISH: Grammar & Punctuation

1 I will visit my uncle this Saturday.
2 My dad has eaten his lunch.
3 Jai is riding his bike into town.
4 Talia can run very fast.
5 Ben was playing in the garden.
6 I will see you tomorrow. (future)
7 Yang is reading a book. (present)
8 We are waiting for Jayne to arrive. (present)
9 Dad was singing in the shower. (past)
10 The two girls were playing in the park. (past)

Unit 14 ENGLISH: Phonic Knowledge & Spelling

1 foot	9 unknown, not known
2 cook, look	10 unhealthy, not healthy
3 book	11 booklet
4 crook	12 bookcase
5 unkind, not kind	13 bookshop
6 unable, not able	14 bookkeeper
7 unsure, not sure	15 bookmark
8 unsafe, not safe	

Unit 14 ENGLISH: Reading & Comprehension

1 b. To make the reader curious about the issue.
2 fact
3 opinion
4 a. to go
5 a. risking death every time we venture into the city
6 b. The author wants cars banned from city centres.
7 b. people concerned about health and safety
8 c. rest
9 a. necessary
10 the Fair Go Party's spokesperson on transport

Unit 14 MATHS: Number & Algebra

1 2356	10 8065	19 15 378	28 a. true
2 4653	11 5576	20 102 458	29 150
3 6048	12 4678	21 b. false	30 400
4 3305	13 6389	22 b. false	31 10
5 4680	14 3700	23 a. true	32 500
6 4678	15 5002	24 a. true	33 100
7 5366	16 4056	25 a. true	34 800
8 2608	17 10 998	26 a. true	35 100
9 7770	18 3056	27 a. true	

Unit 14 MATHS: Measurement & Space

1 Hui	8 4 cm
2 Baby Ling	9 40 cm
3 164 cm	10 Grandma Wen
4 8 cm	11 Tao
5 Zhu	12 100 cm
6 Grandpa Jin	13 95 cm
7 Zhu	14 84 cm

Unit 14 MATHS: Problem Solving

1 m e e t   m e   t o d a y
  3 7 7 6   3 7   6 1 1 4 6
  total = 51
2 b y   t h e   r i v e r
  0 6   6 0 7   9 0 5 7 9
  total = 49
3 d o   n o t   b e   l a t e
  1 1   8 1 6   0 7   2 4 6 7
  total = 43

Unit 15 ENGLISH: Grammar & Punctuation

1 Leo sings in a choir.	(present)
2 The shop will close soon.	(future)
3 Dad washed our clothes on Monday.	(past)
4 I am doing my homework.	(present)
5 A horse galloped through the park.	(past)

6 worked	10 waited	14 will show
7 talked	11 listened	15 will play
8 pushed	12 cleaned	16 will eat
9 asked	13 looked	17 Will (you) carry

Unit 15 ENGLISH: Phonic Knowledge & Spelling

1 moon	5 dwarfs	9 cliffs
2 spooky	6 thieves	10 leaves
3 food	7 loaves	11 thieves
4 pool	8 knives	12 dwarfs

Unit 15 ENGLISH: Reading & Comprehension

1 b. players
2 a. When all players keep to the rules, each team has an equal chance of winning.
3 watches the game carefully and makes sure none of the competitors break the rules
4 a free pass for the other team or being taken out of the game for a short time
5 b. Germs are carried on hands and washing them might prevent people from getting ill after eating the food.
6 a. incorrect
7 to make sure people on a team and people around them are kept safe and happy.

ANSWERS

Unit 15 MATHS: Number & Algebra

1 8	5 18	9 120	13 800	17 1800
2 4	6 14	10 160	14 400	18 1400
3 12	7 80	11 180	15 1200	
4 16	8 40	12 140	16 1600	

19 7 + 7 + 1 = 14 + 1 = 15
20 8 + 8 + 1 = 16 + 1 = 17
21 4 + 4 + 1 = 8 + 1 = 9
22 6 + 6 + 1 = 12 + 1 = 13
23 70 + 70 + 10 = 140 + 10 = 150
24 40 + 40 + 10 = 80 + 10 = 90
25 80 + 80 + 10 = 160 + 10 = 170
26 60 + 60 + 10 = 120 + 10 = 130
27 700 + 700 + 100 = 1400 + 100 = 1500
28 400 + 400 + 100 = 800 + 100 = 900
29 800 + 800 + 100 = 1600 + 100 = 1700
30 600 + 600 + 100 = 1200 + 100 = 1300

Unit 15 MATHS: Statistics & Probability

1 red
2 green
3 c. 2 in 10 chance
4 a. 5 in 10 chance
5 b. likely
6 d. impossible

Unit 15 MATHS: Measurement & Space

1 b. 250 g
2 c. 1 kg
3 1250 g
4 750 g
5 b. 2 kg
6 c. 3$\frac{1}{2}$ kg

Unit 15 MATHS: Problem Solving

Unit 16 ENGLISH: Grammar & Punctuation

1 Who's
2 can't
3 won't
4 We'd, it's
5 That's, I've
6 would've, hadn't
7 doesn't
8 didn't
9 can't
10 He'll, he's

Unit 16 ENGLISH: Phonic Knowledge & Spelling

1 edge
2 porridge
3 dodge
4 trudge
5 trudging
6 smudging
7 dodging
8 judging
9 edging
10 lodging
11–18 a, know, no, led, ledge, edge, gem, me, men
19 prejudge
20 prerecord
21 preview
22 predate
23 reuse
24 return
25 rewrite
26 remake

Unit 16 ENGLISH: Reading & Comprehension

1 b. to make the reader laugh
2 a. to make the reader feel like a friend who will enjoy hearing the funny story
3 a. repairing
4 "I don't have bear feet. I have people feet."
5 c. disagreed
6 b. Georgia's father
7 b. homophones

Unit 16 MATHS: Number & Algebra

1 2

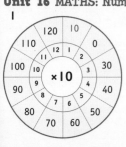

3 6
4 8
5 4
6 13
7 45
8 67
9 600
10 456

---

11 40	13 115	15 600	
12 45	14 250	16 2000	

Unit 16 MATHS: Measurement & Space

1 a. lake
2 c. whale
3 G5
4 b. cooking a fish
5 a. lion
6 b. trees
7 giraffe
8 C5
9 b. C5

Unit 16 MATHS: Problem Solving

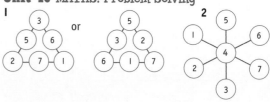

TERM 2 REVIEW

Term 2 ENGLISH: Grammar & Punctuation

1 tiny, old, wet
2 **The singer** sang a song.
3 The tall, black **hat** was stolen from the museum.
4 He, me, him, his
5 "You are walking too fast," moaned Millie.
6 sighed
7 its
8 It's
9 My mother has eaten her lunch. (past)
10 will walk
11 will jump
12 doesn't

Term 2 ENGLISH: Phonic Knowledge & Spelling

1 knew
2 right
3 shiny
4 crispy
5 lazy
6 toys
7 babies
8 cities
9 2
10 I
11 3
12 lives
13 roofs
14 leaves
15 she's
16 won't
17 you're
18 mealworm
19 bookcase
20 booklet
21 bookworm
22 mood
23 judged judging
24 looked looking
25 carried carrying
26 rewrite: to write again

Term 2 ENGLISH: Reading & Comprehension

1 a gift
2 his mum
3 $12.90 ($8.40 + $4.50)
4 $16.80 ($8.40 x 2)
5 b. have enough money for
6 b. past tense of the verb 'see'
7 c. fact
8 a coffee mug

Term 2 MATHS: Number & Algebra

1 one thousand and eighteen
2 twenty-four thousand, five hundred and eighty
3
4 12
5 12
6 5
7 120
8 1240
9 74 300
10 6
11 3
12 6
13 10
14 130
15 45
16 20 ÷ 5 = 4 cupcakes each
17 86
18 56
19 13
20 24
21 $1.40
22 $1.15
23 30
24 70
25 40
26 200
27 300
28 700
29 1000
30 4000
31 5000
32 50
33 400
34 5000
35 6 + 6 + 1 = 12 + 1 = 13
36 8 + 8 + 1 = 16 + 1 = 17
37 2012
38 8437
39 8046

Term 2 MATHS: Statistics & Probability

1 red
2 green
3 c. 3 in 13 chance
4 b. likely
5 d. impossible

TARGETING HOMEWORK 3 © PASCAL PRESS ISBN 9781925726459

Term 2 MATHS: Measurement & Space

1. 3 litres
2. $\frac{1}{2}$ litre
3. $2\frac{1}{2}$ litres
4. 2.10
5. 6.45
6. c. [shape diagram]
7. b. [bench diagram]
8. b. [angle diagram]
9. 3500 g
10. b. E2
11. b. no
12. a. land
13. B4

Unit 17 ENGLISH: Grammar & Punctuation

1. huge
2. large
3. black
4. spindly
5. wooden
6. dusty
7. sticky
8. old
9. dusty
10. moth-eaten
11. loud
12. terrifying

Unit 17 ENGLISH: Phonic Knowledge & Spelling

1. farm
2. garden
3. sharpen
4. bark
5. guard
6. spark
7. dark
8. smart
9. yard
10. far
11. starfish
12. stardust
13. stargaze
14. starship
15. starlet
16. starburst
17. starboard
18. starlight
19. starfruit

Unit 17 ENGLISH: Reading & Comprehension

1. b. bubble
2. b. to give a rhythm to the poem and to create the sounds of the volcano
3. c. tragedy
4. a. calm
5. a. to collapse inwards
6. ash
7. lava
8. bomb
9. vent
10. magma
11. b. a volcano that will erupt again one day

Unit 17 MATHS: Number & Algebra

1. b. 3
2. c. 6
3. b. 5
4. a. 8
5. b. 10
6. a. 2
7. b. 3
8. a. 4
9. b. 5
10. a. 10

Unit 17 MATHS: Statistics & Probability

1. 20
2. Sunday
3. Thursday
4. 30
5. 20
6. true

Unit 17 MATHS: Measurement & Space

1. c. 4 kg
2. b. 8 kg
3. c. 3 kg
4. a. 4, b. 1, c. 2, d. 3
5. b. a family car
6. c. a laptop
7. a. a whale
8. b. false
9. a. true
10. a. true
11. b. false

Unit 17 MATHS: Problem Solving

1. 124 − 12 = 112 cm
2. 3 × 7 = 21 km
3. 5 × 100 = 500 m
4. 30 mins = 2 km
   60 mins = 4 km
   90 mins = 6 km
   90 mins or $1\frac{1}{2}$ hours
5. 65 − 37 = 28 cm

Unit 18 ENGLISH: Grammar & Punctuation

1. wider, widest
2. smaller, smallest
3. louder, loudest
4. longer, longest
5. sweeter, sweetest
6. smallest
7. larger
8. oldest
9. colder
10. best
11. more
12. bad
13. least

Unit 18 ENGLISH: Phonic Knowledge & Spelling

1. Thirteen
2. thirsty
3. girl, skirt
4. circle
5. hungrier, hungriest
6. bigger, biggest
7. prettier, prettiest
8. wetter, wettest
9. hotter, hottest
10. earlier, earliest
11. birdbath
12. birdseed
13. birdsong
14. birdcage

Unit 18 ENGLISH: Reading & Comprehension

1. 3. run errands for his sister and brother
   1. sell herbs at the market with his mother
   2. help his grandfather in the rice paddy field
2. b. chores
3. c. taxi driver
4. b. He wanted to see the monkeys before he started his chores.
5. a. the nearest town to where Nyoman lives
6. Betty
7. b. It was a kitten.

Unit 18 MATHS: Number & Algebra

1. 146, 156, 166, 176
2. 424, 434, 444, 454
3. 5456, 5466, 5476, 5486
4. 12 418, 12 428, 12 438
5. 424, 524, 624, 724
6. 738, 838, 938, 1038
7. 709, 809, 909, 1009
8. 5323, 5423, 5523, 5623
9. 23 638, 23 738, 23 838
10. 4430, 5430, 6430, 7430
11. 9788, 11 788, 12 788, 13 788
12. 27 600, 28 600, 29 600, 30 600

Unit 18 MATHS: Measurement & Space

1. pyramid
2. prism
3. prism
4. pyramid
5. b. pentagonal prism
6. b. hexagonal prism
7. a. heptagonal prism

Unit 18 MATHS: Problem Solving

Vanilla ice-cream

vanilla ice-cream + chocolate topping	vanilla ice-cream + raspberry topping	vanilla ice-cream + strawberry topping

Lime ice-cream

lime ice-cream + chocolate topping	lime ice-cream + raspberry topping	lime ice-cream + strawberry topping

Jackie has 6 combinations of ice-cream and topping to choose from.

Unit 19 ENGLISH: Grammar & Punctuation

1. could/would
2. must/should
3. can
4. must/should
5. couldn't
6. mustn't
7. shouldn't
8. won't
9. can't
10. mightn't
11. couldn't
12. mustn't
13. won't
14. couldn't

Unit 19 ENGLISH: Phonic Knowledge & Spelling

1. her
2. person
3. servant
4. swerve, kerb
5. male, mail
6. flour
7. cheap
8. would, wood
9. serving
10. nervously
11. jerked

Unit 19 ENGLISH: Reading & Comprehension

1. b. a special symbol
2. a. plants and animals that live in the same place they originally came from
3. b. Tasmanian Devil
4. c. Queensland
5. c. unimportant
6. Australian Capital Territory
7. b. represent

Unit 19 MATHS: Number & Algebra

1. $2.99 + $1.99
   $3.00 + $2.00 = $5.00
2. $3.00 + $3.00 = $6.00
3. $3.99 + $2.99
   $4.00 + $3.00 = $7.00
4. $3.50 + $2.50 = $6.00
5. $5.00
6. $4.00
7. $3.00
8. $4.00
9. $4.99 − $1.99
   $5.00 − $2.00 = $3.00
10. $2.99 − $1.99
    $3.00 − $2.00 = $1.00
11. $6.00 − $3.99
    $6.00 − $4.00 = $2.00
12. $3.50 − $2.50 = $1.00

Unit 19 MATHS: Statistics & Probability

1. c. Favourite desserts in our school
2. ice-cream
3. pancakes
4. a. yes
5. b. Year 2
6. 10

Unit 19 MATHS: Measurement & Space

1 b. Ryan	5 no
2 a. Georgia	6 Peter
3 b. Sue	7 a. walk past Mia's desk
4 a. Nat	8 b. walk past David's desk

Unit 19 MATHS: Problem Solving

30 – 6 – 10 – 6 = 8
The baker cooked 8 cookies before 10 o'clock.

Unit 20 ENGLISH: Grammar & Punctuation

(Q 1–6: <u>verb</u>, **adverb**)

1 She <u>spoke</u> **loudly** at the meeting.
2 He <u>crossed</u> the road **quickly**.
3 Mum <u>rode</u> a horse **today**.
4 We <u>will meet</u> you at the restaurant **tomorrow**.
5 I <u>have looked</u> **everywhere** for you.
6 The dog <u>ran</u> **away**.

7 lazily	10 brightly	13 loudly	16 bravely
8 away	11 behind	14 fast	17 angrily
9 yesterday	12 carefully	15 high	

Unit 20 ENGLISH: Phonic Knowledge & Spelling

1 church	5 roughly	9 purse,	11 2
2 nurse	6 lazily	spurt, surf,	12 2
3 purse	7 carefully	turn	13 3
4 purple	8 easily	10 1	

Unit 20 ENGLISH: Reading & Comprehension

1 c. Weather changes daily; climate is weather over a long period of time.
2 b. red/yellow
3 a. temperate
4–7 In any order: summer, autumn, winter, spring
8 a. hot
9 b. distinct
10–11 In any order: temperate, tropical

Unit 20 MATHS: Number & Algebra

1 51	5 a. true	9 a. true	13 149
2 447	6 b. false	10 a. true	14 8196
3 16 350	7 a. true	11 970	15 4624
4 124 567	8 b. false	12 7895	

Unit 20 MATHS: Measurement & Space

1 b. 9:28	4 c. 12:08	7 b. 12
2 b. 10:09	5 b. 4:51	8 a. 4:45
3 c. 1:46	6 a. 5:41	9 a. 12:46

Unit 20 MATHS: Problem Solving

Name	Eyes	Hair
Maddy	brown	brown
Fiona	green	black
James	blue	blonde

Unit 21 ENGLISH: Grammar & Punctuation

1 How	8 How many fish are in the bowl?
2 Why/When	9 When does the party start?
3 When	10 Why
4 Where	11 How
5 How	12 When
6 Where do you live?	13 Where
7 Why are you crying?	

Unit 21 ENGLISH: Phonic Knowledge & Spelling

1 storm	5 saw	9 dairy
2 sore	6 wore	10 brought
3 roar	7 desert	
4 pour	8 quiet	

Unit 21 ENGLISH: Reading & Comprehension

1 c. on the computer	6 opinion
2 a. They give her the latest information on research and treatments.	7 fact
	8 to test for diseases
3 b. It is quick and easy to find information about patients.	9 b. caring
	10 b. to inform readers about the role of doctors today and how science can help patients
4 c. destruction	
5 c. technician	

Unit 21 MATHS: Number & Algebra

1 3	4 4	7 b. false	10 a. true
2 7	5 10	8 b. false	11 a. true
3 3	6 7	9 a. true	

Unit 21 MATHS: Statistics & Probability

1 b. 10	beetles, skaters, larva and tadpoles.
2 a. 8	
3 3T	6 a. Only one class found shrimps.
4 b. 2	
5 b. They both found snails,	

Unit 21 MATHS: Measurement & Space

1 b. Sky Street	4 b. supermarket
2 a. Main Road	5 a. yes
3 b. library	6 a. yes

Unit 21 MATHS: Problem Solving

1 5	2 8		3 3	4 6	
	5 2	6 4		7 2	8 4
9 7		10 2	11 6		5
12 3	13 6		14 1	15 5	
	16 6	17 8		18 5	19 9
	20 3	0			5

Unit 22 ENGLISH: Grammar & Punctuation

1 **D**id Chloe, **L**ily and **T**om get home safely**?**
2 Mrs Jones lives at 49 **W**est **S**treet in **S**andy **B**ay.
3 **L**ook out Max, there's a train coming**!**
4 **"**You're a great goalie!**"** yelled Ben, punching his hands in the air.
5 **"**Why are we going there?**"** moaned Jen.
6 **"**We are going on holiday next week,**"** announced Dad.
7 **"**I'm tired,**"** wailed Peter. **"C**an't we go back now?**"**
8 The car crashed into a tree. **L**uckily, the driver was not hurt.
9 The furniture is stored in a warehouse. **V**ans deliver it to customers.
10 My cousin has a Golden Retriever. **I**ts name is Ginger.
11 The storms caused a lot of damage. **T**hankfully, our house was not damaged.

Unit 22 ENGLISH: Phonic Knowledge & Spelling

1 mountain	6 outside	11 loudly
2 shout	7 roundabout	12 pouches
3 sound	8 mouthwash	13 rounder
4 pouch	9 shouted	14 doubting
5 cloudless	10 cloudy	15 southerly

Unit 22 ENGLISH: Reading & Comprehension

1 b. to present two different points of view about rabbits in Australia
2 c. He thinks all rabbits should be removed from Australia.
3 a. They were brought into Australia from another country.
4 c. They eat native plants and farmers' crops.
5 fact
6 opinion

ANSWERS

156

TARGETING HOMEWORK 3 © PASCAL PRESS ISBN 9781925726459

7 a. an animal or plant that has always lived in a place
8 b. environment
9 encourage people to eat rabbits as a source of food

Unit 22 MATHS: Number & Algebra
1 3 × 9 = 27 pencils
2 8 × 3 = 24 football cards
3 5 × 7 = 35 books
4 3 × 7 = 21 computer games
5 2 × 9 = 18 toy cars
6 9 × 2 = 18
7 5 × 7 = 35
8 3 × 10 = 30
9 5 × 8 = 40
10 100
11 90
12 400
13 50
14 75
15 300
16 160
17 200
18 1000

Unit 22 MATHS: Measurement & Space
1 b. false
2 a. true
3 a. true
4 a. true
5 a. true
6 b. false
7 a. true
8 b. false
9 a. true
10 b. false
11 a. true
12 b. false
13 fifths
14 sixths
15 tenths
16 eighths

Unit 22 MATHS: Problem Solving
1 2, 10
2 The first two and last two numbers in each row total 20 (a total of 40 for each row), except for the first two numbers on the bottom row. 2 and 10 add up to 12, not 20.

Unit 23 ENGLISH: Grammar & Punctuation
1 angry
2 cautious
3 relieved
4 pleased
5 unsure
6 peered
7 glimpsed
8 stared
9 watched
10 noticed

Unit 23 ENGLISH: Phonic Knowledge & Spelling
1 flower
2 town
3 shower
4 b. to use oars to move a boat
5 a. a knot made with loops
6 growl/prowl
7 drown
8 township
9 cowhide
10 cowbell
11 cowgirl
12 cowshed

Unit 23 ENGLISH: Reading & Comprehension
1 b. the inn
2 a. trees and a park
3 b. a petrol station
4 c. Today there are cars, trucks and buses.
5 fact
6 opinion
7 b. remain
8 The building is still in use as an inn (hotel) today.

Unit 23 MATHS: Number & Algebra
1 b. 2
2 4
3 b. 5
4 c. 7
5 b. 6
6 a. 2
7 b. 3
8 a. 4
9 b. 5
10 c. 8

Unit 23 MATHS: Statistics & Probability
1
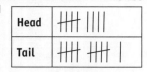

| Head | ||||| |||| |
| Tail | ||||| ||||| | |

2
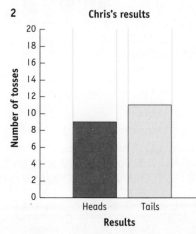

Chris's results

3 a. yes

4 There is an equal chance of tossing a head or a tail so the results should be approximately equal.
5 a. true
6 b. likely
7 d. impossible
8 b. likely

Unit 23 MATHS: Measurement & Space
1 4 cm   2 2 cm   3 5 cm   4 7 cm   5 11 mm

Unit 23 MATHS: Problem Solving
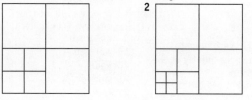

Unit 24 ENGLISH: Grammar & Punctuation
1 the baby's toy
2 the sun's heat
3 Adam's tent
4 girls'
5 Frankie's
6 students'

Unit 24 ENGLISH: Phonic Knowledge & Spelling
1 shawl
2 saw
3 drawer
4 strawberry
5 crawled
6 prawns
7 dawning
8 strawberries
9 oxen
10 teeth
11 geese
12 women

Unit 24 ENGLISH: Reading & Comprehension
1 I C U First
2 *The Lonely Child* or *Whispering Mountain*
3 b. readers over the age of 8
4 opinion
5 fact
6 b. in the park
7 He seems to never learn his lesson and keeps on making the same mistakes.
8 d. dull
9 c. thoroughly
10 b. You will thoroughly enjoy this book.

Unit 24 MATHS: Number & Algebra
1 5 × 16
  5 × 10 = 50
  5 × 6 = 30
  50 + 30 = 80
2 3 × 19
  3 × 10 = 30
  3 × 9 = 27
  30 + 27 = 57
3 2 × 18
  2 × 10 = 20
  2 × 8 = 16
  20 + 16 = 36
4 9 × 17
  9 × 10 = 90
  9 × 7 = 63
  90 + 63 = 153
5 5 × $15
  5 × 10 = 50
  5 × 5 = 25
  50 + 25 = $75
6 3 × 18
  3 × 10 = 30
  3 × 8 = 24
  30 + 24 = 54 chocolate buttons
7 5 × 14
  5 × 10 = 50
  5 × 4 = 20
  50 + 20 = 70 hours
8 3 × $16
  3 × 10 = 30
  3 × 6 = 18
  30 + 18 = $48
9 3 × 14
  3 × 10 = 30
  3 × 4 = 12
  30 + 12 = 42 seashells

Unit 24 MATHS: Measurement & Space
1 a
2 c
3 d
4 d
5 a
6 34 right angles

Unit 24 MATHS: Problem Solving

Term 3 ENGLISH: Grammar & Punctuation

1 huge, rickety, dark, rat-infested, creepy
2 best
3 more
4 bad
5 least
6 couldn't
7 won't
8 mustn't
9 can't

(Q10–12: <u>verb</u>, **adverb**)
10 She <u>spoke</u> **quietly** at the meeting.
11 Liam <u>crossed</u> the street **carefully**.
12 Dad <u>ate</u> a whole cake **today**.

13 Why
14 How
15 **D**id **M**ax, **A**li and **T**im come to your party**?**
16 **"**Come on, you lot,**"** said Maddie.
17 **"**When will we get there?**"** asked Jai.
18 **A** mouse ran into our kitchen. Thankfully, I did not see it.
19 watched
20 heard
21 sniffed
22 Lee's
23 boys'

Term 3 ENGLISH: Phonic Knowledge & Spelling

1 a. to have a noisy quarrel
2 dirtier, dirtiest
3 bigger, biggest
4 prettier, prettiest
5 wetter, wettest
6 heard
7 flour
8 quickly
9 angrily
10 noisily
11 helpfully
12 lives
13 roofs
14 children
15 men
16 soundproof
17 outside
18 mouthwash
19 roundabout
20 3
21 2
22 3
23 cow, coward, down, drown, growl
24 serving
25 herded
26 nervously
27 diary
28 quiet
29 quite
30 dairy

Term 3 ENGLISH: Reading & Comprehension

1 red, yellow, blue
2 b. a board an artist uses to mix colours
3 b. to try out something to see what happens
4 c. few
5 detail work
6 a. clean them well
7–11 In any order: paint, palette, brushes, easel, paper

Term 3 MATHS: Number & Algebra

1 b. 7
2 c. 10
3 a. 2
4 165, 175, 185, 195
5 1332, 1342, 1352, 1362
6 $5.49, round to $5.50
7 $4.50
8 $6.98, round to $7.00
9 $3.00
10 b. false
11 b. false
12 a. true
13 3
14 6
15 7
16 3
17 5 × 9 = 45 books
18 b. 6
19 c. 7
20 a. 3
21 b. 5
22 7 × 13
  7 × 10 = 70
  7 × 3 = 21
  70 + 21 = 91
23 5 × 19
  5 × 10 = 50
  5 × 9 = 45
  50 + 45 = 95

Term 3 MATHS: Statistics & Probability

1 chocolate
2 mint
3 b. banana
4 8
5 b. false
6 b. the chocolate and mint results

Term 3 MATHS: Measurement & Space

1 c. 4 kg
2 a. true
3 b. false
4 c. triangular prism
5 c. square pyramid
6 b. art room
7 b. no
8 b. 6:17
9 a. 11:34
10 b. 12:36

11 a. yes
12 b. no
13 c. 7 cm
14 b

Unit 25 ENGLISH: Grammar & Punctuation

1 swarm
2 pod
3 litter
4 pack
5 herd
6 flock
7 mob
8 colony
9 set of clubs
10 fleet of ships
11 stack of wood
12 block of flats
13 army of soldiers
14 bunch of keys

Unit 25 ENGLISH: Phonic Knowledge & Spelling

1 daughter
2 audience
3 August
4 naughty
5 haul
6 caught
7 sauce
8 paws
9 a, auto, to, ma, mat, at, tic, am, at, cat

Unit 25 ENGLISH: Reading & Comprehension

1 b. vines
2 a. 1957
3 b. early times in a settlement
4 c. failure
5 b. a right given by the government to an inventor, allowing them to be the only person to make or sell an invention
6 hollow plastic
7–8 Spin-a-Hoops, Hoop-d-dos
9 a. estimated

Unit 25 MATHS: Number & Algebra

1 six hundred and forty-three
2 one thousand, seven hundred and ninety-two
3 two thousand and fifty
4 twelve thousand, five hundred and sixty-eight
5 fifty-six thousand, seven hundred and five
6 656
7 405
8 2793
9 13 481
10 82 960
11 b. 80
12 c. 2
13 a. 5000
14 a. 2000
15 a. 50 000
16 3745
17 5607
18 6565
19 9782

Unit 25 MATHS: Statistics & Probability

1 6
2 34
3 28
4 $3.00
5 b. 104
6 c. 52.00
7

Visitors to our Exhibition

Unit 25 MATHS: Measurement & Space

1 a. true
2 a. true
3 b. false
4 a. true
5 b. false
6 =
7 <
8 =
9 >
10 =
11 >
12 $3\frac{1}{2}$ kg
13 $\frac{1}{2}$ kg

Unit 25 MATHS: Problem Solving

1 11
2 7
3 20
4 3
5 9
6 22
7 24
8 35
9 VI
10 X
11 IV
12 XIX
13 XII
14 XXV
15 XXI
16 XXXIV

Unit 26 ENGLISH: Grammar & Punctuation

1 was
2 have
3 are
4 has
5 am
6 action
7 relating
8 relating
9 action
10 relating
11 action
12 Insects **are** small animals with six legs. Insects **have** a hard shell or exoskeleton. Most insects **have** wings and antennae. One of the largest insects in the world **is** the Rhinoceros Beetle.

Unit 26 ENGLISH: Phonic Knowledge & Spelling

1 enjoy	5 sleigh	9 boyhood	13 employee
2 voice	6 tower	10 toyshop	14 poison
3 noise	7 hurt	11 pointless	15 loyalty
4 boy, toy	8 toe	12 voicemail	16 hoisting

Unit 26 ENGLISH: Reading & Comprehension

1 River View Lane
2 b. so he can look out when he wakes up
3 c. next to
4 c. double
5 reading lamp
6 turquoise
7 yellow and orange
8 blue
9 green
10 blue and green

Unit 26 MATHS: Number & Algebra

1 $\frac{1}{2} = \frac{2}{4}$ 2 $\frac{1}{2} = \frac{3}{6}$ 3 $\frac{1}{2} = \frac{5}{10}$ 4 $\frac{1}{2} = \frac{4}{8}$

5

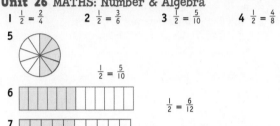

$\frac{1}{2} = \frac{5}{10}$

6

$\frac{1}{2} = \frac{6}{12}$

7

$\frac{1}{2} = \frac{10}{20}$

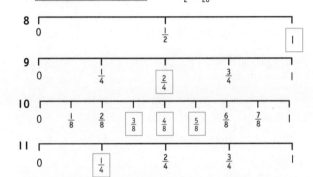

Unit 26 MATHS: Measurement & Space

1 c. 8 litres	5 b. false	9 1400 mL
2 a. 4	6 350 mL	10 1800 mL
3 c. 7 L	7 600 mL	11 1100 mL
4 b. 200 L	8 450 mL	

Unit 26 MATHS: Problem Solving

1 35 minutes
2 35 minutes
3 20 minutes
4 55 minutes
5 7.40 pm
6 100 minutes (1 hour and 40 minutes)
7 2 hours and 35 minutes

Unit 27 ENGLISH: Grammar & Punctuation

1 He ran and ran until his sides started to ache. He dropped down, exhausted, against an old tree. "Phew, I made it," he thought.
2 Mal knocked on the door. When no answer came, he cautiously turned the handle and peered inside. The room was empty.
3 Mal quickly turned around. What was it? The sound made his blood run cold. "Run," he thought. "I've got to run."
4 He stepped further into the room and called Becky's name. No-one replied. Suddenly, he became aware of a strange shuffling sound in the corner.
5 2, 4, 3, 1

Unit 27 ENGLISH: Phonic Knowledge & Spelling

1 stairs
2 share
3 hair
4 spare
5 scared, scaring
6 glared, glaring
7 shared, sharing
8 blared, blaring
9 prepared, preparing
10–19 In any order: airway, airbag, airport, airfare, airline, airship, aircraft, airwaves, airborne

Unit 27 ENGLISH: Reading & Comprehension

1 b. on an angle   2 the Earth's axis   3 c. real
4 c. because the Earth spins around and only one side faces the Sun at any one time
5 sunrise
6 b. a space where two lines meet, measured in degrees
7 because the Earth is always spinning

Unit 27 MATHS: Number & Algebra

1 790	10 99 258	17 <
2 603	11 1248, 2030, 4002, 5706, 6190	18 true
3 488		19 true
4 603		20 false
5 2030	12 <	21 false
6 4002	13 >	22 true
7 1248	14 =	23 true
8 24 500	15 =	
9 4002	16 <	

Unit 27 MATHS: Statistics & Probability

1 b. What is your favourite colour?
2 c. Which do you like better, football or basketball?
3 b. How do you get to school?
4 c. the teachers in her school
5 c. the boys and girls in his class
6 b. the children in her class

Unit 27 MATHS: Measurement & Space

1 a. count to four	4 b. 2	7 Reece
2 c. 120	5 b. 120	8 4:45 pm
3 c. 15	6 b. Jayne	9 75 seconds

Unit 27 MATHS: Problem Solving

1 158, 185, 518, 581, 815, 851
2 851
3 158
4 158, 185, 518, 581, 815, 851
5

Number	×10	×100
158	1580	15 800
185	1850	18 500
518	5180	51 800
581	5810	58 100
815	8150	81 500
851	8510	85 100

Unit 28 ENGLISH: Grammar & Punctuation

1 fell	5 swept	9 hid	13 rang
2 ate	6 spoke	10 sang	14 drank
3 flew	7 gave	11 bit	15 stood
4 caught	8 cleaned	12 told	16 grew

Unit 28 ENGLISH: Phonic Knowledge & Spelling

1 ferry	5 essays	9 pulleys	13 diaries
2 chimney	6 boys	10 days	14 babies
3 copy	7 cowboys	11 puppies	15 cities
4 family	8 kidneys	12 trophies	16 gullies

Unit 28 ENGLISH: Reading & Comprehension

1 c. spring
2–4 In any order: children dance around a maypole decorated with flowers or ribbons; Morris dancers perform folk dances; a May Queen wears a crown
5 b. Walpurgis Night
6 c. celebrated
7 b. a Roman goddess
8 a. a series of activities done to achieve something

Unit 28 MATHS: Number & Algebra

1 add 3, starting at 15
2 subtract 5, starting at 60
3 add 10, starting at 45
4 subtract 3, starting at 133
5 add 5, starting at 254
6 add 10, starting at 578
7 subtract 10, starting at 1345
8 60, 65, 70, 75, 80
9 28, 25, 22, 19, 16
10 62, 72, 82, 92, 102
11 160, 155, 150, 145, 140
12 583, 585, 587, 589, 591
13 346, 356, 366, 376, 386
14 193, 293, 393, 493, 593
15 1640, 1540, 1440, 1340, 1240
16 46, 66
17 62, 82
18 129, 149
19 4358, 4378
20 24 513, 24 533
21 34, 14
22 99, 79
23 550, 530
24 5680, 5660
25 56 351, 56 331

Unit 28 MATHS: Measurement & Space

1 5
2 1
3 5
4 8
5 5
6 2
7 6
8 9
9 8
10 2
11 12
12 18
13 b. pentagonal prism

Unit 28 MATHS: Problem Solving

1 16
2 5 pieces each:

W	W	W	W	W	G	G	G	G	G
J	J	J	J	J	M	M	M	M	M

3 $10 – $5 = $5
  $5 – $3 = $2
4 28 ÷ 4 = 7
  $\frac{1}{4}$ = 7 lollies
  28 – 7 = 21 lollies left
5 $\frac{1}{4}$

Unit 29 ENGLISH: Grammar & Punctuation

1 through   2 under   3 At   4 for
5 The dog ran across the road.
6 We went to the park after school.
7 Our teacher greeted us with a smile.
8 I mixed the cake batter in the bowl.

Unit 29 ENGLISH: Phonic Knowledge & Spelling

1 untidy
2 dislike
3 unclean
4 disconnect
5 untie
6 disbelieve
7 unfold
8 disappear
9 dishonest
10 disobey
11 unafraid
12 disrespect
13 disagree
14 unsafe
15 discontinue
16 unwell
17 unplug
18 disobedient

Unit 29 ENGLISH: Reading & Comprehension

1 c. indecision   2 b. complex
3 c. a decision made after considering all the options
4–6 Any three of the following:
  - What do I have to decide? Why?
  - What are my choices?
  - Gather information. Separate fact from fiction.
  - What are the risks?
  - How does my decision affect others?
  - Will I accept responsibility for my actions?
7 choosing between an apple and a banana for your snack
8 deciding who to be friends with
9 c. unimportant
10 the ability to make wise decisions

Unit 29 MATHS: Number & Algebra

1

×	2	3	4	5	6	7	8	9	10
2	4	6	8	10	12	14	16	18	20
3	6	9	12	15	18	21	24	27	30
5	10	15	20	25	30	35	40	45	50
10	20	30	40	50	60	70	80	90	100

2 12
3 50
4 12
5 45
6 16
7 24
8 70
9 27
10 30
11 7
12 6
13 9
14 4
15 10
16 9
17 7
18 4
19 10
20 10
21 5
22 5
23 10
24 6
25 3
26 3
27 6
28 8
29 2
30 2
31 8
32 7
33 10
34 10
35 7

Unit 29 MATHS: Statistics & Probability

1 b. Snacks eaten by the children in Class 3T last Monday
2 c. 7
3 c. fruit
4 yes
5 no
6 no
7 yes
8 b. Ask the students in your class what they ate when they return to class after break time.

Unit 29 MATHS: Measurement & Space

1 _____
2 _____
3
4

Unit 29 MATHS: Problem Solving

1–4

Name	Region	Height (m)	Order of height
Aconcagua	South America	6961	2
Mount Vinson	Antarctica	4892	6
Mount Kosciuszko	Australia	2228	8
Mount Everest	Asia	8848	1
Puncak Jaya	Asia	4884	7
Mount Elbrus	Europe	5741	5
Denali	North America	6144	3
Kilimanjaro	Africa	5885	4

5 1887 m   6 6620 m

Unit 30 ENGLISH: Grammar & Punctuation

1 Apples, pears and oranges
  ON SALE
2 Come to Bob's Cafe! It's the BEST COFFEE in town!
3 **Sorry!**
  Were CLOSED.
  Please come back tomorrow.

Unit 30 ENGLISH: Phonic Knowledge & Spelling

1 beautiful
2 colourful
3 helpful
4 playful
5 careful
6 cheerful
7 helpful
8 powerful
9 wonderful
10 hopeful
11 painful
12 peaceful
13 pitiful
14 joyful
15 playful
16 plentiful

Unit 30 ENGLISH: Reading & Comprehension

1 a. yes
2 b. investigate the possibility of upgrading Banksiaville playground
3 b. a circular course
4–6 In any order: a skateboard park, a fitness circuit, a basketball court
7 a. They will carry out littering and vandalism.
8 b. beautiful
9 c. surpass
10 a. a reply that says Ms Charge is going to agree to investigate improving the playground

TARGETING HOMEWORK 3 © PASCAL PRESS ISBN 9781925726459

Unit 30 MATHS: Number & Algebra

1 14 + 6 = 20
  20 + 12 = 32
2 15 + 5 = 20
  20 + 17 = 37
3 13 + 7 = 20
  20 + 19 = 39
4 11 + 9 = 20
  20 + 15 = 35
5 16 + 4 = 20
  20 + 18 = 38

6 10 + 10 = 20
  20 + 23 = 43
7 50 + 50 = 100
  100 + 45 = 145
8 30 + 70 = 100
  100 + 23 = 123
9 80 + 20 = 100
  100 + 62 = 162
10 90 + 10 = 100
  100 + 39 = 139

11 45 + 55 = 100
  100 + 20 = 120
12 65 + 35 = 100
  100 + 48 = 148
13 c. 18 + 9 + 2
14 a. 10 + 14 + 10
15 a. 13 + 36 + 7
16 b. 20 + 52 + 80
17 b. 45 + 55 + 98

Unit 30 MATHS: Measurement & Space

1 High Street   2 a. north   3 1, 3, 5   4 Park Street

5

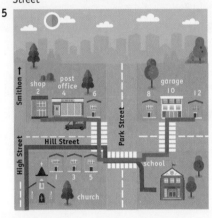

Unit 30 MATHS: Problem Solving

As no cub weighs less than 6 kg, cubs 1 and 2 could weigh:
• 6 kg and 9 kg
• 7 kg and 8 kg
As no cub weighs less than 6 kg, cubs 2 and 3 could weigh:
• 6 kg and 11 kg
• 7 kg and 10 kg
• 8 kg and 9 kg

Trial and error method
If cub 1 weighs 6 kg, then cub 2 must weigh 9 kg (9 + 6 = 15)
If cub 1 weighs 6 kg, then cub 3 would need to weigh 12 kg (6 + 12 = 18) but this would mean that cub 1 would only weigh 5 kg, so this cannot be correct.
Using the same trial and error method, you can work out:
• cub 1 weighs 8 kg
• cub 2 weighs 7 kg
• cub 3 weighs 10 kg.

Unit 31 ENGLISH: Grammar & Punctuation

1 A **boy** with his arm in a sling sat down next to me.
2 The **painting** on the wall was stunning.
3 The **cat** with long, shaggy fur was stalking a bird.
4 The **newspaper** on the table is Dad's.
5 We played a **game** of backyard cricket.
6 The **mouse** under the bed squeaked loudly.
7 of chocolates
8 in a blue dress
9 beside you
10 with hot fudge
11 from small twigs
12 with floppy ears

Unit 31 ENGLISH: Phonic Knowledge & Spelling

1 restless
2 cloudless
3 harmless
4 hopeless
5 tasteless, meaning: without taste
6 lifeless, meaning: without life
7 homeless, meaning: without a home
8 endlessly
9 helplessly
10 senselessly

Unit 31 ENGLISH: Reading & Comprehension

1–4 In any order: snow-capped mountains, glaciers, green pastures, blue waterways
5 b. a hot and dry season followed by a wet season

6–7 Any two of the following: volcano eruptions, earthquakes, tsunamis, floods, cyclones
8 yes
9 islands
10 glaciers
11 mountainous
12 a, c
13 Port Moresby

Unit 31 MATHS: Number & Algebra

1 4 kina
2 5 New Zealand dollars
3 1 pound
4 19 848 rupiah
5 25 yuan
6 12 Solomon Islands dollars

Unit 31 MATHS: Statistics & Probability

1 b. 1 in 6
2 c. 2 in 8
3 b. 2 in 10
4 a. 1 in 6
5 c. 1 in 6
6 a. 2 in 6

Unit 31 MATHS: Measurement & Space

The completed plan should look like this:

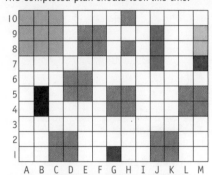

Unit 31 MATHS: Problem Solving

1–3

1	2	3	4	5
6	7	8	9	10
11	12	13	14	15
16	17	18	19	20
21	22	23	24	25
26	27	28	29	30
31	32	33	34	35

4 2, 6, 14, 18, 22, 26, 34

Unit 32 ENGLISH: Grammar & Punctuation

1 sadder, saddest
2 louder, loudest
3 taller, tallest
4 longer, longest
5 smaller, smallest
6 lower, lowest
7 prettier, prettiest
8 funnier, funniest
9 noisier, noisiest
10 busier, busiest
11 drier, driest
12 juicier, juiciest
13 cuter
14 spiciest
15 braver
16 largest

Unit 32 ENGLISH: Phonic Knowledge & Spelling

1 attic
2 magic
3 picnic
4 garlic
5 comically
6 magically
7 sleepily
8 tragically
9 logically
10 angrily
11 automatic
12 photogenic
13 realistic
14 organic
15 Atlantic
16 athletic

Unit 32 ENGLISH: Reading & Comprehension

1 a. sadness
2 b. Mum didn't agree with the things Uncle Andy did.
3 a. His uncle always brought him interesting things to look at.
4 b. some boxes and an orange sleeping-bag
5 c. surprise
6 it fell into a cup of tea at one of her card parties
7 a. an ape
8 b. a snake

Unit 32 MATHS: Number & Algebra

1 1548	6 7069	11 3459	16 700
2 4673	7 2456	12 45 602	17 $4300
3 8239	8 3019	13 9	18 1200
4 5380	9 6554	14 5999	19 7740
5 6506	10 3505	15 7786	20 54 000

Unit 32 MATHS: Measurement & Space

1 4:45
2 3:17
3 1:08
4 10:36
5 2:46
6 2:58
7 3:00
8 12:09
9
10
11
12
13
14

Unit 32 MATHS: Problem Solving

1

9	2	7
4	6	8
5	10	3

2

10	3	8
5	7	9
6	11	4

3

4	9	2
3	5	7
8	1	6

TERM 4 REVIEW

Term 4 ENGLISH: Grammar & Punctuation

1 students
2 flowers
3 lions
4 cards
5 action
6 relating
7 relating
8 fell
9 began
10 gave
11 with
12 At
13 for
14 **Riley's** dog chased after my eldest **sister's** cat.
15 At **Emma's** salon, **we're** open until 7 pm every night, except Sundays.
16 I saw a **man** with a gold walking stick.
17 Mum bought a **basket** of fresh fruit.
18 Who is that **boy** in your class?
19 hotter, hottest
20 older, oldest
21 prettier, prettiest
22 noisier, noisiest
23 b. a group of sentences used to introduce new parts of a story, characters or information
24 climbed
25 ran
26 dug
27 yelled

Term 4 ENGLISH: Phonic Knowledge & Spelling

1 court
2 taut
3 pause
4 neigh
5 tale
6 flour
7 noise
8 scared, scaring
9 dared, daring
10 shared, sharing
11 blared, blaring
12 cowboys
13 stories
14 journeys
15 cities
16 unhappy
17 dislike
18 disobey
19 unsafe
20 playful
21 powerful
22 pitiful
23 plentiful
24 careless (without care)
25 hopeless (without hope)
26 painlessly
27 helplessly
28 easily
29 basically
30 magically
31 sleepily
32 airline
33 airship
34 airport
35 airfare

Term 4 ENGLISH: Reading & Comprehension

1 painting
2 morning
3 b. to move in an awkward way
4 upstairs
5 no
6 I took the long ladder up there yesterday
7 c. paperwork
8 c. started

Term 4 MATHS: Number & Algebra

1 b. 80	14 6	20 + 15 = 35
2 b. 600	15 6	25 50 + 50 = 100
3 a. 2000	16 10	100 + 75 = 175
4 two	17 7	26 20 + 80 = 100
5 four	18 3	100 + 23 = 123
6 <	19 3	27 90 + 10 = 100
7 >	20 7	100 + 46 = 146
8 =	21 13 + 7 = 20	28 18
9 =	20 + 12 = 32	29 10
10 55, 60, 65, 70	22 15 + 5 = 20	30 2
11 18, 15, 12, 9	20 + 19 = 39	31 3423
12 354, 454, 554, 654	23 11 + 9 = 20	32 25 504
13 10	20 + 14 = 34	33 100
	24 12 + 8 = 20	

Term 4 MATHS: Statistics & Probability

1 b. What is your favourite book?
2 8
3 25
4 20
5 $5
6 70
7 d. 1 in 6
8 a. 1 in 6

Term 4 MATHS: Measurement & Space

1 true
2 false
3 true
4 d. 12 litres
5 a. 6
6 a. 60
7 a. Anna
8 6
9 1
10 6
11 10

12
13
14 3:15
15 6:52
16

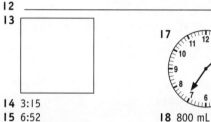

17
18 800 mL
19 32
20 class library
21 3 cupboards at A5, D8 and H2
22 A6, A7, A8

TARGETING HOMEWORK 3 © PASCAL PRESS ISBN 9781925726459